The AMERICAN HERITAGE®
first
dictionary

By the Editors of the American Heritage® Dictionaries

HOUGHTON MIFFLIN HARCOURT
Boston • New York

STAFF

Vice President, Publisher of Dictionaries
Margery S. Berube

Vice President, Executive Editor
Joseph P. Pickett

Vice President, Managing Editor
Christopher Leonesio

Project Manager, Senior Editor
Susan I. Spitz

Senior Editors
Steven R. Kleinedler
Louise E. Robbins
Peter Chipman

Database Production Supervisor
Christopher Granniss

Art and Production Supervisor
Margaret Anne Miles

Editors
Catherine T. Pratt
Patrick Taylor

Associate Production Editor
Sarah Iani

Associate Editors
Erich M. Groat
Uchenna C. Ikonné

Editorial Production Assistant
Katherine M. Getz

Assistant Editor
Nicholas A. Durlacher

Print Production Director
Donna Baxter McCarthy

Editorial Associate
Emily A. Neeves

Lead Print Production Coordinator
Diane Varone

Administrative Coordinator
Darcy Conroy

Text Design
Mazer Creative Services

Copyright © 2016, 2013, 2010, 2007 by Houghton Mifflin Harcourt Publishing Company. All rights reserved.

No part of this work may be reproduced or transmitted in any form or by any means, electronic or mechanical, including photocopying and recording, or by any information storage or retrieval system without the prior written permission of Houghton Mifflin Harcourt unless such copying is expressly permitted by federal copyright law. Address inquiries to Reference Permissions, Houghton Mifflin Harcourt, 222 Berkeley Street, Boston, MA 02116.

ISBN-13: 978-0-544-33663-6

Visit our websites: hmhco.com and ahdictionary.com

Library of Congress Cataloging-in-Publication Data

The American heritage first dictionary.
        p. cm.
    ISBN-13: 978-0-618-67766-5
    ISBN-10: 0-618-67766-6
 1. English language--Dictionaries, Juvenile. I. Title: First dictionary.
    II. Houghton Mifflin Company.
    PE1628.5.A43 2007
    423--dc22

                                        2005031529

Cover: drum Corbis/Ocean; **clownfish** Getty Images/Jeff Hunter; **Rubik's cube** dreamstime/Sr1688; **paint cans** Getty Images/Fuse; **crayons** Getty Images/Photodisc; **sailboat** Getty Images/C Squared Studios; **palette** Getty Images/Ryan McVay; **pinwheel** Corbis/Creativ Studio Heinemann, Westend61; **horse** Getty Images/Gigja Einarsdottir

Manufactured in the United States of America

1 2 3 4 5 6 7 8 9 10-DOW-21 20 19 18 17 16 15

4500530335

TABLE OF CONTENTS

What Is a Dictionary?

A dictionary is a book about words. The dictionary tells you how to spell a word and what a word means. It also shows you how to use a word in a sentence.

How to Find a Word

This dictionary has words in **ABC** order. You have to know the alphabet to find a word in the dictionary.

A B C D E F G H I J K L M N O P Q R S T U V W X Y Z
a b c d e f g h i j k l m n o p q r s t u v w x y z

All of the words that begin with **A** come before all the words that begin with **B** because **A** comes before **B** in the alphabet. And all the words that begin with **B** come before all the words that begin with **C** because **B** comes before **C** in the alphabet.

There are two **guidewords** at the top of most of the pages. They can help you find the word you are looking for. The guidewords are the first and last words you can look for on a page. The other words you can look for come after the first guideword and before the second guideword in **ABC** order. When the guidewords both begin with the same letter as the word you are looking for, look at the second letter of each guideword.

You can also find the letter that words on a page begin with by looking at the **alphabet border** at the bottom of the pages. The letter that every word on the page starts with is white and outlined in blue.

Looking For a Word

Let's look at the letter **D**. All the words that begin with the letter **D** are in **ABC** order. Look at each letter of each word. When words begin with the same letter, you must look at the next letter.

dam comes before **damp** because **damp** has more letters

d a m
d a m p

dark comes before **date** because **r** comes before **t** in the alphabet

d a r k
d a t e

dinner comes before **dinosaur** because **n** comes before **o** in the alphabet

d i n n e r
d i n o s a u r

dinosaur

Let's look up **dive**. Look for the pages that have words beginning with the letter **D**. Then find a guideword that begins with **di** and has a third letter near the end of the alphabet. The guidewords at the top of page 83 are **dish** and **do**. Now read the **D** words on the pages in **ABC** order. **Dive** comes in the ABC's after **distant** but before **divide**:

d i s t a n c e
d i s t a n t
d i v e
d i v i d e
d o

dive

To **dive** means to jump in the water with your hands and head first. Elsa learned how to swim and **dive** at the pool.

> A **diver** is a person who **dives.**

Dive and the other words you look up are in big purple letters. The page numbers are at the bottom corners of the pages.

What You Can Learn About a Word in the Dictionary

What does the dictionary tell you about **dive?**

- The dictionary spells the word.

- The dictionary tells you what the word means.

- The dictionary gives you examples of the word in a sentence.

- The dictionary often gives you a picture of the word.

- The dictionary sometimes has a note that tells you more about the word.

Sometimes a word will have more than one meaning. If you look up the word **orange**, you can see that it has two meanings. A number comes before each meaning when more than one meaning is given.

orange

1. An **orange** is a kind of fruit. It is about the size of a tennis ball. **Oranges** grow on orange trees. **2. Orange** is a color. Pumpkins and oranges are **orange.**

Different Forms of Words

Words can also have different forms. **Plurals** are words that name more than one thing. Most words add **-s** to name more than one.

books	hills	months

Words that end in **x, s, sh, ss,** or **ch** usually add **-es** to name more than one.

boxes	dishes	messes	watches

dishes

Words that end in **consonant-y** change the **y** to **i** and add **-es** to name more than one.

cherry	cherries	jelly	jellies

Some words have special spellings to name more than one. These special spellings are also shown after the meaning or meanings.

child	children	tooth	teeth
mouse	mice	woman	women

Special plurals are shown after the meaning or meanings.

Words that tell what people do also have different forms. **Plays** and **play** are forms of the word **play** that you use to tell about something happening now.

- José **plays** the piano.

- Maggie and Michael **play** in the park.

Played is the form you use to tell about something that happened in the past.

- Anna **played** basketball yesterday with her brothers.

It is usual to add **-ed** to words to show that something happened in the past.

The last **e** in some words is dropped before adding **-ed.** These words usually end with **vowel-consonant-e.**

care	cared	move	moved

The last consonant in some words is doubled before adding **-ed.** These words usually have a short vowel sound followed by one consonant. These forms are shown after the word meaning or meanings in the dictionary.

hop	hopped	nap	napped
hug	hugged	rub	rubbed

hug

Words that end in **consonant-y** change the **y** to **i** and add **-ed.** These forms are also shown after the word meaning or meanings. Some forms of short words like **tried** have their own place in the dictionary.

hurry	hurried	try	tried

Some words have special forms that are not usual. **Go** is a word like this.

- We like to **go** to the zoo.
- Adam **goes** to the zoo often.
- We **went** to the zoo last Saturday.
- We have **gone** to the zoo many times.

Goes, went, and **gone** are all special forms of the word **go.** In the dictionary, special forms like this are shown after the meaning or meanings and usually also have their own place in the dictionary. **Grow** is another word that has special forms.

grow

> **1.** To **grow** is to get bigger. Animals and plants **grow** as they get older. The bush has **grown** so big that I can't reach the top. **2.** To **grow** up means to become a woman or a man. When you **grow** up, you may be taller than your father. **—grew, grown**

If you look for **grew,** the dictionary will tell you that it is a form of **grow.**

grew

> **Grew** is a form of **grow.** Tomatoes **grew** in the garden last summer. Sharon always wanted to be a teacher, and when she **grew** up that is what she became.

Grown is also a special form of **grow,** but it comes right after **grow** in the dictionary. It is given after the meanings of **grow** but does not have its own place in the dictionary's list of words.

Words that describe things also have different forms. These words usually end in **-er** or **-est** to show that one thing is being compared to another.

- My hair is **short.**
- His hair is **shorter** than mine.
- Your hair is the **shortest** of all.

If a word ends in **e,** then only **-r** or **-st** are added to it.

gentle	gentler, gentlest
free	freer, freest

The last consonant in some words is doubled before adding **-er** or **-est.** These words usually have a short vowel sound followed by one consonant. These forms are shown after the word's meaning or meanings.

red	redder, reddest
thin	thinner, thinnest

thin

Words that end in **consonant-y** change the **y** to **i** and add **-er** or **-est.** These forms are also shown after the word's meaning or meanings.

angry	angrier, angriest
happy	happier, happiest

Some of these words have special forms that are not usual. **Good** is a word like this.

- Our team had a **good** score.
- Mimi's team had a **better** score.
- My sister's team had the **best** score. They won the game.

Special forms like these are shown after the word's meaning or meanings. They also have their own place in the dictionary's list of words.

team

Aa

a

A means one. Red is **a** color. Our friends will stay with us for **a** day or two.

able

Being **able** to do something means that you can do it. If you can run fast enough, you will be **able** to win a race.

about

1. **About** means what something tells. The people in this story are Lisa and David. The story is **about** Lisa and David. 2. **About** means nearly. That line is **about** four inches long.

■ above

above

Above means higher. We walked on the bridge **above** the river. ■

absent

Absent means not here. Two students were **absent** because they were sick.

accident

An **accident** is something you did not want or expect to happen. I broke my glasses by **accident.** Being careful can prevent **accidents.**

> The opposite of **absent** is **present.** The students who were **absent** from school yesterday are **present** today.

acorn

An **acorn** is a nut that grows on an oak tree. **Acorns** fall to the ground.

across

Across means from one side to the other. A bridge was built **across** the river. ■

■ across

act

To **act** means to behave in some way. Sometimes Alexander **acts** like a clown.

> People who **act** in plays and movies by pretending to be someone else are called **actors.** The job they do is called **acting.**

actually

Actually means really. Andrea didn't think she would like the party, but when she got there, she **actually** had fun.

add

1. To **add** means to put one thing together with another. Stevie drew a picture of his brother. Then he **added** a funny nose and glasses. **2.** To **add** also means to put numbers together. When you **add** three and one, you get four.

address

An **address** is the name of a place. You put an **address** on a letter to tell the post office where to send it. Some people keep **addresses** in a book.

adventure

An **adventure** is a new or unusual thing that people do. The first time that I went on a train was a big **adventure.** My friends and I like to read about **adventures** in the jungle.

afraid

To be **afraid** means to think something bad will happen to you. The kittens were **afraid** of the dog.

after

After means following. **After** the ball game, we went home. Vince ran fast when his brother came **after** him.

The opposite of **after** is **before**. I always brush my teeth **after** breakfast and **before** going to bed.

afternoon

Afternoon is the part of the day between noon and sunset. **Afternoons** are short in winter and long in summer.

again

Again means one more time. Timmy went skiing on Friday. He went **again** on Sunday.

against

1. Against means touching the side of something. Kathy put her bicycle **against** the wall. **2.** To be **against** someone means to try to beat him or her at a game. Two teams play **against** each other. ■

■ **against**

age

The **age** of something is how old it is. Debra is seven years old. She is tall for her **age.**

ago

Ago means in the past. Dinosaurs lived a long time **ago.**

agree

To **agree** means to share the same idea. Sarah and Kate **agreed** to take turns.

air

Air is a gas that people breathe. **Air** is all around us. We cannot see it, but we can feel it when the wind blows.

airplane

An **airplane** is a large machine. **Airplanes** have wings and fly in the air. **Airplanes** carry people from one place to another. ■

■airplane

Airplanes can fly because their wings have a special shape. When an **airplane** is moving very fast, the air pushes its wings up and lifts it off the ground. **Airplanes** have engines that make them move forward.

airport

An **airport** is a place where airplanes fly up into the air and land. **Airports** are usually near cities.

alike

Alike means almost the same. My hat and yours are **alike,** but mine is red, and yours is blue. ■

■alike

alive

Alive means living and growing. Animals and plants are **alive** until they die.

all

All means each one or each part. **All** horses have four legs. Beth ate **all** of her breakfast.

alligator

An **alligator** is a very large reptile. It has short legs, a long tail, and strong jaws with sharp teeth. **Alligators** live in rivers and swamps where the weather is warm.

allow

To **allow** means to let someone do something. Our parents **allow** us to ride our bicycles on the sidewalk.

almost

Almost means nearly. Marcel's birthday is next week. He is **almost** six years old.

alone

Alone means by yourself. Maggie likes to be **alone** in her room. ■

■ alone

along

1. Along means in a line with. The flowers grow **along** the fence. **2. Along** also means together. Donna went to the store and her brother went **along** with her. ■

aloud

Aloud means so that other people can hear. Camille read a story **aloud** to her friends.

■ along

alphabet

An **alphabet** is the letters that people write with. Our **alphabet** is A, B, C, D, E, F, G, H, I, J, K, L, M, N, O, P, Q, R, S, T, U, V, W, X, Y, Z.

already

Already means before this. Abdul missed the bus today. When he got to the bus stop, it had **already** gone.

also

Also shows something added. Gracie plays the piano. She can **also** play a trombone.

always

Always means every time. Manuel is never late for school. He **always** comes on time.

am

Am is a form of **be**. It is used with the word I. "Are you six years old?" "No, I **am** seven."

amount

An **amount** is how much there is of something. An elephant needs a large **amount** of food. A mosquito makes a small **amount** of noise.

> The **amount** of money that we give when we buy something is called the **price**. The **price** of that hat is ten dollars.

an

An is a form of **a**. It is used before words that begin with A, E, I, O, and before many words that begin with U. A new pen writes better than **an** old one.

anchor

An **anchor** is a heavy object that helps a ship stay in one place. **Anchors** come in many different shapes. ■

■ anchor

and

And joins two things together. Three **and** two are five. Bonnie **and** Jane are best friends.

angry

To be **angry** means to feel very upset with someone. Bill's dad was **angry** because somcone threw a ball through the window. —**angrier, angriest**

> Another word for **angry** is **mad.** When people are **angry,** they sometimes show **anger** by shouting. If there is **anger** in people's voices, they are speaking **angrily.**

animal

An **animal** is a living thing that is not a plant and can usually be seen without a microscope. **Animals** can move and eat plants or other **animals**. Dogs, cats, fish, birds, and insects are all **animals.**

A B C D E F G H I J K L M

another

Another means one more. Lexi ate a carrot. She liked it so much she ate **another** one.

answer

An **answer** is what you give when someone asks a question. The teacher asked some questions. Ari knew the right **answers.**

ant

An **ant** is an insect. **Ants** live in large groups in trees or in tunnels in the ground. ■

■ ant

any

1. **Any** means that it does not matter which one. Take **any** seat you like. 2. **Any** also means some. Do you want **any** of my sandwich?

anybody

Anybody means any person. Steven didn't know **anybody** at the party.

anyone

Anyone means anybody. Invite **anyone** you like for dinner.

anything

Anything means any thing. My brother will eat **anything.**

anyway

Anyway means that something doesn't matter. Diego's foot hurt, but he tried to walk **anyway.**

anywhere

Anywhere means in any place. Sit **anywhere** you like.

apart

1. **Apart** means away from each other. A chicken's toes are far **apart**. 2. **Apart** also means in pieces. Mario likes to take things **apart** to see how they work.

> The opposite of **apart** is **together.** My brother took the puzzle **apart,** but I put it back **together.**

apartment

An **apartment** is a place to live that is part of a bigger building. **Apartments** have one or more rooms.

ape

An **ape** is a kind of animal. **Apes** are like people in many ways. They have long arms and no tail and can stand up straight. ■

■ **ape**

appear

To **appear** means that something can be seen that was not seen before. The magician **appeared** when everyone in the audience sat down.

appetite

Appetite means how hungry you are. My sister has a big **appetite** after she plays soccer. We lose our **appetites** if we eat snacks before meals.

apple

An **apple** is a kind of fruit. **Apples** have red, yellow, or green skin.

April

April is a month of the year. It has thirty days. **April** comes after March and before May.

apron

An **apron** is something you wear to protect your clothes. **Aprons** are useful when you paint or cook. ■

■ apron

aquarium

1. An **aquarium** is a glass box or bowl that is filled with water. People who have fish at home keep them in **aquariums. 2.** An **aquarium** is also a place to look at fish and other animals that live in water. We saw sharks and sea turtles at the **aquarium.** ■

■ aquarium

are

Are is a form of **be.** It is used with you, we, and they. "Where can my shoes be?" "They **are** in the closet."

area

An **area** is a space. The kitchen is an **area** where we cook food. There are two **areas** of the library where we can talk.

aren't

Aren't is a short way to say **are not.** Bananas **aren't** blue. They are yellow.

arm

An **arm** is a part of the body. It is between the shoulder and the hand. Amy used both **arms** to carry wood for the fireplace.

armor

Armor is a hard shell that protects someone's body in a fight. Knights often wore **armor.** ■

■ armor

army

An **army** is a large group of people who protect a country. —**armies**

around

Around means on all sides. Ben's uncle built a fence **around** his yard. Sol looked **around** the room for his shoes. ■

■ around

arrive

To **arrive** is to come to a place. Eric ran all the way to school so he would **arrive** on time. My cousin mailed me a letter, but it never **arrived.**

arrow

1. An **arrow** is a stick with a point at one end. You can shoot **arrows** from a bow. **2.** An **arrow** is a symbol. It is used to point in one direction. ■

■ arrow

art

Art is something made to be beautiful. Pictures, poems, and music are kinds of **art.**

artist

An **artist** is a person who makes art. You can see the work of many **artists** in a museum. ∎

∎ **artist**

> You can also find art outside. Some **artists** paint pictures on buildings in their neighborhoods. Other **artists** make statues for parks.

as

As means in the same way. Dee and Kenny are the same height. Dee is **as** tall **as** Kenny.

ash

Ash is what is left after something burns. It is a soft, gray powder. Ray watched his father clean the **ashes** out of the fireplace.

ashamed

Ashamed means feeling bad because of something you did. I felt **ashamed** when my noise woke up the baby.

ask

1. To **ask** means to say a question. The teacher **asks,** "Who knows the answer?" **2.** To **ask** for something means to say that you want it. Oliver **asked** for more soup because he was hungry.

asleep

Asleep means sleeping. The puppies were **asleep** until a loud noise woke them up. ■

■ **asleep**

> The opposite of **asleep** is **awake.** I thought the baby was **asleep,** but he is **awake** now and wants to eat.

astronaut

An **astronaut** is a person who goes into space. Some **astronauts** have walked on the moon. ■

■ **astronaut**

at

1. At tells where a person or thing is. Elena went to school this morning. She is **at** school now. **2. At** tells when something happens. School begins **at** nine o'clock. **3. At** also means toward. Jerry looked **at** the sky to watch for falling stars.

ate

Ate is a form of **eat.** Chris eats three meals every day. Last night he **ate** pizza for supper.

attention

Attention means looking and listening with care. The crowd watched the magician do tricks with cards. They were interested in what he did. The magician had the crowd's **attention.**

attic

An **attic** is a room at the top of a house. People use their **attics** to store things they don't use every day. ∎

∎ attic

audience

An **audience** is a group of people who watch a show. Neil's parents were in the **audience** when he performed in the school play. I don't like noisy **audiences** when I go to the movics.

August

August is a month of the year. It has 31 days. **August** comes after July and before September.

> **August** comes during the summer. Can you find **August** on a calendar?

aunt

An **aunt** is the sister of your mother or father. An **aunt** is also the wife of your uncle. A person can have many **aunts** and uncles.

author

An **author** is a person who writes a story, a play, or a poem. Many **authors** write books for children.

automobile

Automobile is another word for **car.** People drive **automobiles** on roads. ∎

∎ **automobile**

autumn

Autumn is a season. It comes after summer and before winter. School starts in **autumn.** Another word for **autumn** is **fall.**

> **Autumn** begins in September and ends in December. The leaves on some trees turn colors in **autumn.**

awake

Awake means not asleep. Sanjay tried to stay **awake** all night. ■

■ awake

away

1. **Away** shows distance. The ocean is three miles **away** from here. 2. **Away** also shows direction. Bryan walked **away** from the house and toward the street.

> To give something **away** means to give it to someone else. Dolly gave her bicycle **away** to her younger cousin.

awful

Awful means very bad or terrible. When you have a cold, you feel **awful.**

ax

An **ax** is a tool. It has a flat, sharp metal head and a long handle. **Axes** are used to cut wood. ■

■ ax

Bb

baby

A **baby** is a very young child. **Babies** eat and sleep a lot. —**babies** ∎

∎ **baby**

back

1. The **back** is a part of the body. We like to lie on our **backs** and look up at the sky. **2. Back** is the opposite of **front.** The caboose is at the **back** of the train. **3.** To go **back** or come **back** means to return. Students go **back** to school every fall. We came **back** to our apartment after visiting our grandmother.

backpack

A **backpack** is a cloth bag that you wear on your back so you can carry things. Most of the children in our class have **backpacks.** ∎

∎ **backpack**

backward

1. Backward means in the opposite order. "Saw" spelled **backward** is "was." **2. Backward** also means toward the back. Kendra looked **backward** at Max in the wagon behind her. ∎

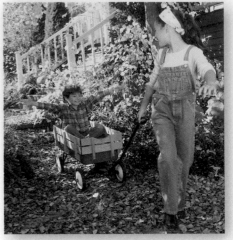

■ **backward**

bad

1. Bad means not good. We couldn't eat the fruit because it was **bad. 2. Bad** also means not nice. Tammy is angry. She is shouting at everybody. Tammy is in a **bad** mood. **3. Bad** can mean able to hurt. Too much candy is **bad** for your teeth. **4. Bad** can also mean serious. Jody had a **bad** cold, so she stayed in bed.

bag

A **bag** is used to hold things. It can be made of paper, plastic, cloth, or leather. Jason brings his lunch to school in a paper **bag.** ∎

■ **bag**

bake

To **bake** is to cook in an oven. John **baked** his pie for an hour.

A person whose job is **baking** is called a **baker.** Some foods that are **baked** are sold in a special store called a **bakery.**

ball

A **ball** is an object that is used in sports and games. Most **balls** are round. They roll or bounce easily so players can throw, kick, or hit them. ∎

balloon

A **balloon** is a kind of bag filled with gas. Some **balloons** are huge and can carry people high into the sky. ∎

ballot

A **ballot** is a piece of paper used to vote for someone or something. Yesterday we had an election to pick our class play. Our teacher collected the **ballots** after we voted.

banana

A **banana** is a kind of fruit. **Bananas** have a long, curved shape and yellow skin.

band

A **band** is a group of people who play music together. Everyone at the parade watched the marching **bands.**

bank

A **bank** is a safe place to keep money. A **bank** can be a small box or jar that you keep at home. **Banks** are also buildings where people can store or borrow money.

A **piggy bank** is a little **bank** shaped like a **pig.** It is used to hold different kinds of coins.

∎ **ball**

∎ **balloon**

barber

A **barber** is a person who gives haircuts. **Barbers** also cut beards. ■

■ barber

bare

Bare means not covered with anything. Luis did not have any socks or shoes on. He was walking around with **bare** feet.

bark

Bark is the skin of a tree. It is thick and rough. **Bark** covers the trunk and the branches.

barn

A **barn** is a kind of building on a farm. The **barn** is where the farm animals stay at night. Farm machines and food for the animals are kept in **barns** too. ■

■ barn

barrel

A **barrel** is used to hold things. It is made of wood or metal. The top and the bottom of **barrels** are flat circles. Some **barrels** have curved sides.

base

1. A **base** is the bottom part of something. The statue in the park has a square **base.** The statue stands on its **base. 2.** A **base** is a place where you are safe in a game. In baseball you try to run to all four **bases.**

baseball

1. Baseball is a sport. It is played by two teams with a bat and a ball.
2. A **baseball** is the hard, white ball used in a game of baseball. Our team hit two **baseballs** over the fence. ∎

∎ baseball

Baseball is played on a special field that is shaped like a diamond. Each team has nine players.

basement

A **basement** is the bottom room of a building. Many families store clothes, books, and other things in their **basements.**

basket

A **basket** is used to hold things. It can be made of strips of wood or grass. **Baskets** are often shaped like bowls and have handles.

basketball

1. Basketball is a sport. It is played by two teams with a large ball and two goals that look like baskets. **2.** A **basketball** is the large rubber ball used in a game of basketball. We keep the **basketballs** in the shed. ∎

∎ basketball

bat

1. A **bat** is a long, thick piece of wood, metal, or plastic. **Bats** are used to hit a ball. **2.** A **bat** is a small animal. It has big wings and a body like a mouse. **Bats** sleep during the day and fly around at night. ■

■ **bat**

In baseball, the player who hits the ball with a **bat** is called the **batter.**

bath

A **bath** is a time to sit and wash your body with water. We gave the dog a **bath** in the back yard. It took a long time to get him clean. ■

bathroom

A **bathroom** is a room where you wash yourself. In Lee's house there are two **bathrooms.**

bathtub

A **bathtub** is used to hold water for a bath. People sit in **bathtubs** to take baths.

be

1. To **be** means to live or fill space. A person cannot **be** in two places at the same time. **2.** To **be** tells what something is like. Dogs can **be** big or small. Tomorrow will **be** sunny. **—am, are, is, was, been**

■ **bath**

beach

A **beach** is an area of sand at the edge of a lake or an ocean. **Beaches** are part of the shore. ■

■ beach

beak

A **beak** is part of a bird's mouth. It is hard and ends in a point. **Beaks** can be large or small. ■

■ beak

bear

A **bear** is a large animal. It has thick fur and strong claws. Many **bears** sleep all winter. ■

beard

A **beard** is the hair on a man's chin and cheeks. The elves in the story all had long, white **beards.**

■ bear

beat

1. To **beat** means to hit. Rich **beats** a drum when he marches in the parade. **2.** To **beat** eggs means to mix them up. You have to **beat** eggs to make a cake. Fred's father **beat** the eggs before he fried them in the pan. **3.** To **beat** also means to win a race or game against someone. Our team has lost all its games this year. We have not **beaten** anyone. —beat, beaten

beaver

A **beaver** is a kind of animal. It has a flat tail and large, strong front teeth. **Beavers** build dams across streams. The dams are made of logs, sticks, and mud. ■

■ **beaver**

became

Became is a form of **become.** Marcie wants to become a pilot one day. Her father **became** a pilot many years ago.

because

Because tells why something happens. Mariah ate an apple **because** she was hungry. People read books **because** they want to learn.

become

To **become** means to change into something. A caterpillar changes into a moth. It **becomes** a moth inside a cocoon. I mopped the floor because it had **become** dirty. —**became, become**

bed

A **bed** is a kind of furniture. People sleep in **beds.**

bee

A **bee** is a kind of insect. It can fly and likes flowers. Some **bees** make honey. ■

■ **bee**

A **B** C D E F G H I J K L M

beef

Beef is a kind of meat. It comes from cattle. Hamburger is made from **beef.**

been

Been is a form of **be**. Van wants to be a farmer when he grows up. His parents have **been** farmers for many years.

beetle

A **beetle** is a kind of insect. It has two pairs of wings. **Beetles** have hard wings on the outside that cover soft wings used for flying.

before

1. Before means that something comes first. Anita washes her hands **before** she eats. **2. Before** also means in the past. Alice rode in a plane for the first time last week. She had never been on a plane **before.**

begin

To **begin** means to start. Grass **begins** to grow in the spring. The birds **began** to sing when the rain stopped. We had **begun** to paint the house when it started to rain. —**began, begun**

> When something **begins,** we say it is at the **beginning.** At the **beginning** of fall, the leaves **begin** to change color.

behave

To **behave** means to do things in some way. Daniel **behaves** well when his family goes to a restaurant.

behind

Behind means at the back. Julio was first in line. All the other children stood **behind** him. ∎

∎ **behind**

believe

1. To **believe** means to think something is true. Anna **believes** everything her sister says. **2.** To make **believe** means to act in a way that is not real. Faye likes to make **believe** she is a doctor.

bell

A **bell** is a hollow piece of metal that rings when you hit or shake it. When the **bells** rang, the horses began the race. ∎

∎ **bell**

A **doorbell** is a button on the door of a house or apartment. The button rings a **bell** when you push it.

belong

1. To **belong** means to feel good in a place. Fish **belong** in the water. **2.** To **belong** also means to be owned by somebody. That shirt **belongs** to Gordon. It is his shirt.

below

Below means under. Roots grow **below** the ground.

The opposite of **below** is **above.**

A **B** C D E F G H I J K L M

belt

A **belt** is a kind of clothes that you wear around the middle of your body. **Belts** are long and thin. They are usually made of leather, cloth, or plastic.

bench

A **bench** is a long seat for two or more people. We sit on **benches** when we wait for the bus.

bend

To **bend** means to make a curve. Eliza **bends** over backward and touches the ground. I **bent** my knees and jumped. Sara's glasses were **bent** after she sat on them. —**bent** ∎

∎ **bend**

berry

A **berry** is a small fruit. **Berries** grow on bushes. Some kinds of **berries** are good to eat, but other kinds make you sick. —**berries**

beside

Beside means at the side of. Chrissy and Jaclyn are sitting together. Chrissy sits **beside** Jaclyn, and Jaclyn sits **beside** Chrissy. ∎

best

Best means better than any other. Susie's **best** friend is the friend she likes most.

∎ **beside**

better

Better means very good, but not the best. Edie swims **better** than Mark. Aviva likes warm days **better** than cold ones.

The opposite of **better** is **worse.** Do you feel any **better,** or is your cold **worse** today?

between

Between means in the middle. The letters **c a t** spell "cat." The **a** is **between** the **c** and the **t.** Nadine stands **between** Allen and Jordan. ■

■**between**

beyond

Beyond means on the other side of something. Luana climbed over a fence and into the field. She went **beyond** the fence.

bib

A **bib** is a piece of cloth or plastic that is worn under the chin. Babies wear **bibs** to protect their clothes when they eat.

bicycle

A **bicycle** is a kind of machine. **Bicycles** have two big wheels, two handles, and a seat. You make a **bicycle** go by moving your legs. ■

■**bicycle**

big

Big means not small. Whales and elephants are **big**. **Large** is another word for **big**. —**bigger, biggest**

bill

1. A **bill** is a bird's beak. Ducks and some birds have big **bills. 2.** A **bill** is also a piece of paper money. A dollar **bill** is equal to one dollar. **3.** A **bill** is also a piece of paper that tells you what you must pay for something. Kim's mother pays the electricity **bill** every month. ■

■ bill

bird

A **bird** is a kind of animal. It has two wings and is covered with feathers. Robins, chickens, eagles, and ostriches are all **birds.** Most **birds** can fly.

A **birdhouse** is a little box where birds can rest and build their nests. **Birdhouses** do not have doors. The birds enter and leave through small holes.

birth

Birth is the moment when a person is born. Most **births** happen in hospitals.

birthday

Your **birthday** is the day of your birth. Lynne's **birthday** is on November 8. **Birthdays** are fun.

bit

1. **Bit** is a form of **bite.** Ed **bit** into an apple. **2. Bit** also means a small amount. Ted put a **bit** of pepper into his soup.

bite

1. To **bite** means to cut with your teeth. Darius **bites** into his apple. Then he chews and swallows. I had **bitten** into the apple when I lost my tooth. **2.** A **bite** is a small amount you can cut off with your teeth. Aliyah has taken some **bites** of her sandwich. She will eat the rest later. — **bit, bitten** ∎

∎ **bite**

bitter

Bitter means having a sharp taste. Debbie tasted the medicine and made a face. It was very **bitter.**

black

Black is a color. It is very dark. This sentence is printed in **black** ink.

> A **blackboard** is a smooth, **black board** in a classroom. The teacher writes lessons on the **blackboard** with chalk.

blacksmith

A **blacksmith** is a person who makes things out of iron. **Blacksmiths** make horseshoes. ∎

∎ **blacksmith**

blanket

A **blankct** is a large, soft cloth. People cover themselves with **blankets** to keep warm. ■

■**blanket**

blend

To **blend** means to mix together. Kwami **blended** the milk and eggs when he made the birthday cake.

> A **blender** is a small machine used to **blend** different foods. What kind of drink can you make by mixing ice cream and milk in a **blender?**

blew

Blew is a form of **blow.** Today it is calm, but yesterday the wind **blew** hard.

blind

Blind means not able to see. A person who cannot see is **blind.**

block

1. A **block** is a piece of wood, plastic, or stone. It has straight sides and is usually shaped like a square or a rectangle. Children play with **blocks.**
2. A **block** is an area of a city. It has four streets for sides. Evan and Rosic walked around the **block.** ■

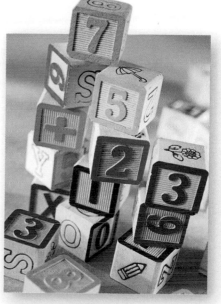

■**block**

blood

Blood is a red liquid inside our bodies. Nobody can live without **blood.**

blossom

A **blossom** is a flower. The **blossoms** on apple trees are white or pink.

blow

1. To **blow** means to push with air. The wind **blows** the leaves around on the ground. Judy **blew** bubbles into the air. 2. To **blow** means to make a sound by pushing air. We heard the whistle **blow.** It has **blown** five times. —**blew, blown** ■

■ **blow**

blue

Blue is a color. The sky is **blue** when no clouds are in it during the day.

> **Blueberries, bluebirds, bluefish,** and **blue sharks** all got their names because they are the color **blue.**

board

1. A **board** is a long, flat piece of wood. **Boards** are used to build houses. 2. A **board** is also a flat surface on which a game is played. Checkers are placed on a **board.** ■

■ **board**

A B C D E F G H I J K L M

boat

A **boat** carries people and things on the water. **Boats** can be made of wood, metal, or plastic. Most **boats** have engines to make them move. Some **boats** have sails. ∎

∎ **boat**

body

A **body** is all the parts of a person or animal. Human **bodies** have a brain, a heart, and two lungs.
—**bodies**

boil

To **boil** is to change from a liquid into a gas. When water **boils** it makes bubbles, and steam rises into the air. ∎

∎ **boil**

bone

A **bone** is a hard part of the body. People and most animals have **bones** under their skin and muscles. ∎

book

A **book** is a group of pages. The pages have words and sometimes pictures on them. The pages are held together with thread or glue. Dictionaries are **books.**

∎ **bone**

boot

A **boot** is a large shoe. **Boots** are made of rubber or leather. Most people wear **boots** in the rain or snow. ■

■ **boot**

border

A **border** is an edge. It is a line where one area ends and another begins. We planted flowers around the **borders** of the garden. The **border** between two states is sometimes a river. ■

■ **border**

born

Born means brought into life. Terry is one day old. She was **born** yesterday.

borrow

To **borrow** means to use something that belongs to somebody else. You can use it for a small amount of time. Wally **borrowed** a book from the library. He has to return it in two weeks.

The opposite of **borrow** is **lend.** Pedro **borrowed** five dollars from Carmen. This means that Carmen **lent** five dollars to Pedro.

A **B** C D E F G H I J K L M

both

Both means two together. Naomi uses both hands to eat a sandwich. ∎

∎ both

bother

To **bother** means to give trouble. The mosquitoes in the yard **bothered** us.

bottle

A **bottle** is used to hold liquids. It is made of glass or plastic. Shoshana got two **bottles** of juice at the store.

bottom

The **bottom** is the lowest part of something. A tree has leaves at the top. It has roots at the **bottom.**

bought

Bought is a form of **buy.** Most people buy food at a store. Fran **bought** some this morning.

boulder

A **boulder** is a very big rock. **Boulders** are found on the ground or in the soil. ∎

bounce

To **bounce** means to move back after hitting something. The ball **bounced** when it hit the street.

∎ **boulder**

bow

1. A **bow** is a curved piece of wood. A piece of string is tied to the ends of it. **Bows** are used to shoot arrows. **2.** A **bow** is also a knot made with ribbon or string. It has two circles and two ends. I tie my shoes with a **bow. 3.** A **bow** can also be a thin, long stick used to play some instruments. A violin is played with a **bow. 4.** To **bow** means to bend the body forward. In the story the knight **bows** to the king. ■

■ **bow**

> A **bow** that you use rhymes with **go** and **blow**. When you **bow** down, **bow** rhymes with **cow**.

bowl

A **bowl** is a kind of dish that is round and hollow. People can eat soup, cereal, and fruit out of **bowls.** ■

bowling

Bowling is a sport. **Bowling** is played with a heavy ball and pieces of wood shaped like bottles.

■ **bowl**

box

A **box** is used to hold things. It has four sides and a flat bottom. Some **boxes** have tops too.

boy

A **boy** is a male child. **Boys** grow up to be men.

braces

Braces are thin, metal wires that a dentist puts on your teeth. **Braces** are worn to make your teeth straight. ■

■ **braces**

braid

A **braid** is a strip of hair. It is made by dividing the hair into three parts and placing each part of loose hair over one of the other parts. My sister wears her hair in **braids** every day. ■

brain

The **brain** is a part of the body. It is inside your head. The **brain** makes our arms, legs, eyes, and ears work. People think with their **brains.**

■ **braid**

branch

A **branch** is a part of a tree. **Branches** grow out from the trunk of a tree. Leaves grow from the **branches.** ■

brave

Brave means without fear. The knight in the story was very **brave.** He did not run away from the dragon.

■ **branch**

bread

Bread is a kind of food. It is made with flour and water and other things mixed together. **Bread** is baked in an oven. ■

■ **bread**

> Some kinds of **bread** taste sweet, like **banana bread.** It is made from flour, bananas, sugar, and chopped nuts.

break

1. To **break** means to divide into pieces. If a window **breaks,** it becomes pieces of glass. A window **breaks** when a ball goes through it. **2.** To **break** also means not to work. If a machine **breaks,** someone has to fix it. Then it will work again. **3.** To **break** the law means to do something against the law. Someone who robs a bank is **breaking** the law. —**broke, broken**

breakfast

Breakfast is a meal. It is the first meal of the day. At **breakfast** Meghan usually eats cereal with milk.

> Some people have eggs for **breakfast.** Other people like pancakes. What is your favorite **breakfast** food?

breath

A **breath** is an amount of air. The air comes through our mouths and noses and into our bodies. The doctor asked Aisha to take deep **breaths.**

breathe

To **breathe** is to take in breaths of air. Jeff **breathes** fast when he runs.

breeze

A **breeze** is a gentle wind. Rhonda enjoys the **breezes** when she goes on a boat.

brick

A **brick** is a very hard piece of clay shaped like a rectangle. Many houses and other buildings are made of **bricks.** ■

■ brick

bridge

A **bridge** is used to cross from one side to the other. **Bridges** are often built over water. ■

bright

Bright means giving a lot of light. The sun is very **bright.**

bring

To **bring** means to take something with you. When Chantal goes to a birthday party, she **brings** a present. —**brought**

■ bridge

broke

Broke is a form of **break**. It is easy for glass to break. Yesterday I dropped a glass. It **broke** into pieces.

broken

Broken is a form of **break.** The glass dish was **broken** into many pieces. The cat knocked it off the table.

broom

A **broom** is a kind of tool. It is a long stick with straw tied to one end. Most people use **brooms** to clean dirt off floors. ■

■ broom

brother

A **brother** is a boy who has the same parents as somebody else. Dave and his **brothers** walk home from school together.

brought

Brought is a form of **bring.** Christine **brought** her dogs when she came to visit.

brown

Brown is a color. Toast and chocolate are **brown.** Some people have **brown** hair.

brush

1. A **brush** is a kind of tool. It looks like a small broom. Some **brushes** are used to paint with. Other **brushes** are used to clean things. 2. To **brush** means to clean with a brush. Alan **brushes** his teeth every morning and every night. ■

■ brush

A **B** C D E F G H I J K L M

bubble

A **bubble** is a round shape with air in it. **Bubbles** can be made in soap and water. **Bubbles** are also made when water boils. ∎

∎ **bubble**

bucket

A **bucket** is used to carry things. It can be made of wood, metal, or plastic. It has a flat, round bottom and a handle. **Buckets** are often used to carry water.

bug

1. A **bug** is an insect. When we go on picnics, **bugs** crawl on our blanket.
2. To **bug** means to bother. The noise from the television **bugs** me sometimes when I am trying to read.

∎ **build**

build

To **build** means to put together. Everyone joined together to **build** a new house. —**built** ∎

building

A **building** is a place that has been built. Houses, hotels, schools, and barns are all **buildings.** ∎

built

Built is a form of **build**. The carpenters **built** that school in one summer.

∎ **building**

■ bull

bull

A **bull** is a large, male animal. It lives on a farm. **Bulls** have horns and eat grass. ■

bulldozer

A **bulldozer** is a very strong tractor. **Bulldozers** push dirt and rocks from one place to another.

bump

1. To **bump** means to hit against something. Duncan **bumped** his head on the table by accident. **2.** A **bump** is a round place that sticks out. The road had a lot of **bumps** in it.

burn

To **burn** is to be changed by fire. We like to watch the logs **burn** in the fireplace. Gasoline and other things are **burned** to make energy and give off heat.

bus

A **bus** is a machine. It has four wheels, an engine, and many seats and windows. **Buses** carry many people from one place to another. ■

■ bus

A **school bus** takes children to and from school.

A B C D E F G H I J K L M

■ bush

bush

A **bush** is a plant. It has many branches and leaves. **Bushes** are not as big as trees. Flowers grow on some **bushes.** ■

busy

Busy means doing many things. Abby has a lot of work to do. She is very **busy** today. **—busier, busiest**

but

1. **But** is used to put two opposite ideas together. The weather was cold yesterday, **but** today it is warm. 2. **But** means except. Tina, Jed, and Liam liked the new car. Albert did not like it. Everybody **but** Albert liked the new car.

butter

Butter is a kind of food. It is made from cow's milk. **Butter** is soft and yellow. Some people eat it on bread.

> **Buttercups** are yellow flowers that have the same color as **butter.** They grow in marshes and meadows.

butterfly

A **butterfly** is kind of insect. It has four thin wings. These wings can have many colors. Some caterpillars change into **butterflies.**
—butterflies ■

■ butterfly

button

A **button** is a small, round piece of wood or plastic. **Buttons** are sewn on clothes. They keep parts of clothes together. ■

■**button**

buy

To **buy** means to give money for something. You can **buy** all kinds of food at a supermarket. —**bought**

buzz

To **buzz** is to make the sound of a bee. The bees **buzzed** around the flowers.

by

1. By shows who or what does something. The question was asked **by** Dana. **2. By** also shows how something is done. We made a garden **by** planting some flowers. **3. By** can mean before some time. Nicki is usually hungry **by** the time she gets home from school.

A B C D E F G H I J K L M

Cc

caboose

A **caboose** is the last car on a train. Trains that have **cabooses** usually carry things that people buy and sell. ■

cactus

A **cactus** is a kind of plant. **Cactuses** grow in hot, dry places. They have thick stems and very thin leaves. —**cactuses, cacti** ■

cage

A **cage** is a kind of box. The sides are made of metal or wood poles. Birds and other animals are sometimes kept in **cages.**

cake

A **cake** is a kind of food. It is made of flour, sugar, eggs, and milk. It is baked in an oven. **Cakes** are sweet.

■ caboose

■ cactus

calendar

A **calendar** is a group of pages that show the days, weeks, and months in a year. Susie and her friends make **calendars** at school when the new year begins.

calf

1. A **calf** is a young cow or bull. I saw a cow and her **calf** at the country fair. **2.** A **calf** is also the back part of your leg that is below your knee. My **calf** hurts sometimes after a long walk. —**calves**

call

1. To **call** means to say in a loud voice. I heard the teacher **call** my name.
2. To **call** means to use the telephone. James **calls** his friends on the telephone when he wants to play. **3.** To **call** means to give a name to. Anne **calls** her doll Emily. **4.** A **call** is a loud sound made by a person. The police heard someone's **call** for help. ■

■ **call**

calm

1. Calm means quiet and not moving. The wind is **calm** today. **2. Calm** means quiet and not bothered. Tim is very **calm** about his first day at school.

calves

Calves means more than one **calf.** They let us feed the **calves** at the farm we visited last week.

came

Came is a form of come. Bill came into the kitchen to eat supper. Our neighbors came outside to see the rainbow.

camel

A camel is a large animal. It has long legs and a long neck. It also has one or two humps on its back. Camels can carry people and things across the desert. ■

■ camel

camera

A camera is a small machine that makes pictures. People often take cameras along on their vacations.

camp

1. A camp is a place where people live outside for a short time. They sleep in tents or huts and cook over a fire. Our family goes to a camp in the woods every summer. 2. A camp is also a place where children play in the summer. Sheryl goes to camp during the day. Her older brother goes away to soccer camp for two weeks. 3. To camp means to live in a camp. Saul and his family camped near the lake. ■

■ camp

A **campground** is a place for **camping.** Some **campgrounds** have tables for picnics, trails for walking, and lakes for swimming and fishing.

can

1. A **can** is used to hold things. It is usually made of metal and comes all in one piece. You can buy paint in **cans. 2. Can** means to be able to. Kelly **can** run fast. Sal **can** speak two languages. —**could** ■

■ can

candle

A **candle** is a stick of wax with a piece of string in it. **Candles** make light when they burn.

candy

Candy is a kind of food. It is made of sugar and is very sweet. **Candies** can be made with chocolate, nuts, or fruit. —**candies**

> **Candy apples** are **apples** covered with melted **candy.**

cannot

Cannot means to be not able to. A dog can run, but it **cannot** fly.

canoe

A **canoe** is a kind of small boat. It is long, narrow, and light. **Canoes** go through the water very quietly. ■

■ canoe

can't

Can't is a short way to say **cannot.** Fish can swim, but they **can't** talk.

cap

A **cap** is a kind of soft hat. People who play baseball wear **caps. Caps** made of wool keep your head warm. ■

cape

A **cape** is a kind of clothes that you wear over your shoulders. **Capes** have no sleeves. ■

■ cap

capital

1. A **capital** is a city where a state or country has its government. Dominic knows the **capitals** of all of the states.
2. **Capital** is also a way that you write letters of the alphabet. The letters **A** and **B** are **capital** letters. The letters **a** and **b** are small letters.

captain

A **captain** is a person who leads other people. Firefighters, sailors, and sports teams all have **captains.**

■ cape

car

1. A **car** is a machine. It has four wheels, an engine, seats, and windows. People travel over roads in **cars.**
2. A **car** is also one part of a train. It is like a big room on wheels. Most trains have many **cars.**

> Babies and young children sit in **car seats** when they ride in **cars.**

card

1. A **card** is a small piece of thick paper. It is shaped like a rectangle. **Cards** have numbers and pictures on them. People play games with **cards. 2.** A **card** is also a small, folded piece of paper with a message on it. You send **cards** to people in the mail. Jada got a **card** on Valentine's Day.

care

1. Care means a slow, steady way of doing things so that nothing bad will happen. You have to handle knives and other tools with **care. 2.** To take **care** of means to keep someone or something safe. Parents take **care** of their children. **3.** To **care** means to have a special interest in something. Nancy **cares** about her pets.

careful

To be **careful** means to use care. Juanita is very **careful** when she crosses the street.

carnival

A **carnival** is a place where people go to have fun. You can win prizes and buy food at **carnivals.** Many **carnivals** have rides and games.

carousel

A **carousel** is a kind of ride you see at a park or fair. It is sometimes called a **merry-go-round. Carousels** have seats shaped like horses and other animals that go around in a circle. ■

■ carousel

carpenter

A **carpenter** is a person who builds things with wood. **Carpenters** also fix the wood parts of houses and ships.

Carpenters use many different tools. They use saws to cut pieces of wood, hammers and nails to hold them together, and ladders to reach high places.

carriage

A **carriage** is a box on wheels that is used to move people from one placc to another. Some **carriages** are pulled by horses. ■

■ **carriage**

A **baby carriage** is a **carriage** that is used to move a **baby** from one place to another. It has four wheels.

carrot

A **carrot** is a kind of vegetable. It is long and orange. **Carrots** grow under the ground. ■

■ **carrot**

carry

To **carry** means to hold something and take it somewhere. Suzie **carries** a big basket of apples. —**carries, carried** ■

cartoon

A **cartoon** is a kind of picture. It is drawn by an artist in a simple way. **Cartoons** are usually funny.

■ **carry**

cash

Cash is another word for **money.** Trisha's mother gets **cash** from the bank every week.

castle

A **castle** is a large building with high, thick walls. **Castles** were built a long time ago. Kings, queens, and knights lived in **castles.** ■

■ **castle**

cat

A **cat** is a small animal. It has four legs, soft fur, and a long tail. Many people have **cats** as pets.

catch

To **catch** means to take and hold something that is moving. Greg throws the ball for Mindy to **catch.** He threw the ball, and she **caught** it.
—**caught**

The **catcher** of a baseball team stays behind the batter. The pitcher throws the ball. If the batter misses it, the **catcher** tries to **catch** it.

caterpillar

A **caterpillar** is a kind of insect. It looks like a worm covered with fur. **Caterpillars** change into butterflies or moths. ■

■ **caterpillar**

cattle

Cattle are large animals that are raised for milk and meat. They have four legs and two horns. Cows and bulls are **cattle.**

caught

Caught is a form of **catch.** Caleb kicked the ball, and Landon **caught** it. ■

■ **caught**

cause

1. To **cause** is to make something happen. When Will dropped the plate, he **caused** it to break. **2.** A **cause** is the person or thing that makes something happen. The storm was the **cause** of the flood.

cave

A **cave** is a hollow place that goes deep under the ground. **Caves** are very dark inside. ■

■ **cave**

ceiling

A **ceiling** is the top side of a room. You walk on the floor. You look up at the **ceiling.**

celebrate

To **celebrate** means to have a good time when something special happens. The city **celebrated** the holiday with fireworks.

cellar

A **cellar** is a room under a house. **Cellars** are a good place to store old clothes.

cent

A **cent** is an amount of money equal to a penny. A nickel is five **cents,** and a dollar is one hundred **cents.**

> The word **cent** sounds the same as **sent.**

center

The **center** is the middle of something. Tiffany stood in the **center** of the room.

century

A **century** means one hundred years. Our country fought a war for independence more than two **centuries** ago. —**centuries**

cereal

Cereal is a kind of food. Many **cereals** are made from corn, wheat, or rice. Most people eat **cereal** with milk in a bowl.

chair

A **chair** is a kind of furniture. It has four legs and a seat. People sit on **chairs.** ■

■ **chair**

> A **chair** that a baby sits in is called a **highchair.**

chalk

Chalk is something you write or draw with. Shane uses blue **chalk** to draw pictures on the sidewalk. The rain washes the **chalk** away. ■

■ **chalk**

chance

1. Chance means luck. I found three dollars by **chance**. **2. Chance** means that something may happen. There is a **chance** it will rain today. **Chances** are it will be sunny tomorrow.

change

1. To **change** means to become different. In the fall, the leaves on many trees **change** from green to red, orange, and yellow. **2.** To **change** means to put on other clothes. After school, Artie and Pablo **change** before they go out to play. **3. Change** means coins. Joyce has a dollar bill and some **change.**

chapter

A **chapter** is a part of a book. The mystery book that I am reading has eight **chapters.**

chase

1. To **chase** means to run after something to try to catch it. Kent's cousin **chased** him around the lake. **2.** A **chase** is when someone follows something quickly. Many car **chases** end in accidents. ■

■ **chase**

cheap

Cheap means not costing a lot. Cole didn't have a lot of money, so he was glad the book he needed was **cheap.**

> **Cheap** is the opposite of **expensive.**

check

1. A **check** is a mark. You make a **check** next to something to show that it is right. A **check** looks like this: ✔ . **2.** To **check** also means to look for something. Mary can't find her shoes. Her mother tells her to **check** under her bed. **3.** A **check** is also a piece of paper that says what a meal costs. **Checks** are given to people in restaurants.

checkers

Checkers is a game for two people. It is played with a board and round, flat pieces. One set of pieces is white or red, and the other is black. Antoinette is very good at **checkers**. ∎

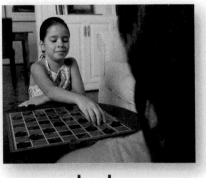

∎ **checkers**

cheek

A **cheek** is a part of the body. Your face has two **cheeks.** They are the wide, soft areas below your eyes.

cheerful

To be **cheerful** means to act happy. Our new neighbor smiles a lot. He says nice things to everybody. He is always **cheerful.**

cheese

Cheese is a kind of food. It is made from milk. Many **cheeses** are yellow or white. ∎

A **cheeseburger** is a hamburger with **cheese** on top.

∎ **cheese**

cherry

A **cherry** is a small fruit. It is round and red. **Cherries** grow on **cherry** trees.
—**cherries** ■

■ **cherry**

chest

1. The **chest** is a part of the body. It is between your neck and your stomach.
2. A **chest** is a strong box. Many **chests** have locks.

chew

To **chew** means to break something into small pieces with the teeth. Our puppy **chewed** an old shoe.

chicken

1. A **chicken** is a large bird. **Chickens** are raised for eggs and meat.
2. **Chicken** is a kind of meat. It comes from a chicken. ■

■ **chicken**

chief

A **chief** is a person who leads other people. **Chiefs** decide how a group of people will do their jobs. Firefighters and the police have **chiefs.**

child

A **child** is a very young person. Boys and girls are **children. —children**

chimney

A **chimney** is a long, hollow part above a fireplace. Smoke and gas from the fireplace go up the **chimney** to the outside. ■

■ **chimney**

chin

A **chin** is a part of the body. It is at the bottom of your face, below your mouth. ■

> **Chin** rhymes with **pin, thin, tin, twin,** and **win.**

■ chin

chocolate

Chocolate is a kind of food. It is usually brown and very sweet. **Chocolate** candies are called **chocolates.**

choice

A **choice** is something you can choose. The restaurant has many **choices** of foods. My father's **choice** for dessert was a bowl of fruit.

choose

To **choose** means to take one thing from a lot of things. There are many books to **choose** from at the library. Abraham **chose** a book about horses. ■

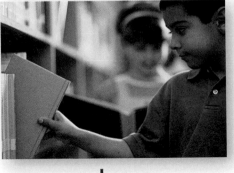

■ choose

chop

To **chop** means to cut into smaller pieces with a sharp tool. Chase's aunt **chopped** vegetables for dinner with a knife. Axes are used to **chop** wood. —**chopped**

chose

Chose is a form of **choose.** Marie and Etta **chose** to play soccer last spring.

chosen

Chosen is a form of **choose.** Annie must choose a kind of sandwich for lunch. She has **chosen** a peanut butter sandwich.

circle

A **circle** is a round shape. It is made by a line that turns until the two ends touch. **Circles** do not have any corners or straight parts. ■

A triangle, a rectangle, and a square are shapes too. They are different from a **circle** because they have straight sides and corners.

■ circle

circus

A **circus** is a kind of show. **Circuses** usually happen in a big tent. You can see clowns, magicians, and animals at the **circus.**

citizen

A **citizen** is a person who belongs to a country. Some people are born in the country that they are part of. Other people become **citizens** after they move to a different country and live there for a long time.

city

A **city** is a place where many people live and work. It has many streets and tall buildings. There are a lot of **cities** in our country. —**cities** ■

■ city

clap

To **clap** means to hit the palms of your hands together. People **clap** after something that they like happens. We **clapped** after we won the game.—**clapped** ∎

∎ **clap**

class

1. A **class** is a group of students who learn together. Our **class** went on a trip to the museum. **2.** A **class** is also what a group of people come together to learn. My mother goes to a tennis **class** every Saturday.

> A **classroom** is a **room** in a school where students learn.

∎ **claw**

claw

A **claw** is a part of the foot of an animal or a bird. It is sharp and curved. Birds hold on to branches with their **claws.** ∎

clay

Clay is a kind of earth. Pots and cups can be made from **clay.** ∎

clean

1. **Clean** means without any dirt. Blake keeps his dog **clean.** He gives her a bath every Saturday. **2.** To **clean** is to take away dirt. Dorie **cleaned** her face with soap and water.

∎ **clay**

clear

1. Clear means easy to see through. The water in the ocean was so **clear** that Leo could see the fish. **2. Clear** also means easy to understand. The directions to school were very **clear.** ∎

∎ **clear**

clever

Clever means able to think quickly. Jaime always invents good stories. She is very **clever** with words.

climate

Climate means what kind of weather a place has. Palm trees grow in warm, wet **climates.**

climb

To **climb** means to move up or down. I like to **climb** the wall at the gym. The elevator **climbed** to the top of the building. ∎

clock

A **clock** is a kind of machine. **Clocks** tell what time it is.

close

1. Close means near. Some flowers grew **close** to that wall. **2.** To **close** something means to move something so that nothing can come in or go out. Amber **closed** the door and the windows. **3.** To **close** means to not allow people inside. The store **closes** at the same time every night.

∎ **climb**

■ closet

closet

A **closet** is a very small room. People keep clothes, shoes, and other things in **closets.** ■

cloth

Cloth is used to make clothes. It comes from cotton, wool, and other things.

clothes

Clothes cover a person's body. Coats, shirts, dresses, pants, and socks are all kinds of **clothes.**

> A **clothesline** is a rope that people put **clothes** on to dry in the air.

cloud

A **cloud** is made up of many drops of water. **Clouds** in the sky have many shapes. Rain comes from **clouds.** ■

■ cloud

clown

A **clown** is a person who makes other people laugh. **Clowns** wear funny costumes. They play tricks. Many **clowns** work in a circus.

coach

1. A **coach** is a person who gives directions to a sports team. Our basketball **coach** practices with us three times each week. **2.** A **coach** is also a large carriage with four wheels, a top, and a seat outside for the driver. In stories, kings and queens ride in **coaches** pulled by horses.

A B C D E F G H I J K L M

coat

A **coat** is something that covers your body. **Coats** are usually made from thick cloth. They keep you warm when the weather is cold. ■

■ **coat**

cocoon

A **cocoon** is a ball of threads made by some caterpillars. These caterpillars live in **cocoons** before they change into butterflies and moths.

coin

A **coin** is a kind of money. **Coins** are usually round. They are made of metal. Pennies, nickels, dimes, and quarters are all **coins.** ■

■ **coin**

cold

1. Cold means having no heat. **Cold** is the opposite of **hot.** Snow and ice are very **cold. 2.** A **cold** is also something that makes you sick. Your head may hurt. You may sneeze a lot and want to rest in bed.

collect

To **collect** means to put things together in a group. We **collected** our toys into a pile.

A person who **collects** things is called a **collector.** Some stamp **collectors** have stamps from around the world.

color

1. Color is the kind of light that comes from a thing. Most things have a **color.** Red, yellow, green, and blue are **colors. 2.** To **color** means to add color to something. Indira **colors** with crayons. ■

■ **color**

comb

A **comb** is a small tool used to make hair smooth and neat. Jesse carries a **comb** to school every day.

come

1. To **come** is to move toward. Billy's mother asked him to **come** to the table to eat supper. He **came** quickly because he was hungry. **2.** To **come** also means to happen or be. Spring **comes** before summer. —**came, come**

comfortable

Comfortable means that something feels good. The new couch we bought yesterday is very **comfortable** to sit on.

The opposite of **comfortable** is **uncomfortable.**

community

A **community** is a group of people who live together. A neighborhood is a small **community.** Cities are large **communities. —communities**

compare

To **compare** means to see how things are alike or different. At camp we **compared** different kinds of leaves.

A B C D E F G H I J K L M

complete

1. Complete means with all the parts together. We worked on the puzzle until it was **complete.**
2. To **complete** means to finish something. After we **complete** our homework, we can go to the movies.

computer

A **computer** is a machine. It helps you find information about things. **Computers** can work very quickly. ■

■ **computer**

concert

A **concert** is a show where people sing or play music on instruments. Our city orchestra plays in two **concerts** every year.

cone

1. A **cone** is a shape that has a circle at one end and a point at the other. Some party hats are shaped like **cones. 2.** A **cone** is a part of some kinds of trees. A pine **cone** has the seeds for new pine trees inside it. ■

■ **cone**

confuse

1. To **confuse** means to cause someone to not understand something. I can't understand my sister. She **confuses** me when she talks. **2.** To **confuse** also means to think one thing is another. My teachers sometimes **confuse** me with my brother.

> When something **confuses** you, it is **confusing.** Is your homework **confusing** sometimes?

consonant

A **consonant** is a kind of letter. B, C, D, F, G, H, J, K, L, M, N, P, Q, R, S, T, V, W, X, Y, and Z are **consonants. Consonants** and vowels make the letters of the alphabet.

container

A **container** is something that is used to store things. Boxes, cans, jars, and barrels are **containers.** In our kitchen we keep flour and rice in **containers.** ■

■ **container**

contest

A **contest** is a kind of game to see who can win. Two or more people can be in a **contest.**

continent

A **continent** is a very large area of land. There are seven **continents** on the earth.

continue

1. To **continue** means to happen without stopping. The rain began in the afternoon and **continued** all night. I **continued** reading the book until I finished it. **2.** To **continue** also means to start again. We played baseball in the morning but stopped for lunch. Then we **continued** the game in the afternoon.

control

To **control** something means to make it do what you want it to do. Amir **controls** his kite with a long string. —**controlled**

cook

1. To **cook** is to heat food to make it ready to eat. We **cooked** the turkey in the oven for six hours. **2.** A **cook** is a person who makes meals. **Cooks** work in kitchens. ■

> A **cookbook** is a **book** that explains how to make different kinds of food. **Cookbooks** have many recipes.

■ **cook**

cookie

A **cookie** is a kind of food. It is like a small, flat cake. **Cookies** arc sweet.

cool

Cool means not very cold. The weather was **cool** this morning, but it got warm this afternoon.

> A **cooler** is a box that keeps food **cool.** Some people put sandwiches and drinks in a **cooler** to take to the beach.

cooperate

To **cooperate** means to work well with someone else. Our whole class **cooperated** in writing a story for the school newspaper.

copper

Copper is a kind of metal. Pennies and wire are made from **copper.**

copy

1. A **copy** is something made to look like something else. Laura drew a picture. Then she made **copies** to give to her friends. **2.** To **copy** something is to make another one like it. Abel prints a poem on a piece of paper. He **copied** the poem out of a book. —**copies, copied**

corn

Corn is a kind of vegetable. It grows on a tall, green plant. **Corn** can be yellow or white. ■

> A **cornfield** is a **field** where **corn** grows.

■ **corn**

corner

A **corner** is the place where two sides come together. Squares and rectangles have four **corners.**

correct

1. Correct means without mistakes. Jack's answer was **correct. 2.** To **correct** means to check for mistakes in something. The teacher **corrects** all our tests.

cost

1. To **cost** means to have a price of some amount of money. The book Jennifer wants **costs** five dollars, but she only has 50 cents. **2.** The **cost** of something is how much money you pay to buy it. The **cost** of the toy I wanted was too great. I didn't have enough money to buy it. —**cost**

costume

A **costume** is a set of special clothes. Stacy and Gillian wore **costumes** in the school play. ■

cottage

A **cottage** is a small house that is usually in the country. Some families have **cottages** where they go on vacation.

■ **costume**

cotton

Cotton is soft, light, and white. It grows on a **cotton** plant. It is made into cloth. People wear clothes made from **cotton** in the summer. ■

couch

A **couch** is a kind of furniture that you sit on. It is wider than a chair so that two or three people can sit at one time. **Couches** are comfortable for reading and watching television.

■ **cotton**

could

Could is a form of **can.** Jimmy can whistle. He **could** whistle when he was five years old.

couldn't

Couldn't is a short way to say **could not.** Last year I **couldn't** read as well as Tyrone, but now I can.

count

To **count** means to add. Katie **counted** the pencils on her desk. There were five pencils.

country

1. A **country** is a large place where a group of people live. There are many cities in each **country** and many **countries** in the world. 2. A **country** is also the group of people who live in a country. Our **country** votes for a president every four years. 3. The **country** is the area away from a city. There are forests, fields, and farms in the **country.**
—**countries**

> Land that is in the **country** is sometimes called the **countryside.**

courage

Courage is what you have when you are brave. The firefighters showed **courage** when they went into the burning building.

cousin

Your **cousin** is the child of your aunt or uncle. Angelina has lots of **cousins.**

cover

1. To **cover** means to put something on top of something else. Wendy **covered** herself with thick blankets to keep warm. 2. A **cover** goes on the top or outside of something. Books have **covers.** Pots and pans also have **covers.** ■

■ **cover**

cow

A **cow** is a large, female animal that lives on a farm. **Cows** are raised for milk and meat.

A B **C** D E F G H I J K L M

cowboy

A **cowboy** is a man who takes care of cattle. **Cowboys** work on big farms. They often ride horses. ■

cowgirl

A **cowgirl** is a woman who takes care of cattle. **Cowgirls** often ride horses and may work with cowboys.

■ **cowboy**

crab

A **crab** is a small animal. It has a hard shell and five pairs of legs. **Crabs** usually live in the ocean.

> There are many types of **crabs.** The **spider crab** has long legs like a **spider.** The **blue crab** has **blue** claws. The **king crab** is one of the largest **crabs.** It weighs more than ten pounds.

crack

1. A **crack** is a broken place that looks like a crooked line. The plate had **cracks** in it. **2.** To **crack** is to break so that cracks are seen. Toby's mirror **cracked** after she dropped it on the floor. ■

■ **crack**

crash

1. To **crash** means to hit something and break with a lot of noise. During the storm, a boat **crashed** into the dock. **2.** A **crash** is a loud noise. We heard a **crash** in the next room.

crawl

To **crawl** is to move on your hands and knees. Babies **crawl** until they learn to walk. ∎

∎ **crawl**

crayon

A **crayon** is a piece of colored wax. It is used to draw and write with. **Crayons** come in many colors.

cream

Cream is a kind of food. It is part of the milk that comes from a cow. Butter is made from **cream.**

crib

A **crib** is a special kind of bed with high sides. Babies sleep in **cribs** so that they are safe. ∎

cricket

A **cricket** is a kind of insect. Some male **crickets** make noises by rubbing their front wings together.

∎ **crib**

cried

Cried is a form of **cry.** My brother **cried** when he fell on the ice.

crocodile

A **crocodile** is a very large reptile. It looks like an alligator with a long, narrow jaw. **Crocodiles** live in rivers and swamps. ∎

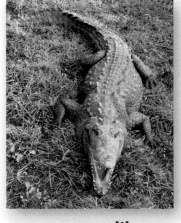

∎ **crocodile**

A B **C** D E F G H I J K L M

■ crooked

crooked

Crooked means not straight. Lightning looks like a **crooked** line in the sky. ■

cross

1. A **cross** is a shape. It is made by two lines that touch in the middle. It looks like this: **+** . **2.** To **cross** means to go to the other side. The bridge **crosses** the river. We **crossed** the street.

crow

A **crow** is a large bird with black feathers. **Crows** can make a loud noise.

■ crowd

crowd

A **crowd** is a large group of people. **Crowds** come to watch football games. ■

crown

A **crown** is a special hat worn by kings and queens. Many **crowns** are made of metal and have jewels on them. ■

cruel

Cruel means not kind. In the story I am reading, the people don't like their **cruel** king.

> **Cruel** is another word for **mean.**

■ crown

crumb

A **crumb** is a very small piece of foods that are baked. Bread, cake, and cookies make **crumbs** when we eat them.

crutch

A **crutch** is a kind of pole that helps people walk when they are hurt. After Isaiah fell, he needed **crutches** to walk. ■

■ **crutch**

cry

To **cry** is to have tears fall from your eyes. People sometimes **cry** when they are sad. —**cries, cried**

cub

A **cub** is a young bear, wolf, or lion. Lion **cubs** weigh only three pounds when they are born. ■

■ **cub**

cup

A **cup** is a small, open container with a flat bottom used for drinking. You can drink milk, juice, or water from **cups.**

A **teacup** is a little **cup** with a handle.

curious

To be **curious** is to want to learn. Hailey asks a lot of questions. She is very **curious.**

curly

Curly means twisting around in small circles. Leigh's hair is **curly,** but Kerry's is straight. —**curlier, curliest** ∎

∎ **curly**

curtain

A **curtain** is a piece of cloth used to cover a window. We have blue, cotton **curtains** on our kitchen windows.

curve

1. A **curve** is a round line. The bottom of a **U** is a **curve.**
2. To **curve** means to follow a round line. This road **curves** back and forth. ∎

cushion

A **cushion** is a kind of soft, cloth pillow. You can sit, lie, or rest on it. Our couch has two large, round **cushions.**

∎ **curve**

customer

A **customer** is someone who buys something. Sebastian helps the **customers** find what they need at his parents' store.

cut

To **cut** is to divide something into pieces with a sharp tool. Dan used scissors to **cut** pictures out of the newspaper. Dina **cut** the carrots before she put them in the soup.—**cut**

Dd

daisy

A **daisy** is a kind of flower. Most **daisies** are white with yellow centers. —**daisies** ■

■ **daisy**

dam

A **dam** is a wall across a river. It causes a lake to form behind it. **Dams** control how fast water goes from the lake to the other side of the **dam.** ■

damp

Damp means not very wet. Erika used a **damp** cloth to wash the table.

dance

To **dance** means to move your body to music. Marta **danced** with her friends at the party.

■ **dam**

dandelion

A **dandelion** is a kind of flower. **Dandelions** are round and yellow. When they become white, their seeds are blown away by the wind ∎

dangerous

Dangerous means not safe. Tornadoes can be very **dangerous.**

> **Danger** is something that is **dangerous.** We are careful to stay out of **danger** when we swim in the ocean.

∎ **dandelion**

dark

Dark means without light. At night it is **dark** outside.

> Where there is no light, there is **darkness.** When the electricity didn't work, we were in **darkness.**

date

A **date** is any one day. July 7 is a **date.** November 20 is also a **date.** Every day has a **date.**

daughter

A **daughter** is a person's female child. Liza and Kit are my teacher's **daughters.**

day

1. A **day** is the time from one morning to the next morning. There are 24 hours in one **day.** There are seven **days** in one week. **2. Day** is the time when it is light outside. Rolf played outside all **day.** He only went in the house when it got dark.

dead

Dead means not alive. Plants and flowers die without water. They become **dead.**

deaf

Deaf means not able to hear. A person who cannot hear is **deaf.**

dear

Something **dear** is something you love. People also use **dear** to begin a letter. Susan's letter to her aunt began with "**Dear** Aunt Sonia."

December

December is the last month of the year. It has 31 days. **December** comes after November and before January.

decide

To **decide** means to choose. Ramona **decided** to wear a red shirt and blue pants to the school picnic.

deep

Deep means that there is much space between the top and the bottom of something. The ocean is **deep.**

> The opposite of **deep** is **shallow.** This end of the pool is **shallow,** but the other end is **deep.**

deer

A **deer** is a kind of animal. It has four legs and soft, brown fur. **Deer** live in forests and fields. —**deer** ∎

∎ **deer**

delicious

Delicious means very good to taste. We enjoyed a **delicious** lunch.

delighted

Delighted means very happy. Kylie was **delighted** when her best friend moved into the house across the street.

dentist

A **dentist** is a kind of doctor. A **dentist** takes care of people's teeth. **Dentists** teach you how to keep your teeth healthy. ■

■ dentist

describe

To **describe** means to tell or write all about something. I **described** my summer vacation to my friends.

> The way something is **described** is a **description.** My book gives a good **description** of how bees make honey.

desert

A **desert** is a large, dry area of land. Not much rain falls there. **Deserts** are covered by sand.

design

A **design** is a group of different lines or shapes. **Designs** are usually drawn or painted. The wheels had pretty **designs** painted on them. ■

■ design

desk

A **desk** is a kind of furniture. It has a large, flat top and legs. People sit at **desks** to read and write. ■

■ **desk**

dessert

A **dessert** is a kind of food. It is the last part of a meal. **Dessert** is usually sweet. Ice cream, pie, cake, and fruit are **desserts.**

diamond

1. A **diamond** is a jewel. **Diamonds** are clear and very hard. **2.** A **diamond** is also a shape. It has four sides and four corners. One corner is at the top, and another is at the bottom. ■

■ **diamond**

dictionary

A **dictionary** is a kind of book. **Dictionaries** show how words are spelled. They also explain what words mean. This book is a **dictionary. —dictionaries**

did

Did is a form of **do.** Alexandra and Joey **did** something together. They went to the movies.

didn't

Didn't is a short way to say **did not.** Ricky was sick. He **didn't** feel well at all. He **didn't** go to school.

die

To **die** means to become dead. The cold weather made all the flowers **die.** The leaves on the trees **died** too.

different

Different means not alike. Birds and fish are very **different** kinds of animals. A dog's tail is **different** from a cat's tail.

> The opposite of **different** is **same.**
> My brother and I live in the **same** house.
> My cousin lives in a **different** house.

dig

To **dig** means to make a hole in the earth. Lester likes to **dig** in the sand. —**dug** ■

■ **dig**

dime

A **dime** is a coin. One **dime** is the same as ten pennies or two nickels. A dollar is the same as ten **dimes.**

dinner

Dinner is a meal. It is usually the biggest meal of the day. Most people eat **dinner** at night.

dinosaur

A **dinosaur** is a reptile that lived a long time ago. Some **dinosaurs** were huge, and some were very small. Some **dinosaurs** ate plants, and some ate meat. ■

■ **dinosaur**

dip

To **dip** means to put something in liquid and then take it out quickly. Dawn **dips** her brush in the bucket of paint. —**dipped**

direction

1. A **direction** is somewhere you can look or point or go. North, south, east, and west are **directions.**
2. **Directions** tell you how to get somewhere. Matt and Arnie gave us the **directions** to their house.
3. **Directions** can also tell you how to do something. Games usually come with **directions.** ∎

∎ **direction**

dirt

Dirt means earth. The ground is made of **dirt** and rocks. Luke gets **dirt** on his clothes when he plays outside. ∎

> **Dirty** means covered with **dirt.** Our dog gets **dirty** when he swims in the swamp.

∎ **dirt**

disappear

To **disappear** means to stop being seen. The sun **disappeared** behind a cloud.

discover

To **discover** means to find out something. I looked down and **discovered** that I was wearing two different socks.

dish

A **dish** is something to put food in. **Dishes** are usually round. Miguel washed all the **dishes** after supper. ■

■ **dish**

distance

Distance is the space between two things. Airplanes can travel long **distances** in a few hours.

distant

Distant means far away. Letters from **distant** countries can take a long time to arrive.

dive

To **dive** means to jump in the water with your hands and head first. Elsa learned how to swim and **dive** at the pool. ■

A **diver** is a person who **dives.**

■ **dive**

divide

To **divide** means to change one big thing into two or more smaller things. Louisa **divided** the apple into two halves. Benjamin **divides** his toys into three piles.

do

To **do** means to make something happen. Hannah always **does** a good job cleaning her room. She has always **done** it without being asked. Bridget and Kimberly **did** some work together. —**does, did, done**

■ dock

dock

A **dock** is a place to tie up a boat. **Docks** are built where land and water meet. Tyler tied his boat to the **dock** so it wouldn't float away. ■

doctor

A **doctor** is a person who helps sick people get well. Many **doctors** work in hospitals. ■

■ doctor

does

Does is a form of **do.** Ben **does** his homework every night. Fatima **does** hers too.

doesn't

Doesn't is a short way to say **does not.** Larry **doesn't** like to eat carrots, but he does like to eat corn.

dog

A **dog** is a kind of animal. It has four legs, fur, and a tail. Many people have **dogs** as pets. There are many kinds of **dogs.** ■

doll

A **doll** is a kind of toy. **Dolls** usually look like babies or small children.

■ dog

dollar

A **dollar** is an amount of money. A **dollar** is usually made of a piece of green paper shaped like a rectangle. One **dollar** is the same as one hundred pennies. My lunch cost five **dollars.**

dolphin

A **dolphin** is a kind of animal that lives in the sea. **Dolphins** are mammals that arc smaller than whales.

done

Done is a form of **do.** Judith and Taryn fed their pets. They have **done** their job for the day.

donkey

A **donkey** is a kind of animal. It looks like a small horse with long ears. **Donkeys** can carry heavy loads. ■

■ **donkey**

don't

Don't is a short way to say **do not.** Fish live in water. They **don't** live in trees.

door

A **door** is a place in a wall where you can walk through. **Doors** usually open and close. ■

dot

A **dot** is a small, round spot. Miranda's skirt has black **dots** on it.

■ **door**

doughnut

A **doughnut** is a small cake. Many **doughnuts** are round and have a hole in the center. Some have jelly inside.

down

1. **Down** means going from a high place to a low place. A big balloon came **down** in our garden.
2. **Down** means in a low place. There is water **down** in the well.

The opposite of **down** is **up.** The balloon was **up** in the sky, but it fell **down** to the ground.

dozen

A **dozen** is a group of 12 things. I bought two **dozen** eggs. —**dozen**

Dr.

Dr. is a short way to write **doctor.** People use **Dr.** with a doctor's name. Our family doctor is **Dr.** Chan.

dragon

A **dragon** is a monster in stories. It is not real. **Dragons** look like huge reptiles with wings and claws. They breathe fire. ■

■ dragon

drank

Drank is a form of **drink.** Sam **drank** his milk quickly. He does not usually drink so fast.

draw

To **draw** is to make a picture. You can **draw** with pencils, pens, or crayons. Abbie has **drawn** many cartoons. —**drew, drawn**

> A picture that you **draw** is called a **drawing.** Myra made a **drawing** of her house.

dream

1. A **dream** is a story or a picture that happens in your mind when you sleep. **2.** To **dream** means to imagine stories while you sleep. One night Fiona **dreamed** she could fly. **3.** A **dream** is also something you wish for. Nick's **dream** is to fly to the moon in a rocket.

dress

1. To **dress** means to put clothes on. Jae's father helped him **dress** for the party.
2. A **dress** is a kind of clothes. It is one piece that covers the top and the bottom of the body. Women and girls sometimes wear **dresses.** ■

■ **dress**

drew

Drew is a form of **draw.** Andy used a red crayon to draw a circle on the paper. Then he **drew** some squares with a blue crayon.

dried

Dried is a form of **dry.** After we washed the car, we **dried** it with old towels.

drink

1. A **drink** is a liquid you can swallow. Orange juice is Troy's favorite **drink**. **2.** To **drink** means to take liquid into your mouth and swallow it. Lydia always **drinks** milk with supper. —**drank, drunk** ■

■ **drink**

drive

To **drive** is to make a car, a truck, or a bus go. Yesterday, my older sister **drove** my mother's car to the beach. She has **driven** to the beach for three years. —**drove, driven**

> A **driveway** is a small road that leads from a street to a house. We park our car in the **driveway.**

drop

1. A **drop** is a very small amount of liquid. I felt **drops** of rain on my nose. **2.** To **drop** something means to let it fall. Tomas **dropped** most of the clothes he was carrying upstairs. —**dropped** ■

drove

Drove is a form of **drive.** When Carla missed the bus, her father **drove** her to school.

drugstore

A **drugstore** is a store where people can buy medicine. **Drugstores** also sell newspapers and other things.

■ **drop**

drum

A **drum** is an instrument. To play **drums,** you beat on them with your hands or with sticks. ■

drunk

Drunk is a form of **drink.** Gerry drinks a lot of water. She has **drunk** nearly a whole bottle today.

■ drum

dry

1. **Dry** means not wet. During the storm we stayed warm and **dry** inside. 2. To **dry** means to take all the water from something. The clothes hang outside to **dry.** The sun **dries** them in a few hours.
—**dries, dried** ■

■ dry

duck

A **duck** is a kind of bird. It has a wide, flat bill and short legs. **Ducks** swim on rivers and lakes. ■

A young **duck** is called a **duckling.** I saw five **ducklings** and their mother in the **duck** pond.

■ duck

dug

Dug is a form of **dig.** Taylor digs in the sand at the beach. She **dug** a big hole with her pail and shovel.

dull

1. Dull means not sharp. It is hard to cut anything with **dull** scissors. **2. Dull** also means not interesting. Tony didn't like the story. He thought it was **dull.**

during

During means for the whole time. It is light outside **during** the day. We stayed inside **during** the storm.

dust

1. Dust is tiny pieces of dirt. **Dust** can make you sneeze. The cowboy's horse left a lot of **dust** behind it. **2.** To **dust** means to take dust off with a cloth or brush. My brother and I **dusted** the furniture yesterday. ■

■ **dust**

Dusty means covered with **dust.** We had to clean the table because it was **dusty.**

A B C D E F G H I J K L M

Ee

each

Each means with none left out. Nan put **each** berry that she picked in her basket.

> **Each** other means one and the other. Karen and Joy gave **each** other presents.

eagle

An **eagle** is a large bird. **Eagles** have curved beaks and strong wings. ■

■ **eagle**

ear

An **ear** is a part of the body. There is one **ear** on each side of your head. People hear with their **ears.**

early

1. **Early** means happening near the beginning. Bobby gets up **early** in the morning. 2. **Early** also means before the usual time. Last night my brother and I went to bed **early. —earlier, earliest**

> The opposite of **early** is **late.**

earn

To **earn** is to get something for what you do. Carly **earns** money sometimes by working in her neighbors' yards.

earth

1. **Earth** means soil. There is good **earth** in the garden for the plants to grow in. 2. The **earth** is our world. The **earth** is covered by land and oceans. ■

■ **earth**

earthquake

An **earthquake** happens when a part of the earth moves suddenly. During **earthquakes,** the ground shakes, and sometimes buildings fall down.

east

East is a direction. The sun rises in the **east. East** is the opposite of **west.** ■

■ **east**

easy

Easy means not hard to do. Frannie thinks it is **easy** to do math. —**easier, easiest**

> The word **easily** means in an **easy** way. Liz swam across the pool **easily.**

eat

To **eat** means to take food into the body through the mouth. People **eat** when they feel hungry. I **ate** some soup for lunch. My grandparents have **eaten** their pizza.—**ate, eaten**

echo

An **echo** is a sound that comes back again. If you shout at a mountain, you may hear **echoes** of your voice. —**echoes**

edge

An **edge** is the line or place where something ends. Ursula swam to the **edge** of the pool. Knives have very sharp **edges.** ▪

▪ **edge**

education

Education means what you learn in school. A good **education** helps you when you look for a job.

egg

An **egg** is a smooth, round shell with a baby animal inside of it. Birds grow inside **eggs** until they are ready to hatch. Many people eat **eggs** from chickens. ▪

▪ **egg**

eight

Eight is a number. **Eight** is one more than seven. **Eight** is written **8.** 7 + 1 = **8.**

either

1. **Either** means one or the other. Becky wants **either** a puppy or a kitten. She would be happy to get **either** of them. 2. **Either** also means that you also do not have something or do not want to do something. Warren did not want to play soccer. He did not want to play basketball **either.**

elbow

An **elbow** is a part of the body. Your arm bends at the **elbow.** Mei sat with her **elbows** on the table. ■

■ **elbow**

election

An **election** is when people vote for someone or something. We have **elections** at school every year for our team captains.

> When we have an **election,** we **elect** someone. My cousin Alexis was **elected** president of her class.

electricity

Electricity is a kind of energy. Lamps make light when **electricity** goes through them. **Electricity** also makes refrigerators, computers, and many other things work.

> Things that use **electricity** are called **electric.** The singer in my favorite band also plays the **electric** guitar.

elephant

An **elephant** is a very large animal. It has thick, gray skin, big ears, and a long trunk. **Elephants** are the biggest animals that live on land. ■

■ **elephant**

elevator

An **elevator** is a machine that takes people up and down in a building. In the library, people use the **elevators** when they don't want to use the stairs.

elf

An **elf** is a tiny fairy in stories. **Elves** often use magic. —**elves**

else

Else means other or different. Molly did not want a turkey sandwich for lunch. She wanted something **else.**

emerald

An **emerald** is a kind of jewel. **Emeralds** are green.

empty

Empty means with nothing inside. Roy ate all of the jelly. He left the **empty** jar on the table. —**emptier, emptiest** ■

> The opposite of **empty** is **full. Empty** boxes are easier to carry than **full** boxes.

■ **empty**

end

1. An **end** is the last part of something. This train has a caboose at the **end. 2.** An **end** is also either side of something long. My brother sat at one **end** of the table, and I sat at the other. **3.** To **end** means to come to the last part. The story **ends** with a surprise.

energy

Energy is something that you need to do work. People, animals, and plants make **energy** from food. Heat, steam, light, and electricity are forms of **energy** that machines make or use.

engine

An **engine** is a kind of machine. It burns oil, gas, or wood to do work. Cars, ships, and planes have **engines** to make them move. ∎

∎ engine

engineer

1. An **engineer** is a person who drives a train. **Engineers** control the engines at the front of trains.
2. An **engineer** is also someone who tells people how to build engines, machines, roads, bridges, and other things.

enjoy

To **enjoy** something means to like it. The first grade class **enjoyed** having a picnic at the end of the year.

enough

Enough means as much or as many as you need. We have **enough** food for everybody.

enter

To **enter** means to go into a place. Tara and P. J. **entered** the building together.

entrance

An **entrance** is where you enter a place. I left my bicycle near the **entrance** of the building. There were two **entrances** to the fair. ■

> The opposite of an **entrance** is an **exit.** Our class walked in through the **entrance** of the museum and left through the **exit.**

■ **entrance**

environment

The **environment** is what is all around a living thing. Air, water, land, and buildings are all part of the **environment.** Cactuses grow best in desert **environments.**

equal

Equal means the same in amount or size. One dime is **equal** to ten pennies. ■

■ **equal**

erase

To **erase** means to make something disappear by rubbing it. I **erased** my math homework after I made a mistake.

especially

Especially means more than anything else. Joellen likes to do a lot of things. She **especially** likes to act in plays.

even

1. Even means all at the same height. Mo made her bed so that the blanket was smooth and **even. 2.** An **even** number is a number that you can get to when you start at zero and count by twos. Two, four, six, eight, and ten are **even** numbers.

evening

Evening is the part of the day between the afternoon and the night. The sun sets during the **evening.** We stay at home most **evenings.**

ever

Ever means at any time. Have you **ever** seen a peacock? Going to the fair last summer is the most fun I have **ever** had.

every

Every means each one. Nobody could read **every** book in the library.

> **Everybody** and **everyone** mean the same as **every** person.

everything

Everything means each thing. After the storm the snow covered **everything.**

everywhere

Everywhere means in every place. Deanna looked **everywhere** for her cat.

evil

To be **evil** is to be very mean. In the story, the **evil** giant would not let people cross the bridge.

> The opposite of **evil** is **good.** In the movie, the **good** king sends the **evil** prince away from the palace.

example

An **example** is something that is chosen because it is like other things of the same kind. Water is an **example** of a liquid.

> We say **for example** when we want to show some **examples.** The zoo has a lot of animals from other countries, **for example,** monkeys and elephants.

excellent

Excellent means very, very good. T. J. makes **excellent** pizza. Brittany had an **excellent** idea.

except

Except means leaving out. Everyone **except** Jane was in school today. She was the only one who did not come to school.

exciting

To be **exciting** is to make people feel a lot of energy. We read an **exciting** story about people who climb mountains. Isabella and I thought the rides were **exciting.** ■

■ **exciting**

excuse

An **excuse** explains the reason for something. Students must bring a written **excuse** from their parents if they are late for school.

exercise

1. Exercise is running and jumping and moving your body around. Grace gets a lot of **exercise** when she goes to the gym. **2.** An **exercise** lets you practice how to do something. We are learning to add by doing the **exercises** in our book. ■

■ **exercise**

exit

An **exit** is the way out of a room or a building. The gym in our school has two **exits.**

expand

To **expand** is to get bigger. A balloon **expands** when you blow air into it. ■

■ **expand**

expect

To **expect** is to think something will happen. Laila **expects** her father to be home in a few minutes.

expensive

Expensive means costing a lot of money. Robert's parents wanted to buy a new car, but it was too **expensive.**

experiment

An **experiment** is a test to find out something. Our class did **experiments** with magnets to find out what they do. We saw how they stick to some metals.

explain

To **explain** means to tell about something so that other people can understand it. Bryce **explained** the rules of the game so we could all play it.

explore

To **explore** means to go into a place you have never been before to see what is there. Some people like to **explore** underwater. ■

■ **explore**

A person who **explores** is called an **explorer.**

extra

Extra means more than what you need or expect. Mr. Chen gave Toni five dollars to clean his car. She got an **extra** dollar for washing the tires.

eye

An **eye** is a part of the body. People and animals see with their **eyes.** Your **eyes** are in the middle of your face, one on each side of your nose.

Ff

face

1. The **face** is the front of the head. The eyes, the nose, and the mouth are all part of the **face.** **2.** The **face** of a clock shows what time it is. Clock **faces** have numbers on them. **3.** To **face** means to look in some direction. Erich **faced** the front of the room. ■

■ face

fact

A **fact** is something that is true. Scientists try to find out **facts.**

factory

A **factory** is a building where people use machines to make things. Many people work at different jobs in large **factories. —factories** ■

■ factory

fair

1. To be **fair** means to treat everyone the same. Breaking the rules is not **fair. 2.** A **fair** is a place where people go to have fun. Some people show animals, vegetables, and other things that they have raised or made. At most **fairs** there are rides and games. ■

■ **fair**

fairy

A **fairy** is a small person in a story. **Fairies** can often perform magic. —**fairies**

fall

1. To **fall** is to go down. Shira still **falls** sometimes when she skates. All the leaves have **fallen** off the trees by December. **2.** To **fall** asleep means to go to sleep. Pascale **falls** asleep easily at night. **3. Fall** is a season. It comes after summer and before winter. **Fall** is another word for **autumn. —fell, fallen**

false

False means not true. It is **false** to say that frogs can fly.

family

Your **family** has in it your parents, sisters, brothers, aunts, uncles, and cousins. There are many different kinds of **families. —families**

fan

A **fan** is an object that can make air move to make a breeze. Some **fans** are machines. Others are made of paper that you wave with your hand. ■

■ **fan**

fancy

Fancy means prettier or better than usual. Janet wore a **fancy** new dress to the festival. **—fancier, fanciest** ■

far

Far means at a great distance. The moon is **far** away from here. It takes a long time to get there.

> The opposite of **far** is **near.** I live **near** my school but **far** from the train station.

■ fancy

farm

A **farm** is an area of land. People grow food and raise animals on **farms.** ■

> A **farmer** is a person who works on a **farm. Farmers** start to work early in the morning.

■ farm

farther

Farther means at a greater distance. The sun is **farther** from us than the moon is.

fast

Fast means quickly. A rocket goes very **fast.**

fat

Fat means big and round. Pigs and hippopotamuses are fat.

> The opposite of fat is thin. My fat puppy became thin when he ate less food.

father

A father is a man who has a child. Fathers and mothers take care of their children.

favorite

Favorite means what you like the most. Holly's favorite color is purple.

fear

1. Fear is what you feel when you are afraid. Sy's fears about school disappeared when he met his new teacher. 2. To fear is to be afraid. Charlie fears the water because he doesn't know how to swim yet.

feast

A feast is a very large meal. Many families have feasts on Thanksgiving and other holidays.

feather

A feather is part of a bird. Most birds are covered with them. Feathers are light and soft. ■

■ feather

February

February is the second month of the year. It has 28 or 29 days. February comes after January and before March.

feed

To **feed** means to give food to. Luisa **feeds** carrots to the horse. —**fed** ∎

■ **feed**

feel

1. To **feel** is to touch. Eve **feels** the dolphin's smooth skin. **2.** To **feel** is also to be some way. When you are happy, you may **feel** like singing. When our friends are sick, we **feel** sorry for them. —**felt** ∎

> A **feeling** is the way you **feel** about something. Joy and love are **feelings.**

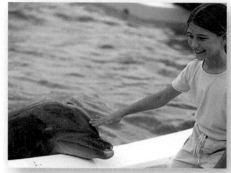

■ **feel**

feet

Feet means more than one **foot.** People have two **feet.** Dogs and cats have four **feet.** Ken is more than four **feet** tall.

fell

Fell is a form of **fall.** Allie **fell** off her bicycle. Evelyn **fell** asleep.

felt

Felt is a form of **feel.** Yesterday Angelo **felt** too sick to go out. The cat's fur **felt** soft when I touched it.

female

Female is a kind of person or animal. It is the opposite of **male.** Girls and women are **female** people.

fence

A **fence** is something that is built outside to keep two places apart. **Fences** can be made of wood, metal, or stone. ■

■ **fence**

festival

A **festival** is a special party where people celebrate something that is important to them. **Festivals** often have food, music, and dancing. ■

■ **festival**

few

Few means not many. Glenn ate a **few** bites of his supper, but he wasn't very hungry.

field

1. A **field** is a large, flat area of land. No trees grow there. Farmers grow corn and other plants in **fields. 2.** A **field** is also where some sports are played. Baseball and football are played on different kinds of **fields.** ■

■ **field**

When you go on a **field trip,** you leave school to visit another place with your teacher and your class. Ms. Carr's class took a **field trip** to the zoo.

fight

1. To **fight** is to get mad at someone when you cannot agree. People often shout when they **fight. 2.** A **fight** is what happens sometimes when people do not agree. Ethan and I had a **fight** yesterday. —**fought**

fill

To **fill** means to make something full. Ron **filled** two glasses with milk. ∎

∎ **fill**

find

1. To **find** is to see where something is. Matt looks around his room for his shoes. He **finds** them under the bed. Yesterday he **found** three socks there. **2.** To **find** out something is to get information about it. In school we **found** out that glass is made from sand. —**found**

fine

Fine means very good. Today is a **fine** day for a walk. Jenny was sick last week, but she feels **fine** now.

finger

A **finger** is a long, thin part of the hand. People have five **fingers** on each hand.

> The **nails** on your **fingers** are called **fingernails.** We must cut our **fingernails** when they grow too long.

finish

To **finish** is to come to the end of something. Tino had so much homework that he couldn't **finish** it.

fire

Fire is flame, heat, and light. It is what happens when something burns. We cut wood for the **fires** at our camp.

■ firefighter

> A **fire engine** is a kind of truck. **Fire engines** carry hoses and ladders to a fire. Firefighters use them to put out the fire.

firefighter

A **firefighter** is a person who puts out fires. **Firefighters** can work in buildings, in forests, or on boats. ■

fireplace

A **fireplace** is a safe place to have a small fire inside a house. It is made of stone or metal. **Fireplaces** must have a chimney for the smoke to go up.

fireworks

Fireworks make light, smoke, and a lot of noise in the sky. **Fireworks** shoot off into the sky on small rockets. ■

■ fireworks

first

1. First means before all others. The letter **A** is the **first** letter in the alphabet.
2. At **first** means in the beginning. At **first** our team was not very good, but we got better as we practiced.

fish

1. A **fish** is an animal that lives in water. **Fish** have tails and can swim very well. **2.** To **fish** means to try to catch fish. When people do this, they are **fishing**. **3. Fish** is a kind of food that comes from a fish. I ate **fish** and rice for lunch. —**fish** ■

■ **fish**

fisherman

A **fisherman** is a person who fishes. Some **fishermen** work on very large boats. Others use a pole and a hook. —**fishermen** ■

fist

A **fist** is a hand that is closed tight. Theo and Jasmine knocked on the door with their **fists.**

■ **fisherman**

fit

1. To **fit** means to be the right size. Leah's favorite shirt **fitted** her last year, but now she is too big for it. **2.** To **fit** is to put something into a small space. Jared could not **fit** all of his toys into one box. —**fitted**

five

Five is one more than four. **Five** is written **5.** $4 + 1 = 5.$

fix

To **fix** is to make something work again when it is broken. Libby's zipper was broken, but her mother **fixed** it.

flag

A **flag** is a piece of cloth with colored shapes on it. Every country has a **flag.** Some **flags** are simple, and others are fancy. The **flag** of our country is red, white, and blue. There are 50 stars, one for each state. There are 13 stripes. ∎

∎ flag

flame

A **flame** is the bright, moving part of a fire. **Flames** are very hot.

flash

To **flash** is to show a bright light for a short moment. The light at the carnival **flashed** on and off all night.

∎ flashlight

flashlight

A **flashlight** is a small lamp that you can carry in your hand. People carry **flashlights** when they go out at night. ∎

flat

Flat means smooth and without any bumps. Floors and tables are **flat.** —**flatter, flattest** ∎

∎ **flat**

flavor

Flavor is what something tastes like. My favorite **flavors** are orange and cherry.

flew

Flew is a form of **fly.** The pilot **flew** his airplane over our house.

float

To **float** is to sit on top of the water. Rob likes to **float** in the pool on a raft.

∎ **flock**

flock

A **flock** is a group of sheep. Some dogs know how to keep **flocks** together. ∎

flood

A **flood** is what happens when water comes up over the edges of a river. **Floods** usually come after there is a lot of rain. Sometimes they happen in the spring when the snow melts. ∎

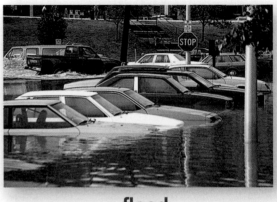

∎ **flood**

A B C D E **F** G H I J K L M

floor

A **floor** is the bottom part of a room. People put rugs on **floors** to cover them.

flour

Flour is a white or brown powder. It is made from wheat or potatoes. **Flour** is used to make bread and cake. ■

> The word **flour** sounds the same as the word **flower.**

■ flour

flow

To **flow** means to move without stopping. Water **flows** in a stream or a river. When I cry, tears **flow** down my cheeks.

flower

A **flower** is part of a plant. Some **flowers** become fruits. **Flowers** come in many colors, shapes, and sizes. People like to smell them and to look at them. ■

■ flower

flown

Flown is a form of **fly.** Neela goes to visit someone in an airplane every year. She has **flown** to many different cities.

flute

A **flute** is an instrument that you blow air into to make music. **Flutes** are tubes made of metal or wood that have holes in them. You put your fingers over the holes to make different sounds. ■

■ flute

fly

1. A **fly** is a kind of insect. It is small and has thin, clear wings. There are many kinds of **flies. 2.** To **fly** is to travel through the air. Most birds can **fly. 3.** To **fly** also means to make something **fly.** A pilot **flies** an airplane. —**flies, flew, flown** ■

■ **fly**

fog

Fog is a cloud that is near the ground. You cannot see very far in the **fog.** ■

Fog rhymes with **dog, frog, jog,** and **log.**

■ **fog**

fold

To **fold** is to bend together. Gail can **fold** paper to make a hat or a bird. ■

follow

1. To **follow** is to go behind. Elena likes to **follow** her brother around. **2.** To **follow** also means to come later. March **follows** February every year.

■ **fold**

food

Food is what people or animals eat. Olivia's favorite **foods** for lunch are hamburgers and peanut butter sandwiches. Cows eat grass for **food.**

foot

1. The **foot** is a part of the body. It is at the end of your leg. The toes and the heel are parts of the **foot.** People and birds have two **feet.** Cats and dogs have four **feet. 2.** A **foot** is an amount of length. One **foot** equals 12 inches. —**feet** ■

■ **foot**

football

1. Football is a sport. It is played by two teams on a field. Onc team tries to throw, carry, or kick a ball down the field. The other team tries to stop them. **2.** A **football** is the ball used in a football game. **Footballs** have a point at each end. ■

■ **football**

for

1. For tells why something is there. A carpenter has a box **for** his tools. I bought this book **for** you.
2. For also means toward. People can reach **for** the sky, but they can't touch it. **3. For** tells how long something continues. We played baseball **for** two hours.

The word **for** sounds the same as the number **four.**

force

A **force** is something that pushes or pulls an object. The **force** of gravity keeps things on the ground.

forest

A **forest** is a place with many trees. Many kinds of animals live in **forests,** but few people live in them. ■

■ **forest**

forget

To **forget** means not to remember. Joseph often **forgets** where he put his shoes. Rebecca **forgot** to put her bicycle in the garage, so it got wet in the rain. Rona has **forgotten** to bring her lunch to school twice this week. —**forgot, forgotten**

fork

A **fork** is a kind of tool to eat with. **Forks** are made of metal or plastic and have sharp points.

form

1. The **form** of something is its shape or what it is like. Clouds have many different **forms. 2.** To **form** something is to give it a shape. Jenna **forms** a piece of clay into a dog. She **formed** another piece of clay into a giraffe. **3.** A **form** is also a kind of something. Ice is another **form** of water. A word can have more than one **form.** "Children" is a **form** of "child."

fort

A **fort** is a building or place with strong walls. **Forts** protect people who are inside them.

forward

1. Forward means in the usual order. Stephanie counted **forward** from one to ten. **2. Forward** also means toward the front. Stuart stepped **forward** when his name was called. The opposite of **forward** is **backward.**

fossil

A **fossil** is an animal that died a very long time ago and turned into stone. The museum has many **fossils** on display. ■

■ **fossil**

fought

Fought is a form of **fight.** Yesterday Bernardo and his brother had a fight, but now they have forgotten what they **fought** about.

found

Found is a form of **find.** Noah always finds something under his bed. Last night he **found** his baseball bat there.

four

Four is one more than three. **Four** is written **4. 3 + 1 = 4.**

fox

A **fox** is a kind of animal. It looks like a small dog. **Foxes** have thick fur, especially on their tails. ■

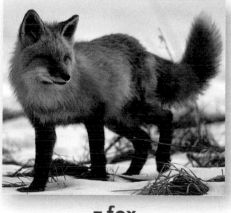

■ **fox**

free

1. To be **free** means that you can do what you like. Benita doesn't have to go to school today. She is **free** for the whole day. 2. **Free** also means that you do not have to pay for something. Air and sunlight are **free.**

freeze

To **freeze** is to change from a liquid into a solid. When water **freezes,** it becomes ice. —**froze, frozen**

fresh

1. **Fresh** means not too old to use. Bread, fruit, and vegetables are best to eat when they are **fresh.**
2. **Fresh** air is air that is clean and good to breathe.
3. **Fresh** water is water that has no salt in it. There is **fresh** water in rivers, ponds, and lakes.

Friday

Friday is a day of the week. **Friday** comes after Thursday and before Saturday.

fried

Fried is a form of **fry.** Many people like to eat **fried** chicken.

friend

A **friend** is someone that likes you and that you like too. Molly and Madison play together and share many secrets. They are best **friends.**

When people are **friends,** they have a **friendship.**

friendly

To be **friendly** means to like to be with people. Some animals are **friendly,** but others are not. —**friendlier, friendliest**

frog

A **frog** is a small animal. It has smooth skin, large eyes, and strong back legs. **Frogs** live near water and eat flies. ■

■ **frog**

from

1. **From** means away. Mackenzie was at school. Then she went to the library. She went **from** school to the library. 2. **From** also means apart. The moon is a long way **from** the earth. 3. **From** also tells where something is found in nature. Apples come **from** trees. 4. **From** also tells what is used to make something. Paper is made **from** wood.

front

Front is the part of something that you see first. Sofia's shirt is blue in **front** and has stripes on the back.

frost

Frost is water that freezes outside into small pieces of ice. You can see **frost** on the leaves on cold days. ■

■ **frost**

frown

1. A **frown** is an unhappy look on a person's face. A **frown** is the opposite of a **smile.** Many **frowns** appeared when it began to rain during the picnic. **2.** To **frown** means to make a frown. Carl **frowned** because he could not go to the playground. ■

■ **frown**

froze

Froze is a form of **freeze.** Last night it was so cold that the lake **froze.**

frozen

Frozen is a form of **freeze.** Ice is water that has **frozen.** ■

fruit

A **fruit** is a part of a plant. It has the seeds of the plant in it. Apples, oranges, and tomatoes are all **fruits.** Many **fruits** are good to eat. ■

■ **frozen**

fry

To **fry** is to cook in very hot oil. On Thursdays Jake's father **fries** chicken for the family's supper. —**fries, fried**

■ **fruit**

full

Full means that something cannot hold any more. Kenneth poured juice into his glass until it was **full,** and then he stopped. ■

> The opposite of **full** is **empty.**

■ **full**

fun

Fun is a happy feeling you get when you do something you like. Lou and his friends wore costumes on Halloween. Everybody had a lot of **fun.**

funny

1. To be **funny** means to make people laugh. Max's uncle tells **funny** jokes. **2. Funny** also means strange. Hana's flute made a **funny** sound. **—funnier, funniest**

fur

Fur is soft, thick hair. Cats, dogs, squirrels, bears, and other animals are covered with **fur.** It keeps them warm in cold weather. ■

> If something has **fur,** we say that it is **furry.** There are a lot of **furry** animals at the zoo.

■ **fur**

furniture

Furniture is objects that people sit on, work on, eat on, and sleep on. Chairs, desks, tables, and beds are all **furniture.**

future

The **future** is the part of time that has not happened yet. Tomorrow is in the **future.** Maybe one day in the **future,** people will be living up in space.

G g

gallon

A **gallon** is an amount of a liquid. It is the same as four quarts. There are **gallons** of milk and juice sold at the supermarket. ■

game

A **game** is a way to play or have fun. Some **games** are played with cards. Others are played with a ball. Every **game** has rules or directions.

■ **gallon**

> A **board game** is a **game** that is played on a board. Checkers is a **board game.**

garage

A **garage** is a building where cars and trucks are kept. Many houses have **garages.** A big **garage** in the city can hold hundreds of cars.

garden

A **garden** is a place where plants are grown. People grow flowers and vegetables in **gardens.** ■

■ **garden**

gas

1. A **gas** is something that is so light that it fills up whatever space it is in. Air and steam are **gases. 2. Gas** also means a group of gases that are mixed together and burned to make energy and heat. Our house is heated by **gas. 3. Gas** is also a short way to say **gasoline.**

gasoline

Gasoline is a kind of liquid that can burn. It is burned in cars and trucks to make them go.

gate

A **gate** is a door in a fence. Some **gates** swing in, and others swing out. ■

■ **gate**

gather

To **gather** means to come together or put together. People often **gather** to listen to music. Ron **gathered** up all his toys and put them in one box.

gave

Gave is a form of **give.** Eva gives her brother some of the books she has read. Last year she **gave** him a book about the stars and planets.

geese

Geese means more than one **goose.** In the fall you can watch **geese** flying south for the winter.

gentle

Gentle means in a soft way that doesn't hurt anything. Pascal was very **gentle** when he held the puppy.

germ

A **germ** is a tiny living thing that can make you sick. **Germs** are too small to see without a microscope.

get

1. To **get** means to have something come to you. Lara **gets** a new sweater from her grandmother every year. **2.** To **get** also means to go and take. Helena was hungry, so she **got** an apple from the refrigerator. **3.** To **get** can mean to become. Doug **gets** tired from running all the way home. **4.** To **get** also means to be able to or be allowed to. My older brother **gets** to stay up later than I do. **5.** To **get** means to arrive. The day the bus broke down, everyone **got** to school late. **6.** To **get** up means to stand up. Burt **got** up to leave after the movie. —**got, gotten**

giant

1. Giant means much bigger than usual. The building had a **giant** statue near the front entrance. **2.** A **giant** is a very tall person. Many children's stories have **giants** in them. ▪

▪ **giant**

gift

A **gift** is something that is given. On her birthday, Caroline got **gifts** from six of her friends.

> Another word for **gift** is **present.**

gigantic

Gigantic means as big as a giant. We saw **gigantic** rocks when we got to the top of the mountain.

giggle

1. To **giggle** is to laugh in a silly way. Keith **giggled** when his father told him a joke.
2. A **giggle** is a time when you giggle. When Rita heard **giggles** in the closet, she knew her brother was hiding in there.

ginger

Ginger is the root of a plant. It is made into a powder and used in some foods.

■ **gingerbread**

gingerbread

Gingerbread is a kind of cake made with ginger. Mona ate a piece of **gingerbread** for dessert. ■

giraffe

A **giraffe** is a very tall animal. It has long legs and a very long neck. **Giraffes** are covered with brown spots. Their necks are long so that they can eat leaves from the tops of trees. ■

■ **giraffe**

girl

A **girl** is a female child. **Girls** grow up to be women.

give

To **give** is to let someone else have something. Logan **gives** his cousins tickets to the school play. Brian has **given** away some of his toys. —**gave, given**

glad

Glad means happy. We went to a ball game yesterday. We were **glad** because the weather was good.
—**gladder, gladdest**

glass

1. Glass is what windows are made from. You can see through **glass.** It feels hard, but it is easy to break. Did you know that **glass** is made from sand? **2.** A **glass** is used to hold liquid that you drink. Dylan can pour his juice into a **glass. 3. Glasses** are made to help people see better. **Glasses** are made of glass or plastic. They fit over your nose and in front of your eyes.

Sunglasses are a special kind of **glasses.** You wear them to protect your eyes when the sun is very bright.

globe

A **globe** is a model of the earth. **Globes** are round and show all of the continents and oceans. ■

■ **globe**

glove

1. A **glove** fits over your hand to protect it. It is made of cloth, wool, leather, or plastic. People usually wear **gloves** to keep their hands warm in cold weather. **2.** Baseball players wear a special kind of **glove** to help them catch the ball. There are several kinds of baseball **gloves.** ■

■ **glove**

glue

Glue is a thick liquid. After it dries, **glue** holds things so they do not come apart.

go

1. To **go** is to move from one place to another. Pam **goes** to school in the morning. She **went** to school late yesterday because the weather was bad. **2.** To **go** also means to leave a place. It is very late, so we have to **go**. **3.** To **go** can mean to lead somewhere. The road **goes** through the forest. It **goes** all the way to the city. **4.** To **go** to sleep means to begin sleeping. Harry closed his eyes, but he could not **go** to sleep. —**goes, went, gone**

goal

1. A **goal** is something you want to do in the future. My **goal** is to become a doctor. People work hard to reach their **goals. 2.** A **goal** is also a space or net where players in some sports try to put a ball. Yoko kicked the ball into the **goal** to win the game. **3.** A **goal** happens when someone puts the ball in the goal. How many **goals** were there in the game?

■ goat

goat

A **goat** is an animal. It has horns, short wool, and hair on its chin. **Goats** are raised for their milk and wool. ■

gold

Gold is a yellow metal. It comes from streams or from underground. **Gold** is used to make rings, coins, and many other things.

goldfish

A **goldfish** is a kind of fish. **Goldfish** are usually small and orange. We keep **goldfish** in a bowl at home. —**goldfish** ■

■ goldfish

gone

Gone is a form of **go.** Marge has **gone** to school. I came to meet her, but she was already **gone.**

good

1. A thing is **good** when people like it. Chuck's bicycle is easy to ride. It is a **good** bicycle. **2. Good** also means doing things well. Kay's mother is a **good** cook. **3. Good** can also mean that something makes you feel healthy. Cold weather is **good** for penguins. —**better, best**

> The opposite of **good** is **bad.** I had a **good** time at the picnic, but the weather was **bad.** It rained all day.

goodbye

Goodbye is the last thing a person says to another person when they finish talking. Jill said "**Goodbye**" to Caitlin and then went home.

gooey

To be **gooey** means to stick to everything. Honey sticks to the spoon you use to get it out of the jar. It sticks to your fingers. Honey is very **gooey. —gooier, gooiest**

goose

A **goose** is a bird. It is like a large duck and has a long neck. Some **geese** fly long distances every winter.
—**geese** ■

■ **goose**

got

Got is a form of **get.** Wesley **got** a magazine in the mail last week. Claire wanted something to read, so she **got** a book from the library. Roseanne almost **got** sick from eating too much. Eddie **got** home late after baseball practice. The next morning he **got** up early to go fishing.

gotten

Gotten is a form of **get.** Lindsey has **gotten** more handkerchiefs than she knows what to do with. I offered to get a banana for my sister, but she had already **gotten** one. Kelsey has never **gotten** too tired to play. Adam had already **gotten** up by seven o'clock.

government

A **government** is a group of people who lead a country, city, or town. In our country we vote for our **government. Governments** make laws and decide many other things.

> Every state has its own **government.** The person who leads a state's **government** is a **governor.**

grade

A **grade** is where you are in school. In her first year Penny was in the first **grade.** This year she is in the second **grade.** There are six **grades** in Penny's school.

grain

1. Grain means the seeds of wheat, rice, corn, and some other plants. Flour and cereal are made from **grain. 2.** A **grain** also means a very tiny piece. **Grains** of sand are very, very small.

gram

A **gram** is a small amount of weight. A penny weighs almost three **grams.**

grandfather

A **grandfather** is the father of your mother or father. Both of my **grandfathers** live in Texas.

> **Grandfathers** and **grandmothers** are called **grandparents.**

grandmother

A **grandmother** is the mother of your mother or father. Both of my **grandmothers** are tall.

grape

A **grape** is a kind of fruit. It is small and round and purple or green. **Grapes** grow on vines in big groups. ■

■ grape

grapefruit

A **grapefruit** is a large, yellow fruit. **Grapefruits** are larger than oranges, and they are not as sweet.

grass

Grass is a kind of plant. It grows in yards, fields, meadows, and parks. There are many different kinds of **grass. —grass** ■

■ grass

grasshopper

A **grasshopper** is a large insect. It has long, strong back legs. **Grasshoppers** can jump many feet in one hop. ■

gravity

Gravity is a force in nature that pulls objects toward the center of the earth. **Gravity** makes things fall to the ground when we drop them.

■ grasshopper

gravy

Gravy is a sauce. It is made from the juice that comes out of meat during cooking. **—gravies**

gray

Gray is a color. Elephants and rain clouds are **gray.**

> When you mix together the colors black and white, they become **gray.**

great

1. Great means very important. Alex has pictures of many **great** people. **2. Great** can mean very good. We had a **great** time on our vacation. **3. Great** also means very large. We stayed inside during the **great** storm last week.

green

Green is a color. Leaves and grass are **green** in the summer.

greenhouse

A **greenhouse** is a special building to grow plants in. **Greenhouses** usually have glass roofs. The air inside is always warm. ■

■ **greenhouse**

grew

Grew is a form of **grow.** Tomatoes **grew** in the garden last summer. Sharon always wanted to be a teacher, and when she **grew** up, that is what she became.

grin

A **grin** is a big smile. Carita cut her pumpkin so that it had a big **grin** for Halloween. She thinks pumpkins with **grins** look funny. ■

grocery

A **grocery** is a store that sells food and other things you need at home. These things are called **groceries. —groceries**

A person who sells **groceries** is called a **grocer.**

■ **grin**

ground

The **ground** is the earth. Jon fell on the **ground** and hurt his knee. Plants grow out of the **ground.**

group

A **group** is a number of people or things together. Two **groups** of students took a trip to the country. Each **group** had a good time. ■

■ **group**

grow

1. To **grow** is to get bigger. Animals and plants **grow** as they get older. This bush has **grown** so big that I can't reach the top. **2.** To **grow** up means to become a woman or a man. When you **grow** up, you may be taller than your father. **—grew, grown**

grownup

A **grownup** is someone who has grown to be a man or a woman. Our parents are **grownups.**

grumble

To **grumble** means to talk about something in an unhappy way. The principal **grumbled** about the students who had bad manners.

grumpy

To be **grumpy** means to be in a bad mood. I was **grumpy** today because I went to bed too late last night. **—grumpier, grumpiest**

guard

1. To **guard** is to watch something so that nothing bad happens to it. Martha **guarded** the picnic basket so that ants and flies would not get inside of it. **2.** A **guard** is a person who watches over something. There are always **guards** in front of the queen's palace. ■

■ **guard**

guess

To **guess** is to try to think of the answer. Shelley does not know where her cat is. She **guesses** that the cat is up in a tree. When she found the cat in the garage, she knew she had **guessed** wrong.

guide

A **guide** is someone or something that shows you what to do. At the museum, the **guides** took us to see the photographs. My mother bought a **guide** and read about the best things to see in the city.

> A **guide dog** is a **dog** that helps blind people know where to go.

guitar

A **guitar** is an instrument that you hold in your arms. **Guitars** are made of wood and have six strings. You hit or pull on the strings with your fingers to make music. ∎

gum

Gum is a kind of sweet, flavored candy that you chew but do not swallow.

∎ guitar

gym

A **gym** is a place inside a building where people play games and exercise. Most schools have large **gyms.**

habit

A **habit** is something you do often. Ryder has a **habit** of drinking a glass of water every night before he goes to bed. People can have good **habits** or bad **habits.**

had

Had is a form of **have.** Ryan and Lucy have four dollars in their bank. Last month they only **had** two dollars.

hadn't

Hadn't is a short way to say **had not.** Justin wanted to watch television, but he **hadn't** done his homework yet.

hair

Hair is what grows on your head. People and some animals have **hair. Hair** can be straight or curly.

> When someone cuts your **hair,** you get a **haircut.** Jackie gets several **haircuts** every year.

half

A **half** is one of two pieces that are the same size. Jeremy gave **half** of his sandwich to me when I forgot my lunch yesterday. —**halves** ■

■ half

hall

A **hall** is a place inside a building. It leads from one room to another room or rooms. Some **halls** are short, and some are long and narrow. ■

■ hall

Halloween

Halloween is a holiday that comes on October 31. People wear costumes on **Halloween.** Sometimes they go out to collect candy in their neighborhoods.

halves

Halves means more than one half. Andrew cut his apple into two **halves.**

ham

Ham is a kind of meat. It comes from pigs. You can buy **hams** at the supermarket. ■

■ ham

hamburger

1. Hamburger is a kind of beef. It has been cut up in very small pieces so you can make it into different shapes. **2.** A **hamburger** is a kind of sandwich. It is made of two pieces of bread with cooked hamburger in between. Denise likes to eat **hamburgers** with onions and ketchup.

hammer

A **hammer** is a tool. It has a handle and a heavy, metal head. It is shaped like a **T. Hammers** are used to hit nails into wood. ■

■ **hammer**

hamster

A **hamster** is a small animal. It is covered with short fur and has a short tail. **Hamsters** make good pets. ■

■ **hamster**

hand

A **hand** is a part of the body. Your **hands** are at the ends of your arms. People use their **hands** to hold things and to use tools. The fingers, the thumb, and the palm are parts of the **hand.**

The parts of a clock or a watch that point to the numbers are called the **hands.** When the big **hand** of the clock is pointing at twelve, and the little **hand** is pointing at four, the time is four o'clock.

A B C D E F G **H** I J K L M

handkerchief

A **handkerchief** is a piece of cloth. You put it over your nose when you sneeze. Many **handkerchiefs** are white.

handle

1. A **handle** is a part of something that you can hold with your hand. Cups, suitcases, and tools all have **handles. 2.** To **handle** something is to hold or touch it with your hands. Sharp tools must be **handled** with care. ∎

∎ **handle**

hang

1. To **hang** is to be held above the ground or floor by something. Priscilla **hangs** from a swing with her legs. **2.** To **hang** is also to put something up so it hangs. I **hung** my coat in the closet. —**hung** ∎

∎ **hang**

happen

To **happen** means to take place. Rana told her parents what **happened** at camp.

happy

To be **happy** means to feel good. Ronnie smiled and laughed at the fair because she was **happy.** —**happier, happiest**

harbor

A **harbor** is a safe area in the water where ships can stay. Ships in **harbors** are protected in storms. ■

■ harbor

hard

1. When something is **hard,** it cannot be shaped with your fingers. Most rocks are **hard. 2. Hard** also means you have to work a lot to do something. **Hard** is the opposite of **easy.** Sometimes homework is **hard.**

> To **harden** means to become **hard.**

hardly

Hardly means almost not at all. There were so many clouds that we **hardly** saw the sun all day.

harp

A **harp** is a tall instrument with many strings. You pull on the strings with your fingers to make melodies. **Harps** are sometimes part of an orchestra. ■

■ harp

harvest

To **harvest** means to gather fruits, vegetables, and other foods from a field when they are ready to eat. Pumpkins and corn are **harvested** in the fall.

has

Has is a form of **have.** Juan **has** two dollars. Aaron **has** two dollars too. Together they have four dollars.

hat

A **hat** is something you wear on your head. **Hats** come in many different shapes and sizes. ▪

▪ **hat**

hatch

To **hatch** is to break out of an egg. Baby crocodiles are very small when they hatch. ▪

▪ **hatch**

hate

To **hate** means to not like something in a very strong way. **Hate** is the opposite of **love.** I **hate** tomatoes, but I **love** strawberries.

have

1. To **have** something means that it is with you. Jamaal **has** a book in his hand. This morning he **had** two books. Cats **have** soft fur. **2.** To **have** to do something means that you have no choice about it. We **have** to brush our teeth every morning. —**has, had**

haven't

Haven't is a short way to say **have not.** Ann and Lynette **haven't** seen their new baby brother yet.

hawk

A **hawk** is a large bird. It has a short, curved beak and strong claws. **Hawks** fly high in the sky and catch small animals on the ground. ■

■ **hawk**

hay

Hay is a kind of tall grass that has been cut and dried. Horses and cows eat **hay.**

he

He means a male person. Edward is a boy. **He** and his brother Freddie are twins.

head

1. The **head** is a part of the body. Your face and your ears are parts of your **head. 2.** A **head** also means a part of a tool. It is the heavy part that does the work. Hammers and axes have **heads.**

A **headstand** is when you put your **head** on the floor and your legs in the air. Clowns in the circus sometimes do **headstands.**

heal

To **heal** is to get better when you are hurt. When you cut your finger, it will **heal** in a few days if you keep it clean.

healthy

Healthy means not sick. Tamiko eats good food and gets exercise so that she will stay **healthy. —healthier, healthiest**

hear

To **hear** is to know what something is like by using your ears. Mick **heard** a loud noise in the other room. **—heard**

heart

The **heart** is a part of the body. It is in the center of your chest. **Hearts** make the blood move through our bodies.

heat

1. **Heat** is a kind of energy that makes things warm or hot. The **heat** from the sun helps plants grow. The **heat** in the oven cooks the food inside it.
2. To **heat** is to make warm. The fire in the fireplace **heated** the whole room.

A **heater** is a machine that can make something warm or hot. A water **heater** makes water warm for washing.

heavy

Heavy means hard to lift. Rocks and bowling balls are **heavy,** but pillows are light. My father and I carried the **heavy** box to the car. **—heavier, heaviest** ■

■ **heavy**

heel

1. The **heel** is a part of the body. It is the back part of the foot. When you put your feet into shoes, your toes go in first, and your **heels** go in last. **2.** The **heel** is a part of a shoe. It is the part that is under the heel of your foot. Some shoes have high **heels.** ∎

∎ **heel**

height

The **height** of something is how high it is. Sandy is five feet tall. Her **height** is five feet. The balloon rose to a **height** of one thousand feet.

held

Held is a form of **hold.** Lana lifted the baby and **held** it in her arms. Colleen tried to put all her toys in one box, but it only **held** half of them.

helicopter

A **helicopter** is a machine. It carries people through the air. **Helicopters** do not have wings like airplanes. They have propellers on the top. The propeller turns around and lifts the **helicopter** off the ground. ∎

∎ **helicopter**

hello

Hello is the first word people say to each other when they talk. When people pick up a telephone that is ringing, they usually say "**Hello.**"

helmet

A **helmet** is a special kind of hat. It is hard and protects your head. My family always wears **helmets** when we ride our bicycles. ■

■ **helmet**

help

To **help** is to give what someone or something needs. Janice **helped** Julia lift the heavy umbrella. The rain **helps** the grass to grow.

hen

A **hen** is a female chicken. **Hens** sit on eggs before they hatch.

her

1. Her means a female person or animal. Corey borrowed a book from Rosa. He gave it back to **her** after two days. **2. Her** also means belonging to a female person or animal. Gina has a room in the house where she keeps **her** things. It is **her** room.

herd

A **herd** is a group of one kind of animal. Cows, sheep, elephants, and other animals live in **herds.** ■

here

Here means in this place. We are waiting for the bus, but it is not **here** yet.

■ **herd**

hero

1. A **hero** is a person who is very brave and does great things to help other people. The firefighters who run into burning buildings are **heroes. 2.** A **hero** is also the most important person in a story or poem. The **hero** of my book is a girl who loves horses. **—heroes**

hers

Hers means belonging to her. Kip has his own room, and his sister has **hers.** Everything in her room is **hers.**

herself

Herself means her and nobody else. Linda looked at **herself** in the mirror. Then she put on her shoes. Nobody helped her. She put them on by **herself.**

hide

1. To **hide** something is to put it where nobody will see it. Gabriel **hid** his mother's present behind the sofa. **2.** To **hide** also means to go where no one can see you. Vic told his sister to **hide** so that he could look for her. She has **hidden** behind the house. **—hid, hidden**

high

1. High means far above the ground or bottom. Brandi stood **high** above the pool before she dived into the water. **2. High** also means greater than usual. On hot days the temperature is **high. ■**

■ **high**

hill

A **hill** is a big bump in the ground. You can climb up one side of a **hill** and down the other side. **Hills** are like small mountains. ■

■ hill

> A **hilltop** is the highest part of a **hill.** It took us a long time to climb to the **hilltop.**

him

Him means a male person or animal. On Dean's birthday, his grandfather took **him** to a baseball game.

himself

Himself means him and nobody else. Michael had a mask on his face. When he looked at **himself** in the mirror, he scared **himself.**

hippopotamus

A **hippopotamus** is a very large animal. It is as big as a small car. **Hippopotamuses** have short legs and large mouths. They swim in lakes and rivers and eat grass. ■

■ hippopotamus

his

His means belonging to him. This watch belongs to Alberto. It is **his** watch.

history

History is what has happened in the past. In school we study the **history** of our state.

hit

To **hit** is to move very hard against something. Baseball players try to **hit** the ball with a bat. An apple fell from the tree and **hit** the ground. —**hit**

hive

A **hive** is a home for bees. Bees make honey inside of **hives.** ∎

∎ **hive**

hobby

A **hobby** is something you like to do when you have time. Some **hobbies** are collecting things, drawing, taking photographs, and playing music. —**hobbies**

hockey

Hockey is the name of two sports. In field **hockey** two teams hit a ball across a field with sticks. In ice **hockey** two teams hit a piece of rubber across the ice. Ice **hockey** players wear skates.

hold

1. To **hold** is to have something in your hands or arms. People can **hold** very large things in their arms. They can **hold** small things in their hands. **2.** To **hold** also means to have room for. A small car will only **hold** four people. —**held** ∎

∎ **hold**

A B C D E F G **H** I J K L M

hole

A **hole** is an empty place in something. Some birds and animals live in **holes** in trees. Two raccoons looked at us from a **hole** in the tree. ■

■ **hole**

holiday

A **holiday** is a special day. Some people do not go to school or work on **holidays.** Sometimes there are parades and fireworks on **holidays.**

> Different countries have their own special **holidays.** In our country, Thanksgiving is a **holiday** that comes in November.

hollow

Hollow means with an empty space inside. Basketballs are **hollow.** Some animals live in **hollow** trees. ■

■ **hollow**

home

A **home** is a place where people or animals live. Most people have **homes** in houses or apartments.

homework

Homework is something that you bring from school to do at home. The next day you bring it back to school for the teacher to correct.

honest

To be **honest** means to tell the truth. Bennett tries to be **honest** so that people will trust him.

honey

Honey is a thick, sweet liquid. It is made by bees. **Honey** is good to eat on toast, in cereal, and with many other foods. ∎

∎ **honey**

hood

A **hood** is a kind of clothes that covers your head and neck. Most **hoods** are parts of shirts and coats. ∎

hook

A **hook** is a curved piece of metal. It is shaped like a J. Some **hooks** have points on the end and are used to catch fish. Other **hooks** are used to keep clothes off the floor. ∎

∎ **hood**

hop

1. To **hop** is to jump up in the air. Rabbits, frogs, grasshoppers, and kangaroos **hop** from place to place. **2.** A **hop** is a jump. Colette jumped over the stream in one **hop.** —**hopped**

hope

To **hope** is to believe something good may happen. We want to swim in the lake tomorrow. We **hope** tomorrow will be sunny. James **hopes** his father will cook something good for dinner.

∎ **hook**

hopped

Hopped is a form of **hop.** The kangaroos **hopped** across the plain.

horn

1. A **horn** is part of an animal's body. Bulls, goats, and some other animals have two **horns** on their heads. **2.** A **horn** is also an instrument. Kaylee blows into her **horn** to make music. **3.** A **horn** is also something that makes a loud noise in the air. We heard the truck's **horn** blow two times. ■

■ **horn**

horse

A **horse** is a large animal with long legs. **Horses** live on farms. People like to ride **horses.** ■

> A **horseshoe** is a piece of iron that is shaped like a **U. Horses** wear **horseshoes** to protect their feet.

■ **horse**

hose

A **hose** is a tube made of rubber or cloth. Firefighters put out fires with water from **hoses.** ■

hospital

A **hospital** is a large building. Doctors and nurses take care of sick people in **hospitals.**

■ **hose**

hot

Hot means something that has a lot of heat. **Hot** is the opposite of **cold.** The sun is **hot** on bright summer days. The inside of an oven is **hot.**

hot dog

A **hot dog** is a kind of food. It is made from meat and other things. People often eat **hot dogs** in long rolls with mustard on them.

hotel

A **hotel** is a big building with many rooms. People who are away from home stay in them. Big cities have many **hotels** because many people come to visit the city.

hour

An **hour** is an amount of time. There are 24 **hours** in one day. One **hour** has 60 minutes in it.

> When you are telling the time, the small hand of the clock points to the **hour.** The big hand points to the minute.

house

A **house** is a building where people live. There are two yellow **houses** in Pilar's neighborhood. ■

■ house

how

1. **How** tells the way something is done. Mercedes wanted to know the way to make a rabbit come out of her hat. "**How** did you make that rabbit come out of your hat?" she asked the magician. He did not tell her **how** he did it. 2. **How** much tells the amount of something. **How** much rain did we get yesterday?

howl

To **howl** means to make a loud cry. The wolf **howled** in the forest. I **howled** when my friend stepped on my foot by accident.

hug

To **hug** is to put your arms around someone and hold that person tight. Some people **hug** each other to show that they are glad to see each other. —**hugged** ∎

∎ **hug**

huge

Huge means very big. Joel made himself a sandwich with turkey, ham, cheese, lettuce, tomato, and three pieces of bread. That was a **huge** sandwich. ∎

∎ **huge**

hugged

Hugged is a form of **hug. I hugged** my grandparents when they arrived at the airport.

human

Human means about people. A **human** body is the body of a person. Girls and boys and men and women are **human.**

hump

A **hump** is a bump on an animal's back. Some camels have two **humps.** Other camels have one **hump.** ∎

∎ **hump**

hundred

A **hundred** is a number. It is written **100.** It takes ten tens to make one **hundred.** There were **hundreds** of people in the audience.

hung

Hung is a form of **hang.** Bert's mother asked him to hang his shirt in the closet. He said he had **hung** it up already.

hungry

To be **hungry** is to want to eat. Betsy has not eaten breakfast yet. She is very **hungry. —hungrier, hungriest**

hurry

To **hurry** is to try to go quickly. When you are late, you have to **hurry. —hurries, hurried**

hurt

1. To **hurt** is to break something or make someone feel bad. If you fall on the sidewalk, you may **hurt** yourself.
2. To **hurt** also means to feel bad. Juana's back was burned in the sun and **hurt** for several days. **—hurt**

husband

A **husband** is a married man. My teacher's **husband** works at the post office. Both **husbands** and wives came to the picnic.

hut

A **hut** is a very simple, small house. **Huts** are usually built in places where the weather is warm. ■

■ **hut**

Ii

I

I is a word you use when you speak about yourself. This coat belongs to me. **I** wear it during the winter to keep me warm.

ice

Ice is water that has frozen. It is hard and cold. Annabel skates on the **ice** that covers the pond. Brandon put **ice** in his drink to keep it cold. ■

■ ice

An **ice skate** is a **skate** with a sharp edge for **skating** on **ice**.

■ ice cream

ice cream

Ice cream is a kind of food. It is a frozen dessert. **Ice cream** is made from cream or milk, eggs, and sugar. There are many different flavors of **ice cream**. ■

idea

An **idea** is something that you think of. You can have an **idea** about anything. Mitch and Mohammed often get **ideas** for new inventions.

if

If tells what might happen. Mack may decide to go to the store, or he may not. **If** he goes, he will buy some bread. **If** it rains today, we will need to use our umbrellas.

igloo

An **igloo** is a kind of house. It is made of blocks of snow. People who live in cold places sometimes build **igloos.** ■

■ **igloo**

ill

Ill means sick. Richard is too **ill** to go outside today. ■

I'll

I'll is a short way to say **I will.** After I finish this book, **I'll** be glad to let you borrow it.

I'm

I'm is a short way to say **I am. I'm** almost as tall as my brother.

■ **ill**

imagine

To **imagine** is to see a picture in your mind. When the snow is falling outside her window, Leora likes to **imagine** that it is summer. She **imagines** herself at the beach in the warm sun.

important

Important things are things you care about or need. Tracy will feel sad if she does not learn to ski. It is **important** to her to learn to ski. Teachers and scientists do work that helps other people. They do **important** work.

impossible

Impossible means that something cannot be. It is **impossible** for the sun to come up in the west.

in

1. **In** tells where something is. Fish swim **in** the water.
2. **In** tells when something happens. Christian's birthday is **in** May. We will have dinner **in** one hour.

inch

An **inch** is an amount of length. There are 12 **inches** in one foot.

independent

Independent means not controlled by anyone else. An **independent** country makes its own laws.

information

Information is facts that you know. You can get **information** from teachers in school, reading books, and listening to other people. My mother gets **information** from reading the newspaper every day.

When you give **information** to people, you **inform** them. The principal **informed** us that our teacher was sick.

injure

To **injure** means to hurt. Two people were **injured** in the accident.

ink

Ink is a liquid that people write with. When you write with a pen, **ink** comes out onto the paper. Many pens have blue or black **ink,** but **ink** can also be other colors. ■

■ ink

insect

An **insect** is a small animal. All **insects** have six legs. Some **insects** can fly. Flies, ants, butterflies, grasshoppers, and bees are all **insects,** but spiders are not. ■

■ insect

inside

1. To be **inside** means to be in something. The sisters stayed **inside** the tent until the weather got cold. Then they went **inside** the house to get warm. **2.** The **inside** of something is what is inside it. The **inside** of a banana is soft. ■

■ inside

instant

An **instant** is a very short amount of time. **Instants** are almost too short to notice. Lightning only flashes for an **instant.**

instead

Instead means in the place of. Melissa wanted to eat an orange. But she only found pears in the refrigerator. So she ate a pear **instead.**

instrument

1. An **instrument** is something that makes music. Pianos, flutes, trumpets, drums, violins, trombones, and guitars are all **instruments.** There are many **instruments** in an orchestra. **2.** An **instrument** is also a small tool that some people use when they work. Doctors and dentists use special **instruments** when they take care of people. ■

■ **instrument**

interest

An **interest** is something you like to learn more about. Elisa has a great **interest** in drawing. She has many other **interests,** too.

> When you are **interested** in something, you want to learn or hear more about it. You think it is **interesting.** My uncle told me many **interesting** stories about his vacation.

into

1. **Into** tells where something goes. My father drives the car **into** the garage. 2. **Into** also tells what something becomes when it changes. Caterpillars change **into** moths and butterflies.

invent

To **invent** means to make something that nobody has ever made before. My uncle has **invented** many useful machines.

> An **invention** is a thing that someone **invents.** Automobiles, radios, and computers are important **inventions.**

invite

To **invite** is to ask someone to come and visit you. Jillian **invited** three of her friends for dinner.

> An **invitation** is a note you write to **invite** someone. Victor gave everyone in the class **invitations** to his party.

iron

1. **Iron** is a kind of metal. It is gray or black. **Iron** is very hard and strong. 2. An **iron** is used to take wrinkles out of clothes. The bottom of the **iron** is flat and gets very hot. Some **irons** make steam. ■

■ **iron**

is

Is is a form of **be.** Last year Ian was six years old. This year he **is** seven. Next year he will be eight.

island

An **island** is an area of land that has water all around it. Rivers, lakes, and oceans can all have **islands** in them. ■

■ **island**

isn't

Isn't is a short way to say **is not.** "Is Karina home?" "No, she **isn't.**"

it

1. It means a thing. Anthony took his bicycle out of the garage. Then he rode **it** to the store. **2. It** also means the way things are. **It** is raining today. If **it** is cold enough tomorrow, **it** may even snow.

itch

1. To **itch** is to make you want to scratch. Mel's head **itches** under his helmet. **2.** An **itch** is what you feel when something itches. I have an **itch** on my nose.

> Something that makes you **itch** is **itchy.** Sometimes sweaters and blankets are **itchy.**

its

Its means belonging to it. Sometimes a dog or cat will chase **its** own tail.

it's

It's is a short way to say **it is.** What a beautiful day it is. **It's** too nice to stay inside.

itself

Itself means it and nothing else. Tom's mother said, "Please clean up your room. It won't clean **itself!**"

I've

I've is a short way to say **I have.** I would like to go to the circus. **I've** never been to one before.

ivy

Ivy is a kind of plant. **Ivies** are vines that can climb up the walls of buildings. They have green leaves. ■

> **Poison ivy** is a plant that has three leaves. If you touch it, it can make your skin itch a lot.

■ ivy

jacket

A **jacket** is a short, light coat.
Jackets are good to wear when
the weather is cool or cold. ■

jail

A **jail** is a kind of building. It has
metal poles on the windows and
doors. People who break the law
have to stay in **jail.**

jam

Jam is a kind of food. It is made from
fruit and sugar boiled together. **Jams**
are thick and sweet.

January

January is the first month of the year.
It has 31 days. **January** comes after
December and before February.

■ **jacket**

jar

A **jar** is used to hold things. It looks like a fat bottle with a wide top. Jam, peanut butter, mustard and other foods come in glass **jars.**

jaw

A **jaw** is a part of the body. It is a bone at the bottom of your face. When you speak, your **jaw** moves. Sharks have large **jaws.**

jelly

Jelly is a kind of food. It is made from fruit juice and sugar boiled together. **Jellies** can be made from many kinds of fruit. —**jellies**

> **Jellybeans** are a type of candy made like **jelly.** They are made by boiling sugar. **Jellybeans** are hard on the outside and soft on the inside.

jellyfish

A **jellyfish** is a kind of animal. It has a soft body and floats in the ocean. **Jellyfish** can hurt you if you touch them. —**jellyfish** ■

■ **jellyfish**

jet

A **jet** is a kind of airplane. Its engines do not use propellers. **Jets** fly faster than other planes. ■

■ **jet**

jewel

A **jewel** is a kind of stone. Light can pass through it. Diamonds, emeralds, and rubies are **jewels.**

> **Jewelry** is things we wear that are made of **jewels.**

job

A **job** is the work someone has to do. It is Wade's **job** to help wash the dishes after supper. When people become grownups, they get **jobs** to earn money. Barbara is a carpenter. That is her **job.**

jog

To **jog** is to run. People who **jog** do not try to run fast. They **jog** to exercise and to keep themselves healthy. —**jogged** ■

join

1. To **join** is to put together. We **joined** the pieces of the puzzle together. 2. To **join** also means become a part of. Both boys and girls can **join** our singing group. 3. To **join** also means to come together. Our families **joined** for the holiday. ■

joke

A **joke** is a short, funny story. Wanda likes to make people laugh by telling them **jokes.**

■ jog

■ join

jolly

To be **jolly** means to laugh and smile a lot. Gabrielle's father was very **jolly** at the school carnival. **—jollier, jolliest**

journey

A **journey** is a long trip. The movie we saw is about some friends and their **journeys** through space.

joy

Joy is the feeling you have when you are very happy. Danny felt great **joy** when the dentist took off his braces.

judge

1. A **judge** is a person who decides things. **Judges** help to decide who is right when people cannot agree. **2.** To **judge** is to decide. Kristen and Trevor asked their teacher to **judge** who drew the better picture.

juggle

To **juggle** means to keep two or more things up in the air at one time by throwing and catching them one after the other. Lea's father can **juggle** five things for a minute. He **juggled** at our family picnic last summer. ■

■ **juggle**

juice

Juice is the liquid inside foods. People drink the **juice** of apples, oranges, grapes, tomatoes, and many other fruits. ∎

When something has a lot of **juice,** we say it is **juicy.** Grapes are **juicy.** Raisins are not.

∎ **juice**

July

July is a month of the year. It has 31 days. **July** comes after June and before August.

jump

To **jump** is to push yourself into the air with your legs. Katya **jumped** up to catch the ball and won the game. Our cat **jumps** down from the chair to the floor.

A **jump rope** is a **rope** that a person **jumps** over for fun or exercise. It is held by one or two people.

June

June is a month of the year. It has 30 days. **June** comes after May and before July.

jungle

A **jungle** is a place where many trees and large plants grow. **Jungles** are found where the weather is warm, and there is a lot of rain. Tigers, birds, monkeys, and snakes live in the **jungle.** ■

■ jungle

junk

Junk is things that people do not want to keep. Old machines and broken furniture are **junk.** ■

■ junk

just

1. Just means only. Catherine thought she heard a monster outside the window, but it was **just** a squirrel. **2. Just** also means a little before. Todd's birthday was yesterday. He has **just** turned seven.
3. Just can also mean the right amount and no more. The kite George wanted cost five dollars. He had five dollars in his pocket. George had **just** enough money to buy the kite.

Kk

kangaroo

A **kangaroo** is a large animal. **Kangaroos** have strong back legs for jumping. **Kangaroo** mothers carry their babies in a pocket in the front of their bodies. ■

■ **kangaroo**

keep

1. To **keep** means to have and not give away. Paula gave Hans a book. She said he could **keep** it as long as he wanted. Hans **kept** the book for three weeks. **2.** To **keep** also means to put in a special place. Mark **kept** his baseball glove in the closet until he needed it. **3.** To **keep** can also mean to continue to be. Reina has to **keep** quiet while her baby sister is sleeping. She **kept** quiet until her sister woke up. **4.** To **keep** a promise means to do what you say you will do. Abe said he would come to the party, and he **kept** his promise. **5.** To **keep** a secret means to not tell it to anyone. I will **keep** the secret that my sister told me. —**kept**

ketchup

Ketchup is a kind of food. It is a thick, red liquid that is made from tomatoes. **Ketchup** is good to eat on hot dogs and hamburgers.

kettle

A **kettle** is a large pot. Water is boiled in **kettles.** ∎

∎ **kettle**

key

1. A **key** is a piece of metal. It opens a lock. People use **keys** to open the doors of their homes and cars.
2. A **key** is also a part of a piano. The **keys** are where you put your fingers to play. There are black **keys** and white **keys** on a piano.

On a piano, the black and white **keys** together are called a **keyboard.**

keyhole

A **keyhole** is the hole in a lock. You put the key into the **keyhole** and turn it to open the lock.

kick

To **kick** is to hit something with your foot. Our neighbor **kicked** the soccer ball all the way across the field. ∎

∎ **kick**

kid

1. **Kid** is another word for **child.** The **kids** in my family like to go skating. 2. A **kid** is also a young goat. There are lambs, **kids,** and calves at the little zoo down the road.

kill

To **kill** is to cause something to die. Poison in the water **killed** the fish.

kilometer

A **kilometer** is an amount of length. One **kilometer** is a thousand meters. A **kilometer** is a little more than one half of one mile.

kind

1. **Kind** means a form of something. Lettuce is one **kind** of vegetable. Carrots and potatoes are other **kinds. 2.** To be **kind** is to try to help others. Sari tries to be **kind** to people who have no home.

kindergarten

Kindergarten is a class in school. It is the year before first grade.

king

A **king** is a man who rules a country. **Kings** are usually the sons of **kings** or queens.

A **kingdom** is a place where a **king** or a queen rules. People do not vote for the rulers in **kingdoms.**

kiss

1. To **kiss** is to touch with the lips. Seth **kissed** his mother before he went to bed. **2.** A **kiss** is a touch with the lips. Shea gives her father **kisses** when he comes home.

kit

1. A **kit** is a set of things that you have to put together. Model cars and airplanes often come in **kits. 2.** A **kit** is also a set of tools or other things that are used to do something. We always pack a sewing **kit** when we go on vacation.

kitchen

A **kitchen** is a room in a house where people cook food. Most **kitchens** have a stove, an oven, and a refrigerator.

kite

A **kite** is a kind of toy. It is made of sticks covered with paper or cloth. You hold on to it with a string. The wind holds **kites** up in the sky. ■

kitten

A **kitten** is a young cat. Most **kittens** like to drink milk. ■

■ **kite**

■ **kitten**

knee

The **knee** is a part of the leg. It bends like an elbow. People bend their **knees** when they sit down.

> When you sit with your **knees** on the ground, you are **kneeling.** The teacher asked the children to **kneel** in a circle.

knew

Knew is a form of **know.** Savannah **knew** how to write her name when she was four years old.

knife

A **knife** is a kind of tool. It has a handle and a piece of metal with a sharp edge. Pete used a **knife** to cut an apple. —**knives**

knight

A **knight** is a person who rode a horse in the army of a king or queen. **Knights** lived long ago. Sometimes they wore armor. ■

■ knight

knives

Knives means more than one **knife.** We cut our meat with **knives.**

knock

To **knock** means to hit. Ellen **knocked** on the door three times before her friend Renee opened it.

knot

A **knot** is a place where two things are tied together. People make **knots** in string, rope, and ribbon. ■

■ **knot**

know

1. To **know** something means to have something that is true in your mind. Our teacher **knows** the names of all the students in the class. We **know** where the train station is. **2.** To **know** someone is to be able to say who he or she is. My brother **knew** all the teachers in his school. Al and Mandy have **known** each other for two years. **3.** To **know** how means to be able to do something. Celine **knows** how to spell "rhinoceros." Marty has **known** how to write for a long time. **—knew, known**

The **k** in words that begin with **kn-** is silent. **Knot** sounds like **not**. **Know** sounds like **no.**

koala

A **koala** is a furry animal that lives in trees. It eats leaves and bark. ■

■ **koala**

Ll

laboratory

A **laboratory** is a room or building used for science experiments or research. In the school science **laboratories,** students look at pond water under microscopes. **—laboratories**

lace

Lace is a fancy kind of cloth. It is made of very thin threads with spaces between them. Maura only wears her **lace** shirt on holidays.

ladder

A **ladder** is used to climb up and down. It is made of wood, metal, or rope. Carpenters use **ladders** to work on high places. ■

laid

Laid is a form of **lay.** The carpenter **laid** some boards on the ground. Then he put nails in them.

■ ladder

lain

Lain is a form of **lie.** Kurt likes to lie on his bed. When he has **lain** there for a few minutes, he usually falls asleep.

lake

A **lake** is a large amount of water that is all in one place. A **lake** has land all around it. **Lakes** are not as big as oceans. ■

> The water in a **lake** is fresh because it does not have salt in it. Water from an ocean is very salty.

■ **lake**

lamb

A **lamb** is a young sheep. Wool from **lambs** is very soft. ■

lamp

A **lamp** is a machine used to make light. Most **lamps** use electricity.

land

1. Land is the part of the world that is not covered by water. **Land** is usually made of rocks and dirt. People live on **land. 2.** A **land** is a country. You can collect stamps from many different **lands. 3.** The **land** is the earth or ground that someone uses. The farmers planted potatoes on their **land. 4.** To **land** is to come down to the ground. The airplane **landed** in a field.

■ **lamb**

language

Language is what people use when they speak or write to each other. Some people can speak several **languages.**

A **language** has many thousands of words. People put words together to make sentences.

lantern

A **lantern** is a container for holding a candle or a lamp to light up dark places. You can carry some **lanterns** in your hand. Other **lanterns** rest on poles or hang from the ceiling. ■

large

To be **large** is to fill a lot of space. Elephants are **large** animals.

The opposite of **large** is **small.**

■ **lantern**

last

1. Last means that there are not any more. The letter **Z** is the **last** letter in the alphabet. **2. Last** also means the one before. **Last** night it was so cold that there is frost on the ground this morning. **3.** To **last** means to stay. The ice on the roof **lasted** for a week.

late

1. Late means after the time when something is expected to happen. We got to the movie after it started. We were **late** for the movie. **2. Late** also means near the end. My sister and I went to bed **late** last night.

later

Later means after more time. We can't come now, but we will see you later.

laugh

To laugh is to make a sound that shows that something is funny. Emmy and her sister always laugh when they hear a good joke. ■

■ laugh

laundry

Laundry is dirty clothes that are ready to be washed. Laundry is also clean clothes that have just been washed. ■

law

A law is a rule that people agree to. Laws are made to tell people what is right for them to do.

■ laundry

lay

1. To lay means to put something down. When it was time for lunch, the carpenter laid down his tools. 2. Lay is also a form of lie. Sylvie was tired. She lay down on her bed and went to sleep. —laid

lazy

To be lazy is to want to do nothing. Yesterday was so nice that Clark did not want to cut the grass. He felt too lazy to work. —lazier, laziest

lead

1. **Lead** is a kind of metal. It is soft and gray. **Lead** is very heavy. 2. **Lead** is the part of a pencil that makes marks on paper. Pencil **leads** are made from a special powder that is pressed together. 3. To **lead** means to go first and show the way. The man **led** his camel through the desert. 4. To **lead** also means to be the person who decides. Our teacher **leads** the class. 5. To **lead** also means to go in the direction of. This road **leads** into the forest. —**led** ■

■ **lead**

> When **lead** means metal or part of a pencil, it rhymes with **head.** When **lead** means to be first, it rhymes with **seed.**

leaf

A **leaf** is part of a plant. **Leaves** are usually green. They are the part that makes food for the plant. **Leaves** come in many different shapes. —**leaves** ■

leap

To **leap** means to jump up quickly. The frog **leaped** over the rock.

■ **leaf**

learn

To **learn** is to get to know something. Jo **learned** how to play the guitar last summer.

leash

A **leash** is a rope or strip used to hold an animal or lead it from one place to another. There are many dogs on **leashes** at the park. ■

■ **leash**

least

Least means less than any other. A car makes some noise. A bicycle makes less noise. Walking makes the **least** noise of all.

leather

Leather is the skin of some animals. It is made into boots, shoes, and gloves. ■

leave

1. To **leave** is to go away. We have to **leave** at five o'clock. **2.** To **leave** also means to put something somewhere and then go away. You can **leave** your books on the chair until dinner is over. **3.** To **leave** out means not to put something or someone in. The cook **left** the salt out of the soup. **—left**

■ **leather**

leaves

Leaves means more than one **leaf.** Some **leaves** change color in the fall.

led

Led is a form of **lead.** Abby **led** her sister by the hand.

left

1. **Left** is a direction. It is the opposite of **right.** We read words on a page from **left** to right. 2. **Left** is also a form of **leave.** I went to Rolf's house on the way to school, but he had already **left.** Allison cannot remember where she **left** her shoes.

leg

1. A **leg** is a part of the body. Animals and people use their **legs** to walk. Insects have six **legs. 2.** A **leg** is also a piece that holds something up. Most furniture has **legs.**

legend

A **legend** is a very old story that people believe but may not be true. The **legends** about King Arthur and his knights have been told for many hundreds of years.

lemon

A **lemon** is a kind of fruit. It is yellow. **Lemons** have a sour taste. ■

■ **lemon**

If you squeeze a **lemon,** juice will come out. You can mix the juice with water and sugar to make **lemonade.**

lend

To **lend** means to let someone borrow something. I **lent** my new helmet to my sister. —**lent**

length

Length is how long something is. Our cat's tail is ten inches long. Its **length** is ten inches.

lent

Lent is a form of **lend.** My mother **lent** our mop to our neighbor.

leopard

A **leopard** is a large animal. It is a kind of wild cat. **Leopards** usually have brown or yellow fur with groups of black spots. ∎

∎ leopard

less

Less means not as much. A quart of milk is **less** than a gallon of milk.

> The opposite of **less** is **more.**

lesson

A **lesson** is something that you learn. Cassie practices hard for her piano **lessons.**

let

1. To **let** means not to stop something. Polly's mother **lets** her have a glass of juice before supper. When Deborah threw an apple to her brother, he didn't catch it. He **let** it fall on the ground. **2.** To **let** also means to cause something to happen. My new glasses **let** me see the boats on the ocean.

let's

Let's is a short way to say **let us.** "**Let's** go to a movie," Connie said to her father when she came home from school.

letter

1. A **letter** is one of the symbols people use to write words. The **letters** of our alphabet are A, B, C, D, E, F, G, H, I, J, K, L, M, N, O, P, Q, R, S, T, U, V, W, X, Y, and Z. **2.** A **letter** is also a message you write on paper. Eli writes **letters** to all of his friends.

> Every **letter** can be capital or small. The **letter** **E** is a capital **letter.** The **letter e** is a small **letter.**

lettuce

Lettuce is a kind of vegetable. It has large, green leaves. Rabbits like to eat **lettuce.** ■

■ **lettuce**

library

A **library** is a place where many books are kept. People borrow books from **libraries** to take home and read. —**libraries** ■

> A person who works in a **library** is called a **librarian.** A **librarian** helps you find the books that you want. Is there a **librarian** at your school?

■ **library**

■ lick

lick

To **lick** means to move your tongue over something. My dog **licked** my chin when I saw him today. ■

lie

1. To **lie** is to say something that is not true. When Cheyenne broke a window, she did not want to get into trouble. So she **lied** and said she had not done it. **2.** A **lie** is something you say that is not true. Carlos told his mother a **lie,** but later he decided to tell the truth. **3.** To **lie** is to be in a place and not move. Faith **lay** on her bed yesterday when she was tired. The cat has **lain** on the sofa all day. **—lay, lain**

life

1. Life is what animals and plants have when they are alive. **2.** A **life** is the time something is alive. Insects have short **lives.** Some trees have very long **lives. —lives**

lift

To **lift** is to pick up. The rock was so heavy that two people together could not **lift** it. Yasmin's father **lifted** her so she could reach the swing at the playground. ■

■ lift

light

1. Light is energy that we can see. The sun, stars, lamps, and candles make **light. 2.** To be **light** is to have light. During the day it is **light** outside. **3.** To **light** is to make something burn. Cara's aunt **lighted** a fire in the fireplace. **4. Light** means easy to lift. It is the opposite of **heavy.** Feathers are **light.**

A **lighthouse** is a tall building with a **light** at the top. **Lighthouses** stand near the shore of the ocean. Their **lights** guide ships in fog and at night.

lightning

Lightning is a big flash of light in the sky. It is a form of electricity. **Lightning** can come from the sky to the ground during storms. ■

■ lightning

like

1. To **like** something means that it makes you feel good. Rafael and his friends **like** pizza. **2. Like** means the same as. Brad and Brent are twin brothers. They look **like** each other. **3. Like** also means in the same way as. The kids pretended to walk **like** elephants. **4. Like** also means for example. Clare loves team sports **like** soccer and basketball.

lime

A **lime** is a kind of fruit. It is green and looks like a small lemon. **Limes** have a sour taste. ■

■ lime

line

1. A **line** is a long, thin mark. **Lines** can be straight, curved, or crooked.

2. A **line** is a group of people where each person stands behind another. Dawn and Marguerite stood in a **line** to buy tickets to a movie. They were waiting in **line**.

> You can make shapes by drawing **lines** in a special way. A square is made from four **lines.** A triangle is made from three **lines.**

lion

A **lion** is a large animal. It is a kind of wild cat. Male **lions** have long, thick hair around their heads. ■

lioness

A **lioness** is a female lion. **Lionesses** are smaller than male lions. They do not have long hair around their heads. ■

■ lion
■ lioness

lip

A **lip** is a part of the face. It is around the outside of your mouth. People have two **lips.**

liquid

A **liquid** is something that you can pour. **Liquid** in a bottle will take the shape of the bottle. Water, milk, and juice are **liquids.**

> You can turn a **liquid** into something that is hard. If you put water in a very cold place, it will freeze and become ice. Ice is a **solid.**

list

A **list** is a group of names that you write down. Patrick's father gave him a **list** of things to buy at the store. He makes **lists** so Patrick can remember what to buy. ■

Buy:
eggs
carrots
bread
milk
tomatoes

■ list

listen

To **listen** is to hear and pay attention to. When she is riding in a car, Marlene likes to **listen** to music. ■

little

1. **Little** means small. Only two people can fit into our **little** car. 2. A **little** means not very much. Sue ate a **little** soup, but she wasn't very hungry.

> The opposite of **little** is **big.**

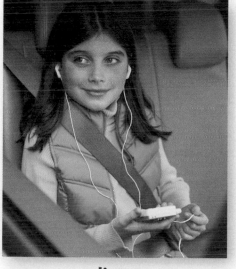

■ listen

live

1. To **live** means to grow and change. Some turtles **live** for more than a hundred years. 2. To **live** means to have a home. Many people **live** in cities. Fish **live** in the water.

lives

Lives means more than one life. Insects have short **lives.** Some people have long **lives.**

load

1. A **load** is something to be carried. Phil brought two **loads** of wood into the house. 2. To **load** is to put something in a place where it can be carried away. Liz and her brother **loaded** boxes into the van.

loaf

1. A **loaf** is an amount of bread. It is baked in one piece. Khalid bought two **loaves** of bread at the store. 2. To **loaf** also means not to work when you should. Darius was **loafing** instead of mopping the garage. —**loaves** ∎

∎ **loaf**

lobster

A **lobster** is a small animal. It lives on the bottom of the ocean. **Lobsters** have hard shells and big claws and tails. ∎

∎ **lobster**

lock

1. A **lock** is an object used to keep something shut. You can open the **lock** only if you have a key. **2.** To **lock** means to put the key in the lock and turn it. Arthur **locked** all the doors to his house before he went away. ■

■ lock

> A **locker** is a place that can be **locked** to keep things safe. My older sister has a **locker** at school.

log

A **log** is a large, round piece of wood. **Logs** are cut from trees. Some **logs** are used in fireplaces. Other **logs** are cut up into boards. ■

■ log

long

1. Long is the opposite of **short.** Swans and giraffes have **long** necks. **2. Long** means how much time something takes. This television show is one hour **long.** ■

look

1. To **look** means to see and pay attention to. Glen and Kirsten **looked** at all the animals in the zoo. **2.** To **look** also means to be the way that something is or how it makes you feel when you look at it. Andrea's friend **looks** nice in her new dress. It **looks** like it's going to rain tomorrow.

■ long

loose

Loose means that something is not tight. Marla tried to walk in her mother's shoes, but they were so big that they fell off her feet. The shoes were too **loose** for her.

lose

1. To **lose** something is to forget where it is. Howie often **loses** his gloves. Last winter he **lost** three pairs. **2.** To **lose** a race or game means that someone else wins. Jason and Nelson ran to the corner in a race. Jason **lost** the race because he tripped. —**lost**

lot

A **lot** means that something has many things to count or measure. There are a **lot** of things to do in the summer. A hippopotamus eats a **lot** of food.

loud

To be **loud** means to make a lot of noise. Thunder in a storm is heard for many miles. Thunder is a **loud** noise.

The word **loudly** means in a **loud** way. The band played so **loudly** that the sound hurt my ears.

love

To **love** means to like something very much. Lina **loves** to swim. Derek **loves** sandwiches for lunch.

low

1. Low means close to the ground or bottom. Nell's uncle has **low** chairs in his house. **2. Low** also means less than usual. Sometimes vegetables do not cost very much in the summer. Then they have a **low** price. ■

■ **low**

luck

Luck is something that you do not plan. If you have good **luck,** you may find a quarter on the ground. If your **luck** is bad, it rains when you go outside to play.

> To be **lucky** means to have good **luck.** To be **unlucky** means to have bad **luck.**

lullaby

A **lullaby** is a song that helps a child go to sleep. When we were babies, my grandmother sang **lullabies** to my brother and me. —**lullabies**

■ **lumber**

lumber

Lumber is wood that has been cut into boards. **Lumber** comes from large trees. ■

lump

A **lump** is a piece of something that has a rough shape. The artist formed the **lump** of clay into a bowl.

lunch

Lunch is a meal. People eat **lunch** in the middle of the day. Many people make **lunch** at home and bring it with them to school or work. ■

■ lunch

> A **lunchbox** is a special box that holds your **lunch.** Do you buy your **lunch** at school, or do you carry it in a **lunchbox?**

lung

A **lung** is a part of the body. You have two **lungs** inside your chest. Air goes in and out of your **lungs** when you breathe.

Mm

macaroni

Macaroni is a kind of food. It is made from flour and comes in the shape of little hollow tubes. ■

■ **macaroni**

machine

A **machine** is an object that does work for people. It may be large or small and may have many parts. Airplanes, computers, and windmills are all **machines.** ■

There are many **machines** in your house or apartment. A refrigerator, a toaster, and a clock are all **machines.** A group of **machines** is called **machinery.**

■ **machine**

mad

Mad means angry. Will slept too late this morning. Now he is **mad** at himself because he missed the bus to school. —**madder, maddest**

made

Made is a form of **make.** Drew **made** breakfast for his family this morning. Cooking **made** him feel good.

magazine

A **magazine** is something that people read. **Magazines** are usually printed every week or every month. They can have stories, poems, photographs, drawings, and cartoons. Gwen's favorite **magazine** is about movies.

magic

Magic is the power to make impossible things seem real. In the story, the wizard changed the prince into a frog by **magic.** Buck learned to do **magic** tricks.

A **magician** is a person who does **magic. Magicians** often pull rabbits out of hats, make things disappear, and do other kinds of tricks.

magnet

A **magnet** is a piece of metal that iron will stick to. **Magnets** are used in many machines. Kent stuck a picture on the refrigerator with a **magnet.** ∎

magnifying glass

A **magnifying glass** is a piece of glass that makes things look bigger. We looked at ants through the **magnifying glass.**

∎ **magnet**

mail

1. The **mail** is the way we send letters and packages from one place to another. I sent some pictures to my cousin Ava by **mail**. **2.** The **mail** is also the letters and packages that are sent to people in the mail. When we came back after vacation, there was a lot of **mail** at our house. **3.** To **mail** something is to send it through the mail. Alex's parents **mailed** her a package at camp last week.

> You can also send letters on a computer. **Mail** that you send on a computer is called **e-mail.**

main

Main means most important. A **main** street is large and holds many cars.

make

1. To **make** means to cause to be. Wes can use flour, water, butter, and apples to **make** a pie. Good music **makes** Franco feel happy.
2. To **make** up means to imagine. Gilbert **makes** up great stories about unicorns and giants. **3.** To **make** a bed means to make the sheets and blanket smooth. Melanie **makes** her bed every morning. **4.** To **make** money is to earn money. Roz **made** a dollar helping her father.
—made ■

■ make

male

Male is a kind of person or animal. It is the opposite of **female.** Boys and men are **male** people.

mall

A **mall** is a large shopping area with many stores. Some **malls** also have restaurants, banks, or theaters.

mammal

A **mammal** is a kind of animal. **Mammals** have hair or fur, and the females make milk to feed their babies. Whales are **mammals** that live in the ocean, but most **mammals** live on land.

man

A **man** is a grown, male person. Boys grow up to be **men. —men**

manners

Manners are ways of acting and speaking with other people. It is good **manners** to say "please" when you ask for something.

many

Many is a large number or amount. There are very **many** grains of sand on the beach.

> The opposite of **many** is **few.**

map

A **map** is a picture that shows where places are. **Maps** can show countries, cities, towns, roads, rivers, lakes, mountains, and many other things.

■ maple

maple

A **maple** is a kind of tree. **Maple** trees turn beautiful colors in the fall. ■

> People collect a sweet liquid from inside **maple** trees and make **maple** syrup. It tastes good on pancakes!

marble

1. Marble is a kind of stone. It is used to make statues and buildings. Most **marble** is white, but it can also be pink, gray, or other colors. **2.** A **marble** is a small, glass ball. **Marbles** are used in several games. ■

■ marble

march

To **march** with someone means to take the same size steps at the same time. The guards **marched** in front of the palace. ■

March

March is the third month of the year. It has 31 days. **March** comes after February and before April.

■ march

mark

1. A **mark** is a spot you can see on something. Pens and pencils leave **marks** on paper. **2.** To **mark** is to put a mark on something. The teacher **marked** the right and wrong answers on our tests.

marry

To **marry** means to join with someone as husband or wife. Men who are **married** are husbands, and women who are **married** are wives. —**marries, married**

marsh

A **marsh** is an area of land that is soft and wet. Frogs, mosquitoes, and some kinds of birds live in **marshes.** ■

■ **marsh**

marshmallow

Marshmallow is a kind of candy. It is soft and white. **Marshmallows** are pieces of this candy. People sometimes roast them over a fire.

mask

A **mask** is something that covers your face. It can be made of paper, cloth, plastic, or rubber. Rosalie wore a purple **mask** with her costume on Halloween. ■

■ **mask**

match

1. To **match** is to be the same. Jana's shirt and shoes are the same color. She bought the shoes because they **matched** the shirt. **2.** A **match** is a short, thin piece of paper or wood used to start a fire. Playing with **matches** is dangerous. **3.** A **match** is also a game or contest between two or more people or teams. My sister won her tennis **match** yesterday.

math

Math is what people know about numbers and shapes. When we add or subtract, we do **math.**

mattress

A **mattress** is the soft, top part of a bed. People sleep on **mattresses.**

may

1. May means that there is a chance something will happen. It **may** snow today. It **might** have snowed yesterday, but it didn't. **2. May** also means you are allowed to do something. Owen's mother says he **may** go to the playground. **—might**

May

May is a month of the year. It has 31 days. **May** comes after April and before June.

maybe

Maybe means that something may be. **Maybe** Jamie will come to visit us this afternoon.

mayor

A **mayor** is a person who leads the government of a city or a town. My parents voted for our **mayor** in an election last year. Our town has had three **mayors** in the past six years.

me

Me is a word I use when I speak about myself. After I bought the kite, it belonged to **me.** My grandmother sent **me** a puzzle when I finished first grade.

meadow

A **meadow** is an area of land that is covered with long grass. Mice, rabbits, and butterflies live in **meadows.** ∎

∎ **meadow**

meal

A **meal** is an amount of food that people eat at one time. Breakfast, lunch, and dinner are **meals.** ∎

You can eat a **meal** at a table in your house or in a restaurant. You can also eat a **meal** outside when you have a picnic. Where do you like to eat your **meals?**

∎ **meal**

mean

1. To **mean** is to say the same thing in different words. Large **means** big. When I said yes, I **meant** that I agree with you. **2.** To **mean** is also to have a message that people understand. A green light **means** "Go." A red light **means** "Stop." **3.** To **mean** is also to be important. Alison wants very much to go to the movies. It **means** a lot to her. It **meant** a lot to her brother to go last week. **4.** To be **mean** is not to be friendly or kind. **Mean** people are not nice to be with. —**meant**

Meaning is what something **means.** Dictionaries tell us the **meanings** of many words.

measure

To **measure** is to find out how big something is. You can **measure** height in inches, feet, or meters. Liquids can be **measured** in quarts. ■

meat

Meat is a kind of food. It comes from animals. Chicken, beef, and ham are all **meats.**

medicine

Medicine is something that helps sick people get well. Many **medicines** are made from plants. Usually a doctor tells you what kind of **medicine** to take.

■ **measure**

meet

1. To **meet** is to get to know someone. You **meet** many new people on the first day of school. **2.** To **meet** also means to be at the same place at the same time. Darrin and Gordon **met** at the corner at three o'clock. —**met**

When people **meet** together to talk about something, they are in a **meeting.**

melody

A **melody** is a group of pleasant sounds that are sung or played on an instrument one after the other. Gavin's grandmother plays beautiful **melodies** on the piano after dinner. —**melodies**

melt

To **melt** is to change from something solid into a liquid. When the weather gets warm, ice **melts** and becomes water.

memory

Memory is what makes people able to remember. People who have good **memories** can remember a lot of things. —**memories**

men

Men means more than one **man.** Three **men** are planting a tree in the yard.

merry-go-round

A **merry-go-round** is a kind of ride you see at a park or a fair. It is sometimes called a **carousel. Merry-go-rounds** have horses and other animals made of wood or plastic. People sit on the horses as they go around in a circle.

mess

A **mess** is something that is not neat. Dennis left clothes, toys, and books on the floor in his room. The room was a **mess.** His little sister makes **messes** all the time when she paints. ■

■ **mess**

If a place has a **mess** in it, or if something is a **mess,** we say that it is **messy.** Tino has to clean his room because it is **messy.**

message

A **message** is a group of words that is sent from one person to another. Many people send **messages** through the mail.

met

Met is a form of **meet.** Pia **met** six new friends at the school picnic. Samantha and Alyssa **met** to have lunch at a restaurant.

metal

A **metal** is something hard that is made from rocks in the ground. **Metals** can bend and not break. Iron, gold, silver, copper, and lead are all kinds of **metal.**

meter

A **meter** is an amount of length. One **meter** is a little more than a yard. There are one thousand **meters** in a kilometer.

mice

Mice means more than one **mouse.** Our cat likes to chase **mice.**

microscope

A **microscope** is used to see things that are too small to see with our eyes alone. **Microscopes** can make tiny things look big.

One way scientists and doctors learn about nature is by looking at things under a **microscope.** They can see very small living things that make people and animals sick.

middle

The **middle** of something is the inside. It is not close to the end. My sister and I sit next to my mother. She sits in the **middle.** ∎

∎ **middle**

midnight

Midnight means 12 o'clock at night. It is dark outside at **midnight.**

might

Might is a form of **may.** Our friends **might** have come to see us last night, but we don't know because we were not home.

mile

A **mile** is an amount of distance. There are 5,280 feet in a **mile.** It takes a man or woman about 20 minutes to walk a **mile.**

milk

Milk is a kind of food. It is a liquid that comes from cows, goats, and other animals. **Milk** can be made into butter and cheese.

million

A **million** is a number. It is written 1,000,000. There are a thousand thousands in a **million.** The sun is **millions** of miles away from the earth.

mind

1. The **mind** is the part of a person that thinks, feels, learns, remembers, wishes, and imagines. If it rains, we might change our **minds** about going to the zoo. **2.** To **mind** means to have bad feelings about something. If we **mind** something, we are sad or angry about it. Melinda doesn't really **mind** when her little brother plays with us. **3.** To **mind** also means to do what you are asked to. Norm **minds** his parents most of the time.

mine

Mine means belonging to me. After I bought the book, it was **mine.**

minus

Minus means you subtract something. If you subtract two from six, you have four. Six **minus** two is four. Six **minus** two can also be written $6-2$.

> The opposite of **minus** is **plus.**

minute

A **minute** is an amount of time. One **minute** has 60 seconds in it. There are 60 **minutes** in one hour.

mirror

A **mirror** is a piece of glass you can see yourself in. Darlene looked at herself in the **mirror.** The old house had lots of **mirrors** on the walls. ■

■ **mirror**

miss

1. To **miss** means not to hit or catch. Wyatt swung his bat, but he **missed** the ball. **2.** To **miss** also means to wish something was there when it is not. Sheena had fun on her vacation, but she **missed** her friends.

mistake

A **mistake** is something you do that is wrong. I made a **mistake** and counted 20 pencils when there were only 18. When I hurry, I make more **mistakes.**

mix

To **mix** is to put two or more things together. Bianca **mixed** flour, eggs, milk, sugar, and chocolate together in a bowl. Then she baked cookies. ■

■ **mix**

model

A **model** is a small copy of a larger object. Marcus and his aunt built three **models** of boats. Each **model** was a few feet long. ■

moment

A **moment** is a very small amount of time. If you will wait a few **moments,** I will help you find your glasses.

■ **model**

Monday

Monday is a day of the week. **Monday** comes after Sunday and before Tuesday.

money

Money is what people use to buy things. When people work, they are paid **money** for what they do. Pennies, nickels, dimes, quarters, and dollars are all kinds of **money.**

> Some **money** is made from paper. Each piece is called a bill. Some **money** is made from metal. Each piece is called a coin.

monkey

A **monkey** is a kind of animal. It has long arms and legs and a long tail. Most **monkeys** live in trees. Some **monkeys** have faces and hands that are a lot like the ones people have. ■

monster

A **monster** is a huge, terrible animal or person that we imagine. Rex was afraid that there were **monsters** in his closet.

month

A **month** is a part of the year. There are 12 **months** in the year. They are January, February, March, April, May, June, July, August, September, October, November, and December.

■ **monkey**

monument

A **monument** is a statue or a building that helps us to remember someone or something. Many cities have **monuments** to people who fought in wars. ∎

∎ **monument**

mood

A **mood** is the way you feel. When the weather is bad, Stefan is in a bad **mood.**

moon

The **moon** is a big, bright object in the sky. The **moon** goes around the earth. It is very far away. ∎

∎ **moon**

mop

A **mop** is a tool used for washing floors. We used **mops** and buckets of water to clean the gym before our class carnival.

more

1. More is the opposite of **less.** There is **more** water in the ocean than there is in a pond. **2.** To do **more** means to keep doing something. I ate a plum. Then I ate another one. I ate **more** because I was hungry.

> **No more** means that there is none of something. We have **no more** paper for making valentines.

morning

Morning is the first part of the day. The sun rises in the **morning.**

> The opposite of **morning** is **evening.** In the **morning** you wake up and get ready for school. In the **evening** you get ready for bed.

mosquito

A **mosquito** is a kind of insect. It is very small and has wings. **Mosquitoes** bite people and animals. —**mosquitoes** ■

■ **mosquito**

most

Most means more than any other. A bicycle makes some noise. A car makes more noise. A train makes the **most** noise of all.

moth

A **moth** is a kind of insect that flies. **Moths** look a lot like butterflies. A caterpillar changes into a **moth** inside a cocoon. ■

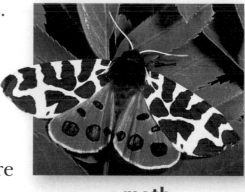

■ **moth**

mother

A **mother** is a woman who has a child. **Mothers** and fathers take care of their children.

motor

1. A **motor** is a machine. It uses energy from electricity to do work. Refrigerators use **motors** to keep things cold. **2. Motor** is also another word for **engine.**

motorcycle

A **motorcycle** is a machine. It is like a big, heavy bicycle with an engine. Some **motorcycles** can go as fast as cars. ■

■ **motorcycle**

mountain

A **mountain** is an area of land that is higher than the land around it. The tops of very high **mountains** are covered with snow. ■

mouse

A **mouse** is a very small animal. It has a long tail, short fur, and sharp teeth. **Mice** live in fields, forests, or houses. —**mice** ■

■ **mountain**

mouth

The **mouth** is a part of the head. It is under your nose. People and animals eat food with their **mouths.**

Inside your **mouth** are your teeth and your tongue. Your lips are on the outside of your **mouth.**

■ **mouse**

move

1. To **move** means not to stay in one place. Plants cannot **move** by themselves, but animals can.
2. To **move** also means to cause something to be in a different place. We **moved** the chair into the basement. **3.** To **move** also means to go to live in another place. Del's family **moved** to a new city last year.

movie

A **movie** is a story made with pictures that move. Moving pictures are made with a special camera. People watch **movies** in theaters or on television.

Mr.

Mr. is a word people use with a man's name. Our teacher in the first grade was **Mr.** Bishop.

Mrs.

Mrs. is a word people sometimes use with a woman's name if she is married. **Mrs.** Berger took her children to the circus.

Ms.

Ms. is a word people use with a woman's name. **Ms.** Cook drives a bus for the city.

much

1. Much means a lot. There is not very **much** food in the refrigerator. **2.** How **much** tells the amount or cost of something. "How **much** is that basketball?" Janna asked.

■ mud

mud

Mud is wet dirt. Many animals like to roll in the **mud.** ■

multiply

To **multiply** is to add a number to itself one or more times. The symbol for **multiply** is ×. 2 × 4 is the same as 2 + 2 + 2 + 2. —**multiplies, multiplied**

muscle

A **muscle** is a part of the body. **Muscles** are under the skin. People and animals use **muscles** to move around.

museum

A **museum** is a place where things are collected so that people can go to look at them. **Museums** can have art, machines, models of animals, and many other things.

mushroom

A **mushroom** is a living thing. It grows from the ground in damp places. Some **mushrooms** look like short, white plants. Some **mushrooms** are good to eat, but others make you sick.

music

Music is sounds that people make with instruments or their voices. There are many kinds of **music** all over the world.

A person whose job is singing or playing a **musical** instrument is called a **musician.** An orchestra is made up of many **musicians.**

must

1. Must means that you have to do something. We **must** leave at noon, or we will be late. **2. Must** also means something is probably true. That saw **must** be on the bench. I left it there yesterday.

mustard

Mustard is a kind of food. It is yellow or brown and has a strong, hot taste. People like **mustard** on hot dogs and sandwiches. ■

> Do you like **mustard** or ketchup on your sandwiches? What other things can you put on a sandwich?

■ **mustard**

my

My means that something belongs to me. This is **my** doll.

myself

Myself means me and nobody else. When I look in a mirror, I see **myself.**

mystery

A **mystery** is something that you do not understand. I do not know how my cap got lost. It is a **mystery** to me. Nature is full of **mysteries. —mysteries**

myth

A **myth** is a story that people made up a long time ago. **Myths** often have heroes and try to explain why things happen in the world.

Nn

nail

1. A **nail** is a piece of metal with a point at one end. **Nails** are usually used to hold two pieces of wood together. **2.** A **nail** is also a part of the body. It is the hard part at the end of your fingers and toes. Chelsea had dirt under her **nails** when she worked in the yard.

name

A **name** is a word that people use to call someone or something by. My parents' **names** are Leslie and Zach.

nap

To **nap** means to sleep for a short time. People usually **nap** during the day. —**napped**

napkin

A **napkin** is a piece of paper or cloth that you use to clean your face and fingers when you eat. **Napkins** also protect your clothes.

napped

Napped is a form of **nap.** The children **napped** during the long ride home.

narrow

Narrow is the opposite of **wide.**
Some city streets are very **narrow.** The buildings on opposite sides are close to each other. ■

■ **narrow**

nation

A **nation** is a group of people who live in one country. Sometimes people from different **nations** meet to talk about problems in the world.

nature

Nature is everything in the world that is not made by people. Animals, plants, the land, the ocean, the sky, and the weather are all parts of **nature.**

near

To be **near** means to be a small distance away. Natalie can walk from her house to school in two minutes. Her house is **near** the school.

neat

Neat means clean and with everything in order. Lorraine likes to keep her room **neat.** ■

The opposite of **neat** is **messy.** Dillon's room is **neat,** but it was **messy** before he cleaned it.

■ **neat**

neck

The **neck** is a part of the body. It is between your head and your shoulders. **Necks** let people turn their heads. ■

■ neck

need

To **need** means that you must have something. Plants cannot live without water. They **need** water to live.

needle

1. A **needle** is a kind of tool. It is a very thin piece of metal with a sharp point. **Needles** and thread are used to sew cloth. **2.** A **needle** is a kind of leaf. It is thin and shaped like a sewing needle. Pine trees have **needles.** ■

■ needle

neighbor

A **neighbor** is someone who lives near you. Many **neighbors** are friends. ■

A **neighborhood** is an area where **neighbors** live. Kimo knows almost everyone in his **neighborhood.**

neither

Neither means not either. Teresa went **neither** left nor right. She kept walking straight up the street.

■ neighbor

nest

A **nest** is what birds build. Birds lay eggs and feed their babies in **nests**. **Nests** are made from grass, mud, sticks, string, and other things. ∎

∎ **nest**

net

A **net** is pieces of string or rope tied across each other with holes in between. Fishermen often use large **nets** to catch fish. **Nets** are also used in sports. Jessica hit the tennis ball over the **net**. ∎

never

Never means not ever. The sun always rises in the east. It **never** rises in the west.

new

1. New means never used or worn before. Alisa's radio came from the store. Nobody ever owned it before. It is a **new** radio. **2. New** also means that something was not there before. The **new** drugstore is across the street.

∎ **net**

> **New** is the opposite of **old.**

news

The **news** is stories about things that are happening. Many people watch the **news** on television. Other people read the **news** in a newspaper or on a computer.

newspaper

A **newspaper** is many large pieces of paper with stories and photographs printed on them. People read the news in a **newspaper.** Many **newspapers** are printed every day. ■

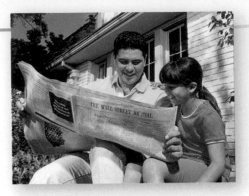

■ newspaper

next

Next means the one after this one. This summer Eduardo stayed at home. **Next** summer he will go to camp.

nice

To be **nice** is to make people feel good. Yesterday the weather was so **nice** that Leah played outside. Our neighbors are **nice,** friendly people.

nickel

A **nickel** is a kind of coin. One **nickel** is the same as five pennies. Five **nickels** are the same as a quarter.

night

Night is the time when it is dark outside. On most **nights** we can see the moon. ■

The opposite of **night** is **day.** You can see stars in the sky at **night.** The sun shines during the **day.**

■ night

nightmare

A **nightmare** is a dream that scares you. Courtney had **nightmares** after she saw a movie about monsters.

nine

Nine is a number. **Nine** is written **9.** $8 + 1 = 9$.

no

1. No means that someone does not agree. Maureen asked if she could have another dessert. Her mother said, "**No.**" **2. No** also means not any. There is **no** snow during the summer. Sonny was sick yesterday, and he is still sick today. He feels **no** better today than he did yesterday.

nobody

Nobody means no person. **Nobody** can fly like a bird.

nod

To **nod** is to move your head up and down. People often **nod** to show that they agree. —**nodded**

noise

A **noise** is a sound. Machines make many different kinds of **noises.**

none

None means that there is not one. **None** of the lunch bags had apples inside.

noon

Noon is 12 o'clock during the day. People usually eat lunch around **noon.**

north

North is a direction. If you look where the sun rises, **north** is on your left. ■

■ **north**

nose

The **nose** is a part of the face. It is below your eyes and above your mouth. People and animals smell with their **noses.**

not

Not means there is no way that something can happen. The sun shines during the day. It does **not** shine at night.

note

1. A **note** is one sound in music. Music is made of many **notes.** The **notes** are written down so that people can read them and play or sing the music. **2.** A **note** is also a short message that you write down. Nora's father put a **note** in her backpack. ■

■ **note**

nothing

Nothing means no thing. An empty box has **nothing** in it.

notice

1. To **notice** is to see or hear something. Lin **noticed** that her brother looked tired yesterday. **2.** A **notice** is also a message that gives people information. The teacher gave the class several **notices** to take home.

November

November is a month of the year. It has 30 days. **November** comes after October and before December.

now

Now means at this time. You are reading these words **now.**

numb

Numb means that part of your body can't feel anything. If you play outside in the snow for too long, your fingers might become **numb.**

number

1. A **number** is a symbol people use when they count things. 12, 52, and 100 are all **numbers. 2.** A **number** is also what you use to call people on the telephone. Kyle's **number** is 555-1324.

nurse

A **nurse** is a person who takes care of sick people. **Nurses** work with doctors. Many **nurses** work in hospitals. ■

■ nurse

nut

A **nut** is a seed or a dry fruit. It has a hard shell. Many **nuts** grow on trees. ■

> The **shell** that covers a **nut** is called a **nutshell.**

■ nut

oak

An **oak** is a kind of tree.
Acorns grow on **oak** trees. ■

object

An **object** is anything that
people can see or touch and
is not alive. Buildings, tables,
chairs, books, scissors, pens,
and pencils are all **objects.**

■ oak

ocean

An **ocean** is a very large area of water. **Ocean** water
has salt in it. **Oceans** cover almost three quarters of
the earth.

Many kinds of animals live in the **ocean.** Some are
very big, like whales. Others are small, like lobsters.

o'clock

O'clock is a word people use to say what time it is.
Nikos gets up at seven **o'clock** in the morning.

October

October is a month of the year. It has 31 days. **October** comes after September and before November.

octopus

An **octopus** is a kind of animal. It lives in the ocean. **Octopuses** have eight body parts that act like arms. —**octopuses, octopi** ■

■ **octopus**

odd

1. An **odd** number is a number that you cannot get to when you start at zero and count by twos. One, three, five, seven, and nine are **odd** numbers. **2. Odd** means strange. Jackson noticed an **odd** smell in the yard. He could not tell what was making it.

> When we talk about numbers, the opposite of **odd** is **even.** Five is an **odd** number. Six is an **even** number.

of

1. Of means that something is part of something else. The walls **of** my room are white. **2. Of** also tells what is used to make something. Most tables are made **of** wood. **3. Of** also tells what something has in it. Hilary was carrying a pail **of** water. **4.** When you tell time, **of** means before. The time is ten minutes **of** four. **4. Of** also means at a distance from. The science museum is seven miles east **of** here.

off

1. **Off** means away from. Please take your books **off** the table before supper. 2. **Off** also means not working. Our house is dark when the lights are **off**.

offer

To **offer** is to say you will give or do something. Joan **offered** to help her father rake the leaves.

office

An **office** is a place where people work. Many people have jobs in **offices**. ■

■ **office**

often

Often means many times. It **often** rains in April.

oil

Oil is a liquid. It floats on water. **Oils** from vegetables are used in foods. **Oil** from the ground is used in cars and machines. ■

If something has **oil** on it, or if something feels like **oil**, we say that it is **oily**. My hair felt **oily** after I played outside all afternoon.

■ **oil**

old

1. Old is the opposite of **new.** Travis puts on his **old** jacket when he goes out to play football. **2.** To be **old** means to have been alive a long time. **Old** is the opposite of **young.** My grandmother is **old,** but she still walks several miles every day. **3. Old** also tells how long something has been alive. Some trees are thousands of years **old.**

on

1. On tells where something is. The dishes are **on** the table. **2. On** means that something is working. The room is bright when the light is **on. 3. On** means about. Thea has a book **on** dinosaurs. **4. On** also tells what day something happens. We play ball **on** Sundays.

once

1. Once means one time. Birthdays only come **once** every year. **2. Once** also means after. **Once** Gary was in the third grade, he had homework to do every night.

one

1. One is a number. **One** is written **1. One** is the first number when you count. **2. One** is used for something you have already talked about. Suzanne likes green grapes, but she doesn't like purple **ones.**

onion

An **onion** is a kind of vegetable. It is round and has a strong smell and taste. **Onions** grow in the ground. ■

■ onion

only

Only means one and no more. There is **only** one sun that we see in the sky.

open

1. Open means that something can move in or out of a space or container. The breeze came in through the **open** window. **2.** To **open** means to take off the cover. Maggie **opened** a jar to get the peanut butter out. **3.** To **open** also means to allow people to enter. The factory **opens** at nine o'clock.

> **Open** is the opposite of **close.** My father **opens** the store in the morning, and he **closes** it at night.

opposite

1. Opposite means different in every way. Tall is the **opposite** of short. **2.** To be **opposite** also means to be on the other side of something. The swimmers stood at **opposite** sides of the pool. ■

■ **opposite**

or

Or shows that only one thing out of two can happen. You can have a turkey sandwich **or** a ham sandwich.

orange

1. An **orange** is a kind of fruit. It is about the size of a tennis ball. **Oranges** grow on **orange** trees. **2. Orange** is a color. Pumpkins are **orange.**

orchestra

An **orchestra** is a large group of people who play instruments together. **Orchestras** can have more than a hundred people. ■

During a concert an **orchestra** performs for an audience. People buy tickets so they can go to the concert. Many musicians work for **orchestras.**

■ **orchestra**

order

1. Order is the way one thing follows another. The letters of the alphabet always come in the same **order. 2.** To **order** means to ask for something that you will pay for. Ashley **ordered** a hamburger at the restaurant. **3.** To **order** also means to tell someone what to do. The firefighters **ordered** everyone to leave the building. **4.** In **order** means everything is the way it should be. Tabitha always keeps her room in **order.**

ostrich

An **ostrich** is a very large bird. It has long legs and a long neck. **Ostriches** cannot fly. ■

■ **ostrich**

other

1. **Other** means one of two. One of Vicki's socks has a hole in it. The **other** one has no holes. 2. **Other** also means different. Keiko has no time to play today. She will have time some **other** day.

ounce

An **ounce** is an amount of weight. There are 16 **ounces** in one pound.

our

Our means belonging to us. These are **our** clothes. The people who live next door are **our** neighbors.

ours

Ours means belonging to us. Those are your books and crayons. These are **ours.**

ourselves

Ourselves means us and nobody else. When Alana and I looked in a mirror, we saw **ourselves** there.

out

1. **Out** tells where something is or is going. **Out** is the opposite of **in.** A bird flew in one window and **out** the other. José went **out** the door. 2. **Out** also means that something stops making light. The lights were **out** in the kitchen, so we used flashlights to make sandwiches. I blew **out** the candle before I went to sleep.

> When you are **out** of something, there is no more of it. We are going to the store because we are **out** of milk.

outside

1. Outside is the opposite of **inside.** Leo stayed **outside** until it was dark. Then he went into the house. **2.** The **outside** of something is the part that goes around things on the inside. The **outside** of an apple is the skin. Eggs are smooth on the **outside.**

oval

An **oval** is a shape. It looks like a circle that has been stretched. Hens' eggs are shaped like **ovals.** ∎

∎ oval

oven

An **oven** is a metal box that uses heat to cook food. **Ovens** can become very hot. Talia and her mother baked cookies in the **oven.** ∎

∎ oven

over

1. Over means above. A helicopter flew **over** our house. **2. Over** also means on top of. Jacqueline wore a sweater **over** her shirt. **3. Over** can also mean more than. Lily's father is **over** six feet tall. **4. Over** can also mean down. Paulette knocked **over** a glass of milk. **5. Over** also means again. The band played a song. Then they played it **over** because everyone liked it. **6. Over** can mean finished. After the meeting was **over,** we went home.

owe

To **owe** means that you must give someone something. Timothy **owes** the store a quarter for his apple.

owl

An **owl** is a kind of bird. It has a large head and large, round eyes that look straight ahead. **Owls** can see well at night. ■

■ owl

own

1. To **own** means to have and keep something. Janie **owns** a lot of books and toys. 2. **Own** also means that something belongs only to you. Like the other kids, I brought my **own** snack on the field trip.

> Someone who **owns** something is an **owner.** The **owner** of the restaurant let us enter early.

ox

An **ox** is a large, male animal. **Oxen** are used to pull heavy loads. **—oxen**

pack

To **pack** is to put something in a suitcase or a box to take with you. Walter **packed** his clothes and some books for his vacation. ∎

∎ **pack**

package

A **package** is a box that you put something in and send through the mail. People bring **packages** to the post office to mail.

page

A **page** is a piece of paper. There are words on both sides of this **page.** Books are made of many **pages** held together.

paid

Paid is a form of **pay.** Milo **paid** six dollars for a movie ticket.

pail

A **pail** is used to hold things. It is made of metal or plastic and has a flat, round bottom. **Pail** is another word for **bucket.** ■

■ pail

> **Pails** are useful for many things. You can make castles from sand when you take a **pail** and a small shovel to the beach. When farmers get milk from a cow, they put the milk in a **pail.**

pain

Pain is what you feel when you are hurt. When I fell on the ice, I had **pains** in my leg.

paint

1. **Paint** is a liquid with color in it. People put **paint** on things to make them look new. Artists make pictures with **paints. 2.** To **paint** is to cover with paint. April and her mother **painted** one room pink and one room blue. ■

■ paint

> A **painting** is a picture that is made with **paint.** Many art museums have **paintings** you can look at.

pair

A **pair** is two things that match each other. Shoes, socks, and boots come in **pairs.** ■

■ pair

pajamas

Pajamas are a kind of clothes. People wear them when they sleep. Most **pajamas** are warm and soft.

palace

A **palace** is a huge building where kings and queens live. Some **palaces** have more than one hundred rooms.

palm

1. A **palm** is the flat part of your hand that your fingers touch when you bend them. There are many lines on the **palms** of our hands. **2.** A **palm** is also a kind of tree. **Palm** trees grow in warm climates. ■

■ palm

pan

A **pan** is something to cook in. It is made of metal. My father used two **pans** to make eggs and pancakes for breakfast.

pancake

A **pancake** is a kind of food. It is a thin, flat cake that is cooked in a hot pan. **Pancakes** are made of flour, eggs, and milk. ■

■ pancake

panda

A **panda** is a large animal that looks like a bear. **Pandas** have thick fur that is black and white. ■

■ **panda**

pants

Pants are a kind of clothes. People wear **pants** over their legs. Most **pants** have pockets in the sides. ■

paper

Paper is something people use to write on. It is made from wood. My aunt's desk has lots of **papers** on it.

> **Paper towels** are **towels** that are made of **paper.** They can be used only once.

■ **pants**

parade

A **parade** is a group of people who march together down the street. Most **parades** have bands that play music as they march. **Parades** often happen on holidays. ■

parent

A **parent** is a mother or father. Men and women who have children are **parents.**

■ **parade**

park

1. A **park** is a place where people go to enjoy being outside. Most **parks** are full of grass and trees. **2.** To **park** is to put a car somewhere and leave it there. Cheng's father **parks** the car in the garage every night.

parrot

A **parrot** is a kind of bird. It has a large beak and feathers in bright colors. Some **parrots** can learn to say a few words. ■

■ **parrot**

> Can you think of a word that rhymes with **parrot?**

part

1. A **part** is one piece of something. Leaves, branches, roots, and the trunk are **parts** of a tree. **2.** A **part** is also the person that someone pretends to be in a movie or play. Alyson got a big **part** in the school play this year. **3.** To **part** means to leave someone. Vincent didn't like **parting** from his family when he went to camp.

partner

A **partner** is someone who works or plays with another person or with a group of people. During dance class, Deb is my **partner.** Everyone in the first grade has two **partners** in his or her reading group.

party

A **party** is a time when people get together to have fun. Margaret invites many friends to her birthday **parties. —parties** ■

■ **party**

pass

1. To **pass** means to go past. My teacher **passes** my house when he walks to school. **2.** To **pass** also means to give to someone with your hands. Brianna **passed** the bread to her father at the table. **3.** To **pass** also means to get a score on a test that is good enough. You have to **pass** a test to drive a car.

passenger

A **passenger** is a person who travels in a car, boat, train, or airplane. The **passengers** on the train looked out the windows at the mountains.

past

1. The **past** is the part of time that has already happened. Yesterday is in the **past. 2.** To go **past** means to go beside. A big river goes **past** many towns and cities.

paste

Paste is something used to stick paper or light cloth together. **Paste** is not as strong as glue.

pasture

A **pasture** is a field of grass where animals eat. Horses and cows eat grass in **pastures.**

patch

1. A **patch** is a small piece of cloth. People sew **patches** on clothes to cover up holes. **2.** A **patch** also means an area of ground. Vegetables are growing in a **patch** behind the barn. ∎

∎ **patch**

path

A **path** is a place where you can walk through a field or a forest. There are two **paths** to the lake through the woods. ∎

paw

A **paw** is the foot of some animals. Dogs, cats, bears, and rabbits all have four **paws.** ∎

∎ **path**

Paw rhymes with **claw, law,** and **saw.**

pay

1. To **pay** is to give money for something. Louise **paid** five dollars for a book. **2.** To **pay** attention means to look or listen carefully. Philippe **pays** attention when his teacher talks to the class. —**paid**

pea

A **pea** is a kind of vegetable. It is small, round, and green. **Peas** are the seeds of **pea** plants.

∎ **paw**

peace

Peace is a time when people are not fighting. When the war was over, everyone was glad to have **peace.**

peach

A **peach** is a kind of fruit. It is yellow and red and has a lot of juice inside. **Peaches** grow on peach trees.

peacock

A **peacock** is a very large, male bird. It has blue and green feathers on its head and body. **Peacocks** have long back feathers that can spread out like a large fan. These feathers have spots that look like eyes. ■

■ **peacock**

peak

A **peak** is the top of a mountain. Some mountain **peaks** are covered with snow.

peanut

A **peanut** is a kind of food. It comes in a shell and looks and tastes like a nut. **Peanuts** grow in the ground.

Peanut butter is made by breaking **peanuts** into very small pieces and making them soft. There is no real **butter** in **peanut butter,** but it is soft and smooth like **butter.**

pear

A **pear** is a kind of fruit. **Pears** are yellow, green, brown, or red. They are round at both ends, but one end is smaller than the other. ▪

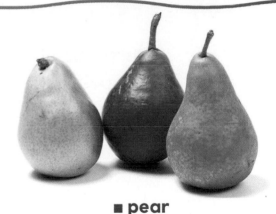

▪ **pear**

pebble

A **pebble** is a small rock. Trish likes to collect **pebbles** when she goes to the beach.

peek

To **peek** is to look at something quickly. After my mother told me to cover my eyes, I **peeked** and saw the new car. ▪

▪ **peek**

peel

1. A **peel** is the skin of some fruits or vegetables. Bananas and oranges have **peels. 2.** To **peel** means to take the skin off a fruit or vegetable. My sister and I help my father **peel** potatoes for dinner.

pen

A **pen** is a tool to write with. **Pens** are filled with ink. They are usually made of plastic or metal.

pencil

A **pencil** is a tool to write with. **Pencils** are made of wood or plastic. The part that writes on paper is called the lead.

penguin

A **penguin** is a kind of bird. It lives near the ocean in places where it is very cold. **Penguins** cannot fly. They use their wings to swim in the water. ■

■ **penguin**

> **Penguins** can swim for a long time under the water, but they need to come up for air. Fish do not need to breathe air.

penny

A **penny** is a coin. One **penny** is one cent. There are 25 **pennies** in a quarter and one hundred **pennies** in one dollar. —**pennies**

people

People means more than one person. No two **people** are the same.

pepper

1. Pepper is a kind of food called a spice. It is a black powder that is made from a tiny fruit. **2.** A **pepper** is also a vegetable. **Peppers** are usually red, yellow, or green. ■

■ **pepper**

perfect

Perfect means that everything is just right. Miles did a **perfect** job cleaning his room.

perform

To **perform** means to do something in front of an audience. My piano teacher **performs** at a concert twice each year.

perhaps

Perhaps means maybe. **Perhaps** we will have time for a walk after dinner.

period

A **period** is a dot that is at the end of a sentence. **Periods** are not used after sentences that are questions.

person

A **person** is a man, woman, boy, or girl.

pet

A **pet** is a small animal that lives with people. Many people have dogs, cats, or birds as **pets.** ■

■ pet

phone

Phone is another word for **telephone.** Craig called his friend Jen on the **phone.** We have two **phones** in our apartment.

photograph

A **photograph** is a picture that cameras make. People like to have **photographs** of special times like vacations and holidays.

piano

A **piano** is an instrument. **Pianos** have 88 black and white keys. You push down on the keys with your fingers to make music. ■

■ piano

pick

1. To **pick** means to take something off a tree or another plant. Aidan **picked** the highest apple he could reach. **2.** To **pick** also means to choose. Stu **picked** out a tie to go with his shirt. ■

■ pick

picnic

A **picnic** is a meal that people eat outside. We have **picnics** near the lake on summer afternoons. ■

picture

1. A **picture** is something you draw or paint. Harris drew a **picture** of his house. **2.** A **picture** can also be a photograph. Many people like to take **pictures** of their pets.

■ picnic

pie

A **pie** is a kind of food. **Pies** are baked in an oven. The outside of a **pie** is often made with flour and butter. The inside can be fruit, cheese, meat, or other things.

piece

1. A **piece** of something is less than the whole thing. Carrie gave Deirdre a **piece** of her peach. When the baseball hit the window, the glass broke into many **pieces.**
2. A **piece** is also something that is one of a group of things used together. We picked up all of the **pieces** of the game after we finished playing. ■

■ **piece**

pig

A **pig** is a kind of animal. It is short and fat and has a flat nose. **Pigs** are raised for their meat.

A young **pig** is called a **piglet.**

pile

A **pile** is a lot of something all in one place. Zachary and I dug a hole at the beach. We left big **piles** of sand. ■

pill

A **pill** is a solid piece of medicine that you swallow. When my brother was sick, he took **pills** every day.

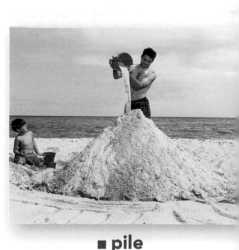

■ **pile**

pillow

A **pillow** is a cloth cover filled with feathers or something else that is soft. People put their heads on **pillows** when they sleep or rest.

pilot

A **pilot** is a person who flies an airplane or a helicopter. **Pilots** have to practice many hours before they can fly alone.

pin

A **pin** is a short, thin piece of metal with a sharp point. **Pins** are used to hold clothes together while they are being sewn.

pine

A **pine** is a kind of tree. **Pines** have needles on their branches. **Pine** needles stay green all winter.

pineapple

A **pineapple** is a large fruit. It has thick skin and long leaves. The inside is yellow and sweet. **Pineapples** grow in warm places. ■

■ pineapple

pink

Pink is a color. You can mix red paint and white paint to make **pink.**

pint

A **pint** is an amount of liquid. Two **pints** are the same as one quart.

pipe

A **pipe** is a tube made of metal, clay, or glass. **Pipes** are used to carry liquids from one place to another. ■

■ pipe

pirate

A **pirate** is a person who robs people on ships. Hundreds of years ago, **pirates** sailed all over the world.

pit

1. A **pit** is a hard seed in the center of some fruits. Peaches and cherries have **pits. 2.** A **pit** is also a hole in the ground. Sometimes people cook food in **pits.**

pitch

To **pitch** means to throw. In baseball, a player from one team **pitches** the ball. A player from the other team tries to hit the ball with a bat.

pitcher

1. A **pitcher** is a container that is used to hold and pour liquids. **Pitchers** usually have a handle. **2.** A **pitcher** is also a person on a baseball team who pitches a ball. The **pitchers** on my brother's team can throw the ball very fast. ■

■ **pitcher**

pizza

Pizza is a kind of food. It is flat bread with tomatoes, cheese, and other foods on top. **Pizzas** are baked in an oven. ■

■ **pizza**

place

1. A **place** is somewhere for something to be. Rooms, fields, and countries are all **places. 2.** To **place** something is to put it somewhere. Shannon **placed** the forks on the table.

> Some words that rhyme with **place** are **base, face,** and **race.**

plain

1. **Plain** means simple. The opposite of **plain** is **fancy.** I bought a **plain,** white dress for the concert. **2.** A **plain** is a large, flat area of land with few trees. **Plains** often have grass that cows can eat.

plan

1. A **plan** is an idea or information about how to do something. Our vacation **plans** are to travel and to ski. **2.** To **plan** is to have a plan to do something. Our family **plans** to go to the beach this summer. —**planned**

plane

Plane is another word for **airplane.** Robby's father knows how to fly a **plane.**

planet

A **planet** is a very large object in space that moves around a star. There are eight **planets** that move around the sun. ∎

∎ planet

planned

Planned is a form of **plan.** We **planned** to go to the baseball game, but when it started raining, we decided not to go.

plant

1. A **plant** is a living thing that is not an animal and can make its own food. Most **plants** grow in the ground. Flowers, trees, and vegetables are all **plants.**
2. To **plant** means to put seeds or small plants in the ground. The seeds that my neighbor **planted** in the spring grew into big pumpkins by the fall. ■

■ **plant**

plastic

Plastic is something that things are made of. Some kinds of **plastic** are easy to bend, and some are very hard. **Plastic** can be any color. It is less easy to break than glass.

> **Plastic** is not something that you can find in nature. Instead, people make **plastic** from oil found in the ground.

plate

A **plate** is a thin, flat dish that you put food on. Paige put **plates,** glasses, forks, and spoons on the table before dinner.

play

1. To **play** is to have fun. Most people like to **play** games. You can **play** alone or with other people.
2. To **play** is also to make music with an instrument. Larry can **play** the trombone. **3.** A **play** is a kind of story. People act in **plays** while other people watch them. **Plays** are seen in theaters and on television.

> A **player** is someone who **plays**. There are nine **players** on a baseball team.

playground

A **playground** is a place to play outside. **Playgrounds** usually have swings, seesaws, and other objects for people to play on. Most schools have **playgrounds.** ■

■ **playground**

pleasant

Pleasant means nice. The picnic we went to was **pleasant.** Ms. Greenberg is always **pleasant** when we give her our money for lunch.

please

1. Please is a word people use when they ask for something. Paco asked, "May I have an apple, **please?**" **2.** To **please** means to make someone happy. The students **pleased** their teacher when they behaved so well.

plum

A **plum** is a kind of fruit. **Plums** are usually purple and grow on small trees. ■

■ **plum**

plural

A **plural** is the form of a word that means more than one person or thing. "Cats" is the **plural** of "cat." Most **plurals** are made by adding the letter **s** to a word.

plus

Plus means added to. If you add two and three, you get five. Two **plus** three is five. Two **plus** three can also be written 2 + 3.

pocket

A **pocket** is a small bag of cloth. **Pockets** are sewn into jackets, coats, shirts, and pants. You can carry all kinds of things in your **pockets.** ■

■ **pocket**

poem

A **poem** is a group of words that are put together in a special way. People write **poems** to say things that can be hard to say with usual language. The words in many **poems** rhyme.

> Another word for a **poem** or a group of **poems** is **poetry**. **Poets** write **poetry**.

point

1. A **point** is a sharp end. Pins, needles, and arrows have **points. 2.** To **point** is to show where something is. When Marco's brother asked where the boat was, Marco **pointed** to the ocean with his finger. ■

■ **point**

poison

A **poison** is something that can hurt people or animals if they swallow or breathe it. Some medicines that you put on your skin are **poisons** if you eat or drink them.

pole

A **pole** is a long piece of wood or metal. Telephone **poles** hold wires up in the air. ■

■ **pole**

police

The **police** are people whose job is to protect other people. But if people break the law, the **police** can put them in jail.

polite

Polite means acting kind and pleasant to other people. People who are **polite** have good manners.

pollution

Pollution is bad things that people put into the environment. **Pollution** can make people, animals, and plants sick.

pond

A **pond** is a large amount of water that is all in one place. Some **ponds** are big enough to swim in. A **pond** is smaller than a lake.

pony

A **pony** is a kind of horse. **Ponies** are not as big as most horses.
—**ponies** ■

■ pony

pool

A **pool** is a container filled with water that you can swim in. Some **pools** are large holes that are dug into the ground. Others are made of plastic and sit on the ground. ■

poor

Poor is the opposite of **rich**. **Poor** people do not have much money.

■ pool

popcorn

Popcorn is a kind of food. It is made from the seeds of corn. Pieces of **popcorn** get big and soft when they are cooked. They make a loud sound when they get hot. ■

■ popcorn

porch

A **porch** is a covered area at an entrance to a building. People like to sit on their **porches** and rest during the summer. ∎

∎ **porch**

port

A **port** is a harbor or a city that has a harbor. Boats and ships come and go at **ports.**

possible

Possible means that something can happen. It is **possible** that it will rain tomorrow.

> The opposite of **possible** is **impossible.** It is **possible** to teach dogs to sit, but it is **impossible** for dogs to fly.

post office

A **post office** is a building. When you mail a letter, it goes to the **post office.** From there, it goes to the person you are sending it to.

pot

A **pot** is a deep, round pan to cook food in. **Pots** are made of metal, glass, or clay. Most **pots** have handles. ∎

∎ **pot**

potato

A **potato** is a kind of vegetable. It has brown skin that is covered with bumps. **Potatoes** grow in the ground.
—**potatoes**

> Can you think of another food whose name rhymes with **potato?**

pound

A **pound** is an amount of weight. One **pound** is 16 ounces. Three apples weigh about one **pound.** Madison's new baby sister weighs seven **pounds.**

pour

To **pour** is to make liquid go from one place to another. Lena **poured** juice from a bottle into her glass. ■

■ **pour**

powder

A **powder** is a lot of very tiny pieces of something. Flour is a kind of **powder.**

power

1. Power is being able to do work. A bulldozer has enough **power** to move big piles of dirt. **2.** To have **power** means to be able to decide things. The president of our country has a lot of **power. 3. Power** is another word for **electricity.** Our house had no **power** after the storm.

practice

To **practice** is to do something many times so that you can do it well. People who play music well have to **practice** a lot.

prepare

To **prepare** is to get ready. Ernie **prepared** to go to camp by packing his clothes in a suitcase.

present

1. A **present** is a gift. People often get **presents** on their birthdays.
2. The **present** is the part of time that is here now. This minute is part of the **present. 3.** To be **present** means to be somewhere. My parents were **present** when I won the race. ■

■ **present**

> The opposite of **present** is **absent.** Only ten students were **present,** and the rest were **absent** because they were sick.

president

A **president** is a person who leads a group of people. The people in our country elect a **president** every four years. We remember two of our **presidents** on **Presidents'** Day every year.

pretend

To **pretend** is to make believe. When Joni acted in the school play, she **pretended** to be a princess.

pretty

Pretty means nice to look at. Everyone likes **pretty** flowers. **—prettier, prettiest**

prevent

To **prevent** means to stop something from happening. The rain will **prevent** us from having our picnic today.

price

A **price** is how much money you have to pay for something. The **price** of Vickie's skirt was eight dollars.

prince

A **prince** is the son of a king or a queen. Some **princes** become kings.

princess

A **princess** is the daughter of a king or a queen. Some **princesses** become queens.

principal

1. A **principal** is a person who leads a school. School **principals** work with teachers to help students learn.
2. Principal also means something that is most important. The **principal** problem in our building is noise.

print

1. To **print** means to write with care so that none of the letters touch each other. Deval **printed** his name at the top of his paper. **2.** To **print** also means to put letters on paper with a machine. Large machines are used to **print** books and newspapers.

prize

A **prize** is something that you win. **Prizes** can be cups, ribbons, money, or many other things. ■

probably

Probably means that something is expected to happen. Roland comes to my house every Saturday. He will **probably** come this Saturday too.

■ **prize**

problem

A **problem** is something that you have trouble with. My brother had **problems** with reading last year.

project

A **project** is something you do or make that shows what you have learned. Students often work on special **projects** at school. This year Andrea's science **project** is about magnets.

promise

1. To **promise** is to say you will do something. When Les borrowed Josh's baseball glove, he **promised** to return it the next day. **2.** A **promise** is something that you say you will do. People should always keep their **promises.**

pronounce

To **pronounce** means to speak the sounds of letters or words. Cal could not **pronounce** his new teacher's name.

propeller

A **propeller** is a part of a machine. It is made of wood or metal. **Propellers** make planes and boats move by spinning in the air or water. ∎

protect

To **protect** means to keep safe. An umbrella **protects** you from the rain or the sun.

∎ **propeller**

proud

To be **proud** is to be glad to have people see what you have or what you have done. Alice was **proud** of the picture she made.

> When you feel **proud** of something, you have **pride** in it. We say "**proud** as a peacock" because some people think peacocks have **pride** in their fancy tails.

pudding

Pudding is a kind of food. **Pudding** is sweet and smooth. You can eat it with a spoon. Tamara's family likes vanilla **pudding** for dessert.

puddle

A **puddle** is a small amount of water that has collected in one place. Rain makes **puddles** in the street. ∎

∎ **puddle**

pull

To **pull** is to make something move toward you. Charlene and her friends **pulled** on the rope. ∎

∎ **pull**

pumpkin

A **pumpkin** is a very large fruit. It is yellow or orange and grows on a vine. We place **pumpkins** on our porch in the fall. ∎

∎ **pumpkin**

punch

To **punch** means to hit hard with your fist. In gym class we learned how to **punch** the ball over the net.

puppet

A **puppet** is a toy that looks like a small person or animal. Some **puppets** fit on your hand. Others are moved by strings from above.

puppy

A **puppy** is a young dog. **Puppies** have soft fur and big feet. They like to play with everything. —**puppies** ∎

> Another word for **puppy** is **pup.**

∎ **puppy**

purchase

To **purchase** means to buy. Our teacher **purchased** new books for our class this year.

purple

Purple is a color. Grape juice and grape jelly are usually **purple.**

purse

A **purse** is a bag that girls and women carry. They can keep keys, money, pens, and other things in their **purses.**

push

To **push** is to make something go ahead of you. Lydia's mother **pushed** her across the snow. ∎

■ push

put

1. To **put** is to find a place for something and leave it there. Diana **put** a sandwich in her lunch box to take to school. **2.** To **put** out a fire means that you stop the fire from burning. My mother **put** out the candles before we went to bed. **3.** To **put** on clothes means to cover your body with them. Josie **put** on a new vest.

puzzle

1. A **puzzle** is a game. **Puzzles** are pieces of paper or wood that you have to put together to make pictures. **2.** A **puzzle** is also something that is hard to understand. It was a **puzzle** to Tess how her sister got home before she did.

quart

A **quart** is an amount of liquid. There are four **quarts** in one gallon.

quarter

1. A **quarter** is a kind of coin. One **quarter** is the same as five nickels. Four **quarters** is the same as one dollar.
2. A **quarter** is one of four pieces that are the same size. You can cut a pie into **quarters.**

queen

A **queen** is a woman who rules a country. **Queens** usually rule for as long as they live. A **queen** can also be the wife of a king.

question

A **question** is a group of words that ask something. Sometimes the teacher asks **questions** that are hard to answer.

When a **question** is asked, there is usually an **answer.** The teacher asked the **question** "What is two plus three?" The correct **answer** is "Five."

quick

Quick means fast. The mouse was so **quick** that we almost did not see it.

> **Quickly** means in a **quick** way. Ronald ate lunch **quickly** because he was late for the game.

quiet

To be **quiet** means to make very little sound. Our neighborhood is very **quiet** at night.

> **Quietly** means to do something in a **quiet** way. When we are in the library, we speak **quietly.**

quilt

A **quilt** is a kind of blanket. **Quilts** are made of two pieces of cloth sewn together with cotton, wool, or feathers between them. Each piece may be made of other smaller pieces. ■

■ **quilt**

quit

To **quit** means to stop doing something. My brother **quit** the swim team because he has a job after school. —**quit**

quite

1. Quite means very. The weather can get **quite** hot here in the summer. **2.** Not **quite** means almost. Davy has three more pages to read. He has not **quite** finished the book.

Rr

rabbit

A **rabbit** is a small animal. It has long ears and soft fur. **Rabbits** hop using their long back legs.

raccoon

A **raccoon** is a small animal. It has short legs and dark marks like a mask over its eyes. **Raccoons** live in forests and fields. ■

■ raccoon

race

A **race** is a contest to find out who is fastest. People have **races** on foot, in cars, on horses, and in many other ways. ■

■ race

radio

A **radio** is a machine that uses electricity to make sounds. A **radio** station uses electricity to send the sounds to **radios** in homes and cars. You can hear music or news on the **radio.** ■

■ radio

raft

A **raft** is a kind of flat boat. **Rafts** are made of logs, boards, rubber, or plastic. ■

■ raft

rag

A **rag** is a piece of cloth used for cleaning, washing, or dusting. My mother uses **rags** to wash the car.

railroad

A **railroad** is the metal path that trains ride on. **Railroads** can go across bridges, through tunnels, and over mountains. ■

■ railroad

rain

1. Rain is water that falls in drops from clouds. Plants need **rain** to grow. **2.** To **rain** means to fall as drops of water. When it **rains,** everything gets wet.

rainbow

A **rainbow** looks like a ribbon of many colors across the sky. **Rainbows** appear when the sun shines after it rains. ■

The color red is on the top of a **rainbow.** The color purple is at the bottom. The colors orange, yellow, green, and blue are in the middle.

■ **rainbow**

raise

1. To **raise** is to lift up. Ella **raised** her hand to answer the question. **2.** To **raise** means to take care of something while it grows. Farmers **raise** vegetables. Parents **raise** children.

rake

1. A **rake** is a tool. It is made of long, thin pieces of metal or plastic joined together like fingers. The fingers are at one end of a long pole. **Rakes** are used to gather grass and leaves into piles. **2.** To **rake** is to gather into a pile with a rake. Geraldo helps his father **rake** the leaves in the fall. ■

■ **rake**

ran

Ran is a form of **run.** Michele **ran** to school in the morning.

rang

Rang is a form of **ring.** The bell **rang** at the end of the day.

rat

A **rat** is a kind of animal. It has a long tail, short fur, and sharp teeth. **Rats** are bigger than mice.

> **Rat** rhymes with **bat, cat,** and **that.**

reach

1. To **reach** means to put your hand out toward something. Annette **reached** across the table. **2.** To **reach** also means to get all the way to. The big storm did not **reach** our part of the country. ∎

∎ **reach**

read

To **read** means to look at words and know what they mean. June is learning to **read.** She often **reads** stories with her friends. —**read** ∎

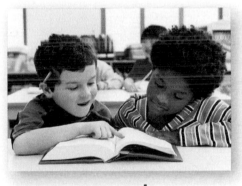

∎ **read**

> A **reader** is someone who **reads.** The teacher is happy that the students are good **readers.** A **reader** is also a book that helps people learn how to **read.** There is a story about a rabbit and a turtle in our **reader.**

ready

1. When something is **ready,** people can use it. "Dinner will be **ready** when the food is cooked."
2. When people get **ready,** they are prepared to do something. After we packed, we were **ready** to go on vacation. **—readier, readiest**

real

Real means the way the world is. When something is **real,** people did not make it up. Maya likes to pretend, but Corinne likes stories about **real** people.

really

Really means that something is actually true. Pine needles do not look like other leaves. But they **really** are leaves.

reason

A **reason** is why something is so. Bad weather is the **reason** there was no school yesterday. There are many **reasons** why I like the city better than the country.

recipe

A **recipe** is a set of directions for making food. My uncle borrowed my mother's **recipes** for tomato sauce and pizza.

rectangle

A **rectangle** is a shape. **Rectangles** have four sides and four corners. ∎

∎ **rectangle**

recycle

To **recycle** means to make trash into something that can be used again. Our city **recycles** old newspapers, cans, and glass.

red

Red is a color. Some apples and fire engines are **red. —redder, reddest**

> **Redden** means to become **red.**
> The sky **reddens** as the sun sets.

refrigerator

A **refrigerator** is a kind of machine. It is a box that is cold inside. **Refrigerators** keep food and drinks cold. Most people have **refrigerators** in their kitchens. ■

■ **refrigerator**

remember

To **remember** is to be able to think of something again. Laurie **remembers** the phone numbers of all her friends.

remind

To **remind** means to cause someone to remember something. My mother **reminded** me to bring an umbrella to school.

repeat

To **repeat** is to do or say again. "I did not hear you. Would you please **repeat** what you said?"

reptile

A **reptile** is a kind of animal. Snakes, turtles, and alligators are **reptiles.** ■

■ **reptile**

research

To **research** is to study something. People **research** things to learn about them. Our teacher asked us to go to the library so we could **research** the history of our state.

rest

1. To **rest** is to be still. People and animals need to **rest** when they are tired. 2. The **rest** of something is what has not been used. Louis ate half of his sandwich for lunch. He saved the **rest** for after school.

> The word **rest** rhymes with **best, chest, nest, test, vest,** and **west.**

restaurant

A **restaurant** is a place where people pay for meals. Most **restaurants** have many different kinds of food. **Restaurants** have kitchens where cooks make the food.

return

1. To **return** is to come back. Birds that have gone south in the winter **return** every spring. 2. To **return** also means to bring back. Megan **returned** the books to the library after she read them.

rhinoceros

A **rhinoceros** is a very large animal. It has short legs and gray skin. **Rhinoceroses** have one or two horns on their faces. ■

■ rhinoceros

rhyme

To **rhyme** means to end with the same sound. Cook **rhymes** with book. Group **rhymes** with soup. Tall **rhymes** with small. Many poems use words that **rhyme.**

ribbon

A **ribbon** is a long, thin piece of cloth or paper. **Ribbons** come in many colors. Presents are often wrapped in paper and tied with a **ribbon.** ■

■ ribbon

rice

Rice is a kind of food. Grains of **rice** are soft when they are cooked. **Rice** is the seeds of a kind of grass. ■

rich

To be **rich** means to have a lot of money. The **rich** princess had everything that she wanted.

The opposite of **rich** is **poor.** The **rich** king rode in a carriage past the **poor** farmers.

■ rice

ridden

Ridden is a form of **ride.** Trina likes to ride her bicycle. She has **ridden** it every day this week. Have you ever **ridden** a horse?

riddle

A **riddle** is a kind of joke. **Riddles** are questions that have funny answers. "When does Thursday come before Wednesday?" is a **riddle.** The answer is "In a dictionary."

ride

1. To **ride** is to sit in or on something that moves. Cowboys **ride** horses. Some children **ride** to school on a bus. 2. A **ride** is a time when you ride in something. Every Sunday our family goes for a **ride** in the country. 3. A **ride** is also a kind of machine at a carnival or a fair. **Rides** turn people around or upside-down or carry them through the air. —**rode, ridden** ■

■ ride

right

1. **Right** means correct. Robin usually knows the **right** answer. 2. **Right** also means the way something should be. **Right** is the opposite of **wrong.** It is always **right** to tell the truth. 3. **Right** is the opposite of **left.** In this country, people drive cars on the **right** side of the road. 4. A **right** is something that the law allows a person to do. Every citizen has the **right** to vote.

ring

1. A **ring** is a metal circle that people wear on their fingers. Many **rings** are made of gold or silver. Some **rings** have jewels on them. **2.** To **ring** is to make the sound of a bell. The school bell **rings** every morning when school starts. —**rang, rung** ∎

∎ ring

rink

A **rink** is a place where you skate. There are **rinks** for ice skating, roller skating, and ice hockey. ∎

∎ rink

rise

1. To **rise** is to go up. The sun **rises** in the east every morning. I like to watch bubbles **rise** to the top of my glass. **2.** To **rise** is also to become more in amount. The temperature outside **rises** on hot days. It has **risen** every day this week. **3.** To **rise** also means to stand up. We **rose** when the parade passed by. —**rose, risen**

river

A **river** is a wide path of water that has land on both sides. Some **rivers** are hundreds of miles long. ∎

∎ river

road

A **road** is a wide path. **Roads** can go through fields, forests, and towns. People travel over **roads** in cars, trucks, and buses. ∎

∎ road

roast

To **roast** is to cook with hot air in an oven or over a fire. Shari and her friends **roasted** marshmallows on Sunday. ∎

∎ roast

rob

To **rob** means to take from someone something that does not belong to you. Three people **robbed** the bank on Tuesday. They took all the money. —**robbed**

> A **robber** is a person who **robs** someone. The police caught the **robbers** and put them in jail.

∎ robin

robin

A **robin** is a kind of bird. **Robins** are red in front. ∎

robot

A **robot** is a machine that does a job. Many **robots** do the same jobs over and over again. ∎

∎ robot

rock

A **rock** is a hard object in the ground. Some **rocks** have metal in them.

rocket

A **rocket** is a kind of machine. It is a tube that flies up when something inside burns very fast. Astronauts are carried into space on large **rockets.** ■

■ **rocket**

rode

Rode is a form of **ride.** Len **rode** to school on the bus this morning, but he walked home.

> The word **rode** sounds the same as the word **road.**

roll

1. To **roll** is to keep turning over and over. When you kick a ball, it **rolls** away. 2. A **roll** is a kind of bread that is round or curved. People usually eat hamburgers and hot dogs in **rolls.**

roof

A **roof** is the top of a building. Some **roofs** are flat. Others have sides that join at the top. ■

■ **roof**

room

1. A **room** is an area in a building. **Rooms** usually have four walls, but they can be many different shapes or sizes. 2. **Room** means space. There is **room** for one more person to sit on the couch.

rooster

A **rooster** is a male chicken. **Roosters** make a lot of noise early in the morning. ■

■ **rooster**

root

A **root** is a part of a plant. It usually grows under the ground. Plants get water and food from the ground through their **roots.**

rope

Rope is made of several pieces of string twisted together. **Rope** can be tied in knots and used to hold things together. Sailors use **rope** to raise sails and tie their boats to docks. ■

■ **rope**

rose

1. A **rose** is a kind of flower. **Roses** are usually red, pink, yellow, or white. They grow on bushes and have a wonderful smell. **2. Rose** is a form of **rise.** The sun **rose** this morning at six o'clock. ■

rotate

To **rotate** means to turn in a circle. The earth **rotates** in space. The picture was upside-down, so we **rotated** it.

■ **rose**

rough

Something that is **rough** does not feel even. The bark of most trees is **rough.**

> The opposite of **rough** is **smooth.** The edge of the rock was **rough.** The front of the mirror is shiny and **smooth.**

round

Round means having the shape of a circle. A **round** object has no points or corners. Balls, wheels, and coins are **round.**

route

A **route** is the area that you go through to go from one place to another. On my **route** to school, I pass a grocery store and a post office. There are two different bus **routes** from the library to my house.

rub

To **rub** means to press against something with your hand and move back and forth. Pat **rubbed** the window with a cloth to clean the dirt off. **—rubbed**

rubber

1. Rubber is something that is strong and easy to stretch. Water cannot go through **rubber.** Tires for cars are made of **rubber. 2. Rubbers** are like shoes. They are made of rubber. People wear them over their shoes to keep their feet dry.

ruby

A **ruby** is a kind of jewel. **Rubies** are red. **—rubies**

rug

A **rug** is used to cover all or part of a floor. It is made of cloth or yarn. **Rugs** can be one color or many colors. ■

■ **rug**

rule

1. A **rule** tells how people must behave. To play a game right, you have to follow the **rules. 2.** To **rule** is to make laws and decide things. Sometimes wars are fought about who will **rule** a country.

ruler

1. A **ruler** is a strip of wood, metal, or plastic used to measure lengths or to draw straight lines. During our lesson, we used **rulers** to measure our books. **2.** A **ruler** is also a person who rules. The **ruler** of some countries is a king or queen.

run

1. To **run** is to go somewhere by moving your legs quickly. Rudy has **run** in races with her friends. **2.** To **run** also means to work. The washing machine makes a noise when it is **running. —ran, run** ■

■ **run**

rung

Rung is a form of **ring.** We know we are late for school because the bell has already **rung.**

rush

To **rush** means to hurry. Angie **rushed** home because she did not have much time to get dressed for the party.

Ss

sack

A **sack** is a bag made of cloth, plastic, paper, or string. We stored two **sacks** of potatoes in the cellar. ■

■ sack

sad

Sad means not happy. Jonah is **sad** because his best friend moved to another town. Everybody feels **sad** sometimes. —**sadder, saddest**

safe

Safe means that you will not be hurt. **Safe** is the opposite of **dangerous.** There was a terrible storm outside, but inside the house everyone was **safe.**

said

Said is a form of **say.** When Erica called her friend Michelle on the phone, the first thing Erica **said** was, "Hello!"

sail

1. A **sail** is a large piece of cloth on a boat. Boats move when the wind hits their **sails. 2.** To **sail** is to move over water. The boat **sailed** to a small island. **3.** To **sail** also means to make something sail. The captain **sailed** the ship on the ocean. ∎

> A **sailor** is a person who **sails** a boat. **Sailors** know a lot about wind and water.

∎ **sail**

salt

Salt is something people put on food. It looks like white grains of sand. Ocean water has **salt** in it.

> **Salty** means something has a lot of **salt** in it. My soup tastes too **salty.**

same

To be the **same** means to be alike in every way. **Same** is the opposite of **different.** The huts on the beach are all blue and yellow. The colors are the **same.** ∎

∎ **same**

sand

Sand is made of tiny grains of rock. It covers beaches at lakes and oceans. **Sand** can feel rough or soft. Tovah and her friend built a castle made of **sand.** ∎

∎ **sand**

sandwich

A **sandwich** is a kind of food. It is two pieces of bread with meat, cheese, peanut butter, or other foods in between. Many students in our class eat **sandwiches** for lunch. ■

■ **sandwich**

sang

Sang is a form of **sing**. Elizabeth learned a new song yesterday. She **sang** it all day long. Her friends liked it so much they **sang** it too.

sat

Sat is a form of **sit**. Perry **sat** on the floor while he played with marbles.

Saturday

Saturday is a day of the week. **Saturday** comes after Friday and before Sunday.

sauce

Sauce is a thick liquid that is put on food to make it taste better. Cheese **sauce** tastes good on macaroni. Other **sauces** are made from tomatoes and apples.

saucer

A **saucer** is a small dish that isn't very deep. It usually fits under a cup. People sometimes put milk into **saucers** for cats to drink. ■

■ **saucer**

save

1. To **save** means to make someone or something safe. Firefighters often **save** people's lives. **2.** To **save** also means to keep and not use. Lila **saves** a little money every week. She has **saved** enough to buy a kite.

saw

1. A **saw** is a tool. It is made of a flat piece of metal with a handle at one end. The edge of the metal piece has sharp points that are called teeth. **Saws** are used to cut wood, metal, and plastic. **2. Saw** is a form of **see.** Erin looked out the window and **saw** two squirrels in the front yard. ▪

■ **saw**

say

1. To **say** means to speak words. When Jacob answers the telephone, he **says,** "Hello!" **2.** To **say** also means to tell us something that is not spoken. The clock **says** it is time for us to go. The recipe **says** to add salt. —**said**

scale

A **scale** is an object that weighs people or things. The **scales** at the supermarket are for weighing fruits and vegetables. ▪

scare

To **scare** means to make afraid. The loud noise **scared** the baby, but we calmed her down.

■ **scale**

scarecrow

A **scarecrow** is something outside that looks like a person wearing old clothes. **Scarecrows** are put in fields of corn or other vegetables to scare birds away. ■

school

School is a place where students learn from teachers. Most **schools** are open from September until June.

■ **scarecrow**

> A **schoolyard** is the area around a **school** where children can play. The students in Ms. Kelly's class played baseball in the **schoolyard.**

science

Science is what people know about nature and about how things in the world work. Facts about the earth, oceans, weather, stars, plants, and electricity are all parts of **science.**

> A **scientist** is a person whose job is to learn about **science. Scientists** do experiments to find out what is true.

scissors

Scissors are a kind of tool. They are used to cut paper or cloth. Two pieces of metal are joined to make one pair of **scissors.** Each piece has a sharp edge and a hole for your fingers. ■

■ **scissors**

score

A **score** is a number that tells how well you perform at a game or on a test. Our football team had the winning **score** at the end of the game.

> A **scoreboard** is a large sign that shows the **score** of a game.

scrap

A **scrap** is a small piece of something. There were **scraps** of paper on the floor after we used scissors to make paper stars.

scratch

1. To **scratch** means to make marks with something hard. A rock can **scratch** a piece of glass. **2.** To **scratch** also means to rub hard with fingernails or claws. Ariel **scratched** her skin when it itched. The cat is **scratching** herself with her claws.

scrub

To **scrub** means to clean by rubbing hard. My parents **scrubbed** the plastic pool before we went in to swim. —**scrubbed**

sea

Sea is another word for **ocean.** Many years ago, pirates sailed the **seas** looking for treasure.

> The **seashore** is the land that is at the edge of an ocean or **sea.** Some **seashores** are covered with rocks, and others are covered with sand.

seal

1. A **seal** is a kind of animal. It has smooth fur. **Seals** swim in the ocean and eat fish. **2.** To **seal** means to close tight. My mother **sealed** the bag so that the cereal inside would stay fresh. ■

■ seal

search

To **search** for something is to look for it in many places. We **searched** for the ball in the tall grass beside the field.

season

A **season** is a part of the year. There are four **seasons** that come every year. They are winter, spring, summer, and fall.

seat

A **seat** is anywhere you can sit. Matthew found a **seat** at the back of the room. ■

■ seat

second

1. A **second** is a very short amount of time. Lightning flashes in about a **second.** There are 60 **seconds** in one minute. **2. Second** is next after first. The **second** letter of the alphabet is **B.**

secret

A **secret** is something nobody else knows. Jordana kept the **secret** about who won the class election. It is not easy for her to keep **secrets.**

see

1. To **see** is to know what something is like by using your eyes. Did you **see** the beautiful sunset yesterday? Have you **seen** the new movie? **2.** To **see** also means to understand. I **see** why my teacher said the test would be hard. —**saw, seen**

> **See** sounds the same as **sea.**

seed

A **seed** is a hard part of a plant. Many fruits have **seeds** inside them. New plants grow from **seeds.** ■

■ **seed**

seem

To **seem** means to be the way that something is or how it makes you feel. This **seems** like a good place to have a picnic.

seen

Seen is a form of **see.** Danielle likes to look at birds. She has **seen** several dozen different kinds of birds.

seesaw

A **seesaw** is something to play on. **Seesaws** are long boards with one person sitting on each end. When one end goes up, the other end goes down. ■

■ **seesaw**

sell

To **sell** means to give something for money. Donald **sells** glasses of juice outside his house on hot days. —**sold**

> The opposite of **sell** is **buy.** When my friends **sell** lemonade, my mother **buys** some for me.

send

To **send** means to make someone or something go somewhere. Susan likes to **send** letters to her friends. Frank's mother **sent** him to the store to buy some bread. —**sent**

sentence

A **sentence** is a group of words. Books are usually written in **sentences.**

separate

To **separate** means to put things apart. Ezra **separated** the white clothes from the colored clothes in the laundry.

September

September is a month of the year. It has 30 days. **September** comes after August and before October.

serious

1. Serious means that you are not being funny. Brett was **serious** when he said I couldn't borrow his new book. **2. Serious** also means being very interested in something. Kayla is a **serious** student who always does well in school.

set

1. A **set** is a group of things that go together. Casey's mother has one **set** of blue dishes and two **sets** of white ones. **2.** To **set** means to put somewhere. Rafi **set** the plate on the table. **3.** To **set** also means to go below the part of the sky that you see. It was such a fine evening that everyone went out to watch the sun **set.**

settler

A **settler** is one of the first people to live in an area. The **settlers** liked the land because it was good for farming.

seven

Seven is one more than six. **Seven** is written **7.** $6 + 1 = 7.$

several

Several means more than two or three. Stacey has **several** hobbies.

sew

To **sew** is to put pieces of cloth together with a needle and thread. Graham **sewed** a button on his shirt. Miriam has **sewn** a patch on her pants. —**sewn** ■

■ **sew**

shade

1. Shade is a place that is not in the sun's light. It is usually cooler in the **shade. 2.** A **shade** is a cover for a window that keeps light out. When we go to sleep, we pull down the **shades** in our room.

shadow

A **shadow** is a dark area where the sun cannot shine. When there is a light behind you, you see your **shadow** in front. When the light is in front of you, your **shadow** is behind. ■

■ **shadow**

shake

1. To **shake** means to make something go up and down or from side to side very quickly. Sid **shakes** the jar to mix up the orange juice. After he has **shaken** the jar, he pours the juice into a glass. **2.** To **shake** your head is to move your head from side to side or up and down. People **shake** their heads from side to side to say no. —**shook, shaken**

A **saltshaker** is a small container that holds **salt** and has small holes on top. When you turn it upside-down and **shake** it, **salt** falls out.

shall

Shall is another word for **will**. We **shall** go to the carnival if it doesn't rain.

shallow

Shallow means that there is little space between the top and bottom of something. The opposite of **shallow** is **deep**. My cousins like to swim where the water is **shallow**. ■

■ **shallow**

shape

1. The **shape** of something is what it is like on the outside. Baseballs and basketballs have round **shapes.** A box has the **shape** of a square or rectangle. **2.** To **shape** is to give a shape to something. Dane's uncle **shaped** a piece of clay into a ball.

share

To **share** means to let someone have or use something. Rick **shared** his crayons with me.

shark

A **shark** is a kind of large fish. **Sharks** have many sharp teeth and eat smaller fish. ■

■ **shark**

sharp

To be **sharp** is to have a point or a thin edge that cuts. Some knives have **sharp** edges. ■

she

She means a female person. Mrs. Perez lives on our block. **She** is our neighbor.

■ **sharp**

shed

A **shed** is a small building used to store things. Many people keep shovels and other tools in **sheds** in their yards.

sheep

A **sheep** is a kind of animal. It is covered with wool. **Sheep** are raised for their wool and their meat. —**sheep** ■

■ **sheep**

sheet

1. A **sheet** is a large cloth shaped like a rectangle that you put on a bed. I have green, cotton **sheets** on my bed. **2.** A **sheet** is also a single piece of paper. We need ten **sheets** of white paper for our writing project.

shell

A **shell** is a hard cover on the outside of something. Eggs, nuts, crabs, and turtles all have **shells.** ■

■ **shell**

A **seashell** is a **shell** that you find on the beach. **Seashells** were once part of small animals.

shelter

A **shelter** is a safe place for a person or an animal to stay. **Shelters** protect us from rain, wind, and other kinds of bad weather.

shine

To **shine** is to send out a bright light. The sun **shines** every day when there are no clouds. —**shone**

ship
caption: ■ ship

ship

A **ship** is a big boat. It sails in deep water. Large **ships** can carry many people across the ocean. ■

shirt

A **shirt** is a kind of clothes. People wear **shirts** on the top part of their bodies. Many **shirts** have buttons. ■

shoe

A **shoe** is something that covers a foot. It can be made of leather, cloth, or plastic. **Shoes** come in pairs.

■ shirt

A **shoelace** is a string that helps a **shoe** fit on your foot. Allegra knows how to tie her **shoelaces.**

shone

Shone is a form of **shine.** The moon **shone** in the sky all night.

shook

Shook is a form of **shake.** Stan **shook** the jar until the juice was all mixed up. When he asked Sophia if she wanted any, she **shook** her head to say no.

shoot

1. To **shoot** is to go up or out quickly. Rockets **shoot** up into the air. **2.** To **shoot** also means to make something go quickly toward something else. Ross **shoots** a basketball at the basket. —**shot** ■

■ **shoot**

shop

1. A **shop** is a small store. There are book **shops,** flower **shops,** hat **shops,** barber **shops,** and many other kinds of **shops. 2.** To **shop** is to go to a store to buy things. My aunt **shops** at the supermarket for food. —**shopped** ■

> A **shopper** is a person who **shops.** Cho was one of the first **shoppers** at the new mall.

■ **shop**

shore

The **shore** is the land at the edge of the water. Oceans, lakes, ponds, and rivers all have **shores.** ■

■ **shore**

short

1. Short is the opposite of **tall.** Ponies are **short** horses. **2. Short** is also the opposite of **long.** Toni likes **short,** curly hair. **3. Short** means a small amount when we talk about time. It only took Jean and Kevin a **short** time to make their beds because they worked quickly.

shot

1. Shot is a form of **shoot.** Ross **shot** the ball into the basket. **2.** A **shot** is something you shoot. Ross tried three **shots** before he hit the basket.

should

Should means that people want something to happen. Everyone **should** be in the room when class starts.

shoulder

A **shoulder** is a part of the body. It is between your neck and your arm. My father put the jacket over one of his **shoulders.** ■

■ shoulder

shout

To **shout** is to talk in a loud voice. Ken **shouted** so that his friend could hear him across the street.

> The opposite of **shout** is **whisper.**
> Jim **shouted** in the library, and his teacher asked him to **whisper** instead.

shovel

A **shovel** is a tool. It is made of a wide piece of metal joined to a long handle. **Shovels** are used to dig holes and to move dirt and snow. ■

■ shovel

show

1. To **show** means to let someone see. Meredith **showed** Rina her books. **2.** To **show** also means to teach. Lizzie **showed** Edwin how to skate. **3.** A **show** is a story that you see or hear on television or radio, at the movies, or in a theater. I watch my favorite television **shows** on Friday afternoons. —**shown**

shut

To **shut** means to close. Marina opened the door and came into the house. Then she **shut** the door behind her. —**shut**

shy

To be **shy** means to find it hard to talk to people. **Shy** people are often quiet. —**shier, shiest**

sick

To be **sick** is to have something wrong with you. Sometimes when you are **sick,** your head or your stomach hurts. Doctors and nurses take care of **sick** people.

side

A **side** is a flat part of the outside of something. A piece of paper has two **sides.** A square has four **sides.**

sidewalk

A **sidewalk** is a narrow path or road where people can walk. Usually there are **sidewalks** along the sides of streets. ■

■ **sidewalk**

sign

1. A **sign** is a symbol. The **signs** for plus and minus are + and −.
2. A **sign** is also a flat piece of metal, wood, or plastic with a message printed on it. Road **signs** warn that people should be careful. ■

■ **sign**

> There are many **signs** that you can make with your arms and hands. One kind is called **sign language**. **Sign language** is sometimes used by people who are deaf.

silent

To be **silent** is to make no sound at all. Nat tried to stay **silent** so his sister would not find him hiding behind the door.

> **Silent** letters are letters in words that are written but not spoken. The **g** in the word **sign** is **silent**.

silk

Silk is a soft, fancy kind of cloth. Becca has a **silk** shirt that she only wears on special days.

silly

To be **silly** means to act funny. Raj and his friends were giggling and running around the room. They were acting **silly**. —**sillier, silliest**

silver

Silver is a kind of metal. **Silver** is used to make coins, jewelry, and other things. ■

■ silver

simple

Simple means not fancy. Helen can make a **simple** drawing of a person with only four lines and a circle.

since

Since means after. We have not had any rain **since** last month. The weather has been dry **since** then.

sing

To **sing** is to make music with your voice. Blair likes to **sing** lullabies to her little sister. —**sang, sung**

A **singer** is a person who **sings.** Most bands have **singers** and people who play instruments.

single

Single means only one. Our class walked in a **single** line when we entered the gym.

sip

To **sip** means to drink in small amounts. I **sip** hot drinks so that I don't burn my mouth. —**sipped**

sister

A **sister** is a girl who has the same parents as somebody else. Alec and his **sisters** made supper for their parents.

sit

To **sit** is to rest your weight on something. Shawn has his own chair to **sit** on at his desk. Last night he **sat** there so he could use his computer. —**sat**

six

Six is one more than five. **Six** is written **6.** 5 + 1 = **6.**

size

The **size** of something is how big it is. All tennis balls are the same **size.** People and clothes come in many different **sizes.**

skate

1. A **skate** is a kind of shoe. It has a long piece of metal or small wheels on the bottom. People wear **skates** to go fast on ice, on the sidewalk, or on the floor. **2.** To **skate** is to move on skates. Ruth can **skate** in a circle on one leg. ■

■ skate

A **roller skate** is a **skate** with wheels that is used to **skate** on floors or sidewalks. **Ice skates** have a sharp edge for **skating** on ice.

ski

1. A **ski** is a long, narrow piece of wood, metal, or plastic. People wear **skis** on their feet to go fast on snow.
2. To **ski** means to move over the snow on skis. Connor **skied** down a hill. ■

■ ski

skin

The **skin** is the outside part of people, animals, and many plants. The **skin** protects what is inside. Banana **skins** are yellow.

skip

1. To **skip** means to move by hopping on one foot and then the other. We like to **skip** to the playground after school. 2. To **skip** also means not to do something that you usually do. I **skipped** the school picnic because I visited my cousins. —**skipped**

skirt

A **skirt** is a kind of clothes that hangs down from the middle of the body. **Skirts** are usually worn by girls and women. The girls wear black **skirts** and red shirts when they dance at school. ■

■ skirt

skunk

A **skunk** is a small animal. It has a big tail and a white stripe on its back. **Skunks** can make a very strong smell that protects them from other animals. ■

■ skunk

sky

The **sky** is the air far above the ground. It is blue during the day when there are no clouds. We see the sun, the moon, and the stars in the **sky. —skies**

skyscraper

A **skyscraper** is a very tall building. Most big cities have many **skyscrapers.**

sled

A **sled** is something you ride on to go over the snow. **Sleds** are made of wood, metal, or plastic. ∎

∎ **sled**

sleep

Sleep is a time when your body is resting. Most people **sleep** in beds at night. This morning Angela **slept** until nine o'clock. —**slept** ∎

> When you are **sleepy,** you are awake but very tired.

∎ **sleep**

sleeve

A **sleeve** is a part of a shirt, sweater or coat that covers your arm. In the winter Sheila wears shirts with long **sleeves,** but in the summer she likes to wear shirts with short **sleeves.** ∎

∎ **sleeve**

slept

Slept is a form of **sleep**. Ginny **slept** at her friend's house last night.

slice

A **slice** is a piece that you cut from something. In the fall, my family likes to eat **slices** of pumpkin pie. ■

■ **slice**

slip

To **slip** means to slide by accident. People often fall down after they **slip**. My father **slipped** and fell because the floor was wet. **—slipped**

> When something can make you **slip**, we say that it is **slippery**.

slipper

A **slipper** is a kind of shoe. **Slippers** are usually worn inside the house.

slow

To be **slow** means to take a long time. **Slow** is the opposite of **fast**. Turtles are very **slow**.

small

1. Small means filling not much space. **Small** is the opposite of **big**. We would like two **small** jars instead of one big one. Mice are **small** animals. **2. Small** also means letters of the alphabet that are not capital letters. The letters **a** and **b** are **small** letters. The letters **A** and **B** are capital letters.

smell

1. To **smell** is to know what something is like by using your nose. Billy **smelled** the smoke in the kitchen when the food burned in the oven. **2.** A **smell** is what something is like when you smell it. Flowers often have a pleasant **smell.** Many nice **smells** come from my garden. **3.** To **smell** also means to have a smell. The bread that we bake in the oven **smells** wonderful.

smile

1. A **smile** is a happy look on a person's face. The ends of the mouth turn up, and the skin near the eyes wrinkles. When I told the jokes, there were a lot of **smiles** in the room. **2.** To **smile** is to put a smile on your face. Tomas **smiled** when I took his picture. ■

■ **smile**

smoke

Smoke is something made by things that burn. It looks like a cloud. **Smoke** can be white, gray, or black.

> A room that is full of **smoke** is called **smoky.** It is hard to breathe in a **smoky** room.

smooth

To be **smooth** is to feel even and have no rough spots. A piece of glass in a window is **smooth.**

snack

A **snack** is something you eat sometimes between meals. My favorite **snacks** are carrots and peanuts.

snail

A **snail** is a very small animal. It has a soft body and a hard shell. **Snails** move very slowly on land or on the bottom of the sea.

snake

A **snake** is a kind of reptile. It has a long, narrow body and no arms or legs. Most **snakes** are short, but some can be very long. ■

■ snake

sneaker

A **sneaker** is a kind of shoe. It has rubber on the bottom and cloth on the top. People wear **sneakers** when they run or play sports. ■

sneeze

1. A **sneeze** happens when your nose itches. The air comes out of your nose and mouth very fast. Some people have three or four **sneezes** at a time. 2. To **sneeze** is to make a sneeze. Nita **sneezed** because she has a cold.

■ sneaker

snow

1. **Snow** is tiny pieces of frozen water that fall from the clouds. In some places, **snow** covers the ground in winter. 2. To **snow** means to fall as pieces of frozen water. When it **snows,** we like to go skiing. ■

When there is **snow,** it is fun to build a **snowman**. The **snowman** looks funny when it begins to melt.

■ snow

so

1. So means very. Jamie thought of a joke. It was **so** funny that he could not stop laughing for several minutes. **2. So** can mean also. Isabel and Patty read the same book. Isabel liked it, and **so** did Patty. **3. So** also means that one thing causes another thing to happen. Tanya forgot her umbrella, **so** she got wet when it rained.

■ soap

soap

Soap helps take dirt off things when it is mixed with water. Rochelle uses **soap** and water to wash her hands. ■

soccer

Soccer is a sport. In **soccer** two teams kick a ball up and down a field. They may not touch the ball with their hands. ■

■ soccer

sock

A **sock** is a kind of clothes. People wear **socks** on their feet, inside their shoes. ■

■ sock

sofa

A **sofa** is a kind of furniture that you sit on. **Sofas** are wider than chairs. **Sofa** is another word for **couch.**

soft

1. When something is **soft,** it is easy to change its shape with your fingers, and it does not scratch other things. **Soft** is the opposite of **hard.** Fur and cotton are **soft. 2. Soft** also means quiet. **Soft** is the opposite of **loud.** When Henry is in the library, he tries to be quiet. He speaks in a **soft** voice.

> **Soften** means to become **soft.** The clay **softened** when we added water to it.

soil

Soil is the top part of the ground. Most plants grow in **soil.** ■

■ **soil**

sold

Sold is a form of **sell.** Chico's father sells cars. Last week he **sold** four cars.

solid

1. Solid means hard. Things that are **solid** always have a shape of some kind. Things made of wood and steel are **solid. 2.** A **solid** is something that is hard. Ice is a **solid,** but air is a gas.

solve

To **solve** means to find the answer. After a few minutes we **solved** the mystery of my lost glasses. I had left them in the car.

some

Some means an amount that is more than a little but less than a lot. Brenda has not read most of the books in the library. But she has read **some** of them. The high mountains have **some** snow on them.

somebody

Somebody means a person, but you don't know or don't say who it is. **Somebody** from our school won first prize.

somehow

Somehow means in some way or another. Rain is getting through the roof **somehow.**

someone

Someone is another word for **somebody. Someone** turned on the radio in my room while I was outside.

something

Something means a thing, but you don't know or don't say what it is. The baby is hungry. She wants **something** to eat. **Something** is making a noise outside.

sometimes

Sometimes means at some times but not all times. **Sometimes** it rains during the winter, and **sometimes** it snows.

somewhere

Somewhere means a place, but you don't know or don't say where it is. I left my jacket **somewhere** in the park.

son

A **son** is a person's male child. Don's parents have two **sons.** One is Don, and the other is Robert.

> **Son** sounds the same as **sun.**

song

A **song** is what someone sings. Some **songs** are written for a lot of voices singing together.

soon

Soon means in a short time. It is almost time for supper. We will be eating **soon.**

sorry

To be **sorry** is to feel sad about something. Maryam was **sorry** that Nathaniel was sick. —**sorrier, sorriest**

sound

Sound is anything that you hear. Wind, thunder, dogs, and trains all make different **sounds.**

> Words have **sounds** when you say them. When two words **sound** the same, they have the same **sound.** To **sound** out a word means to say the **sounds** of the letters slowly.

soup

Soup is a kind of food. It is made with water and pieces of vegetables, meat, or other things. We eat **soup** in bowls. ∎

∎ soup

sour

Sour is a kind of taste. Lemon juice tastes **sour.**

south

South is a direction. It is the opposite of **north.** If you look at where the sun rises, **south** is to your right. ∎

∎ **south**

space

1. A **space** is a place where nothing is. There are **spaces** between the words on this page.
2. **Space** is everywhere outside of the earth. The sun, the moon, and the stars are in **space.** ∎

∎ **space**

speak

To **speak** is to make the sounds of words with your mouth. Sometimes Phil **speaks** in a soft voice. Other times he **speaks** loudly so that everyone can hear. —**spoke, spoken**

special

Special means important and not like all the rest. Holidays and birthdays are **special** days.

spell

To **spell** is to put letters together to make words. Nan knows how to **spell** most of the words in this book.

> A **spelling bee** is a contest where people take turns **spelling** words.

spend

To **spend** means to pay money to buy things. Andreas often **spends** his money on books. Irene **spent** most of her money on gifts. —**spent**

spice

A **spice** is something that adds flavor to food. Ginger and pepper are **spices.**

> Something that has lots of **spice** in it is called **spicy.**

spider

A **spider** is a very small animal with eight legs. **Spiders** are not insects. But they catch insects in the webs they make. ■

■ spider

spin

1. To **spin** means to turn around in a circle. The wheels of my bicycle were still **spinning** when it fell on the street. 2. To **spin** also means to make a web or cocoon. The spider **spun** a big web near the shed. —**spun**

spoke

Spoke is a form of **speak.** We could not hear the teacher in the back of the room, so he **spoke** louder.

spoken

Spoken is a form of **speak.** Eleni has **spoken** with a lot of people about the winter concert today.

spoon

A **spoon** is a tool to eat with. It looks like a tiny bowl with a handle. People eat soup and cereal with **spoons.**

sport

A **sport** is a kind of game. Baseball, football, hockey, tennis, basketball, and soccer are all different **sports.**

spot

1. A **spot** is a small mark that is a different color from the area around it. Some animals are covered with **spots. 2.** A **spot** is also a place. Lance found a very nice **spot** to sit down. ■

■ **spot**

spread

1. To **spread** means to put something over a wide area. My uncle **spread** the blanket on the sand. **2. Spread** also means to put over a surface in a smooth and even way. My sister used the knife to **spread** jelly on her bread. —**spread** ■

■ **spread**

spring

Spring is a season. It comes after winter and before summer. The weather gets warmer and flowers begin to grow in the **spring.**

The days of **spring** are called **springtime.** Our baseball team plays its first game in the **springtime.**

spun

Spun is a form of **spin.** The propeller of the helicopter **spun** when the helicopter rose off the ground.

square

A **square** is a shape. All four sides of a **square** are the same length. ■

■ **square**

squeeze

To **squeeze** means to push on the outside of something. Callie **squeezed** the tube until toothpaste came out. ■

■ **squeeze**

squirrel

A **squirrel** is a small animal. It has gray or red fur and a big tail. **Squirrels** live in trees. ■

stable

1. A **stable** is a building on a farm where horses, cows, or other animals are kept. The animals sleep in the **stable** when it is cold outside. **2. Stable** also means that something will not fall down. The shed we built is strong and **stable.** We will have it for many years. ■

■ **squirrel**

stack

A **stack** is a pile of things, one on top of another. We put the magazines in **stacks** on the desk.

■ **stable**

stairs

Stairs are a group of steps. People walk up and down **stairs** to get from one floor of a building to another. ∎

∎ **stairs**

stamp

A **stamp** is a small piece of paper with words and numbers and a picture on it. People buy **stamps** to stick on letters and packages they send through the mail.

stand

To **stand** is to keep your body straight and rest all your weight on your feet. Objects can **stand** on their legs or bases. Nate's desk **stands** by the door. —**stood**

star

1. A **star** is a large amount of burning gas that is very far away. It looks like a tiny dot of light in the sky at night. There are millions and millions of **stars.** Our sun is a **star** too. **2.** A **star** is also a shape. It has five or six points. Our country's flag has 50 **stars. 3.** A **star** can also be an important person in movies, plays, or shows. **Stars** are people that almost everybody knows about. ∎

∎ **star**

stare

To **stare** is to look for a long time at something. Marcia and Felix **stared** at the rainbow that appeared yesterday afternoon.

start

1. To **start** is to do something when you have not been doing it before. I **started** to walk home at three o'clock. **2.** To **start** also means to begin working. The engine in a car **starts** when you turn a key.

> The opposite of **start** is **finish**. Heidi **started** her project on Monday, and she **finished** it on Friday.

state

1. A **state** is a part of a country. Our country is divided into 50 **states**. **2.** A **state** can also mean an independent country. It is not divided into other **states**. **3.** To **state** means to say. The mayor **stated** that the roads would be closed after the storm.

station

A **station** is a special place or building. A train **station** is a place where trains stop. A gas **station** is where people buy gasoline for their cars. Television shows come from television **stations**. The police can be found at a police **station**. ■

■ **station**

statue

A **statue** is an object that is a kind of art. **Statues** usually look like people or animals. **Statues** are made from stone, clay, wood, or metal and can be small or large. ■

■ **statue**

stay

To **stay** means to be in a place and not go away. Janis and Mickey **stayed** at school in the afternoon to play baseball with some other children.

steady

Steady means not shaking. Jake's father held the ladder **steady** while Jake climbed up to the tree house. —**steadier, steadiest**

steak

A **steak** is a piece of meat. Most **steaks** are made of beef. They are cooked over a fire outside or in the oven.

steam

Steam is water that has become a gas. Water changes into **steam** when it becomes hot. ■

■ **steam**

> A place that is full of **steam** is called **steamy.**

steel

Steel is a metal made from melted iron. **Steel** is hard and strong. It is used to make bridges, buildings, and other things. ■

stem

A **stem** is a part of a plant that usually grows up from the ground. **Stems** are long and thin. They let water go up to the leaves.

■ **steel**

step

1. A **step** is lifting one foot and putting it down. Tall people with long legs can take big **steps. 2.** A **step** is also a flat place where you can put your foot to go up or down. Carla walks down the **steps** to the basement. **3.** To **step** is to move one foot in front of the other and walk. Erik **stepped** forward and raised his hand. —**stepped** ■

■ **step**

stick

1. A **stick** is a piece of wood. Many **sticks** are old, dry branches of trees. Bob's dog likes to play with **sticks. 2.** To **stick** is to push into. Ellie **sticks** her foot into the water to see how cold it is. **3.** To **stick** out means not to be in all the way. The branches **stick** out from the trunk of a tree. **4.** To **stick** together means to put two things against each other so they do not come apart. Ricardo used glue to **stick** two pieces of paper together. —**stuck** ■

■ **stick**

still

1. Still means that something has not stopped. My sister was mad at me yesterday. She is **still** mad at me today. **2. Still** also means not moving. When there is no wind, the water in the lake is very **still.**

stomach

A **stomach** is a part of the body. The food we eat goes into our **stomachs.**

stone

A **stone** is a small piece of rock. When the water in the river gets low, we can see a lot of **stones**. ∎

∎ **stone**

stood

Stood is a form of **stand.** Athena's mother **stood** on a chair to reach some dishes.

stop

1. To **stop** means not to move. Buses **stop** at different places to let people get on and off. **2.** To **stop** something means that you were doing it, but you don't do it now. We **stopped** playing tennis when it started to rain. **3.** To **stop** also means to not let someone do something. The teacher **stopped** us before we put more food in the aquarium. —**stopped**

store

1. A **store** is a place where things are sold. Shoes are sold in shoe **stores.** You can buy toys in a toy **store.** Some **stores** are very big and have all kinds of things to buy. **2.** To **store** something is to put it away and save it. We **store** furniture in our attic.

storm

A **storm** is a strong wind. **Storms** usually bring rain or snow. Some also have thunder and lightning. ∎

∎ **storm**

> After a **snowstorm,** there is a lot of **snow** on the ground. After **rainstorms,** there are many puddles.

A B C D E F G H I J K L M

story

A **story** is a group of words that tell what happened to people and places. **Stories** can be real or they can be made up. —**stories**

stove

A **stove** is a machine that makes heat. Food is cooked in pots or pans on top of some **stoves.** ■

■ **stove**

straight

To be **straight** is to have no turns or curves. The opposite of **straight** is **crooked.** We drove all the way through the desert on a **straight** road. ■

■ **straight**

strange

Strange means different and hard to understand. New things often feel **strange** to us until we learn more about them.

stranger

A **stranger** is someone you do not know. Julie's family moved to a new town. They were **strangers** there until they met some new friends.

straw

A **straw** is a long tube made of paper or plastic. People can drink juice, water, or milk through **straws.** ■

■ **straw**

stream

A **stream** is a narrow path of water. It moves in one direction. **Streams** are not as big as rivers. ■

■ **stream**

street

A **street** is a road in a city or a town. Large cities have many **streets.**

A **streetlight** is a **light** at the top of a pole outside. **Streetlights** are usually on during the night.

stretch

1. To **stretch** is to change the shape of something by pulling it. Rubber and some kinds of plastic are easy to **stretch. 2.** To **stretch** also means to reach with your arms or legs. Marcy **stretches** her legs before playing soccer. ■

■ **stretch**

string

String is used to tie things. It is made from long, strong plants or from a special kind of plastic. **String** comes in different sizes and colors. Rope is made of many **strings** twisted together. ■

strip

A **strip** is a narrow piece of something. Ribbons are made from **strips** of cloth or paper.

■ **string**

A B C D E F G H I J K L M

stripe

A **stripe** is a line of color. Some fish are covered with **stripes.** Clyde has a shirt with **stripes** on it. ■

■ **stripe**

strong

1. To be **strong** is to have a lot of power. Morty is so **strong** that he can lift two full suitcases. **2. Strong** also means hard to break. Things made from steel are very **strong.**

> The opposite of **strong** is **weak.** If you exercise, you can turn **weak** muscles into **strong** ones.

stuck

Stuck is a form of **stick.** Brianne **stuck** a pin into the cushion by accident. Omar **stuck** two pieces of paper together with paste.

student

A **student** is a person who goes to school to learn. **Students** learn from teachers in classes.

study

To **study** means to try to learn. People usually read when they **study.** Francie is **studying** for a test. —**studies, studied**

submarine

A **submarine** is a kind of boat that can travel underwater. **Submarines** are long and narrow. ■

■ **submarine**

subtract

To **subtract** is to take away one number from another number. When you **subtract** four from nine, you get five. The symbol for **subtract** is −.

subway

A **subway** is a train that travels through tunnels underground. **Subways** carry people through large cities. ∎

∎ **subway**

such

1. Such means so much. Rod went to see his sister dance. He did not know she was **such** a good dancer.
2. Such as means for example. I like places that have rides, **such** as fairs and carnivals.

sudden

To be **sudden** is to happen quickly without anyone expecting it. The **sudden** noise was a surprise to us.

> **Suddenly** means that something happens in a **sudden** way. We were having a good time at the picnic, when **suddenly** it began to rain.

suds

Suds are many tiny bubbles made by soap and water. Margie likes to have a lot of **suds** when she washes the dishes. ∎

∎ **suds**

sugar

Sugar is something people put on or in food. It is made of small white or brown grains that are sweet. Many desserts are made with **sugar.**

suit

A **suit** is a set of clothes that match. A jacket and pants or a jacket and a skirt made from the same cloth are a **suit.** Some people wear **suits** on special days. ■

■ **suit**

suitcase

A **suitcase** is a kind of box to carry clothes in when you travel. All **suitcases** have handles, and many have small wheels. ■

sum

A **sum** is a number that you get when you add two other numbers together. The **sum** of 11 and 9 is 20. We made **sums** of the numbers the teacher gave us.

summer

Summer is a season. It comes after spring and before fall. The weather is often hot during the **summer.** Many schools are closed in **summer.**

■ **suitcase**

sun

The **sun** is a yellow star. It shines in the sky during the day. The **sun** gives us heat and light.

A **sunny** day is a day when the **sun** is shining.

Sunday

Sunday is a day of the week. **Sunday** comes after Saturday and before Monday.

sung

Sung is a form of **sing.** Hala has been singing all morning. She has **sung** the songs she knows from many shows.

sunlight

Sunlight is light from the sun. **Sunlight** is good for plants and animals.

sunrise

Sunrise is when the sun comes up. There is a **sunrise** every morning, but we can't see it if there are too many clouds. ■

■ **sunrise**

sunset

Sunset is when the sun goes down. Many people like to go out to watch a beautiful **sunset.**

supermarket

A **supermarket** is a very big store where food is sold. **Supermarkets** sell all kinds of food.

supper

Supper is a meal. People eat **supper** in the evening.

suppose

To **suppose** means to think when you do not know for sure. When five students were late, we **supposed** it was because the school bus broke down.

sure

To be **sure** is to know. Addie was **sure** she had time to take the dog for a walk before dinner.

surface

A **surface** is the outside or top part of something. Boats sail on the **surface** of the ocean. The **surfaces** of a desk and table are smooth.

surprise

1. A **surprise** is something you do not expect. We thought it would rain today. It was a **surprise** to see the sun in the sky. Mia loves **surprises. 2.** To **surprise** someone is to do something he or she did not expect. Joe's friends **surprised** him with flowers when he was sick.

If you give someone a **surprise party,** that person does not know about the **party.** We had a **surprise party** for my father on his birthday. When he entered the room, we yelled "**Surprise!**"

swallow

To **swallow** is to make food go from your mouth to your stomach. Bart's mother tells him to chew his food before he **swallows** it.

swam

Swam is a form of **swim.** Rusty **swam** all the way across the pool. Then he **swam** back.

swamp

A **swamp** is an area of land that is soft and wet. Frogs, mosquitoes, snakes, and alligators live in **swamps.**

swan

A **swan** is a large bird. It is usually white and has a long neck. People like to watch **swans** swimming on ponds and lakes. ■

■ swan

sweater

A **sweater** is a kind of clothes. People wear **sweaters** over their shirts. **Sweaters** are often made of wool or cotton. ■

■ sweater

sweet

Sweet is a kind of taste. Apple juice, cake, and pudding are **sweet.**

swim

To **swim** is to go through the water by moving your arms and legs. Nathan's brother **swims** in races every month. Some people can **swim** long distances. —**swam, swum** ■

■ swim

swing

1. To **swing** something is to move it from one side to the other while holding it at one end. Phoebe **swings** her bat to hit the ball. **2.** A **swing** is a seat held up by ropes or chains. Children play on **swings** in playgrounds or in their yards. —**swung** ■

■ swing

swum

Swum is a form of **swim.** Asher has been swimming all morning. He must have **swum** about a mile.

swung

Swung is a form of **swing.** Howard **swung** the rope and Felicia jumped over it.

symbol

A **symbol** is a mark or design that means something. Letters of the alphabet are **symbols** for sounds. Words are **symbols** for things.

The colors of a traffic light are **symbols.** Red means "stop" and green means "go."

syrup

Syrup is a thick, sweet liquid. It is made from sugar or the juice from some plants. **Syrup** is good to eat on waffles. ■

■ syrup

T t

table

A **table** is a kind of furniture. It has a flat top and legs. My family sits at the **table** to eat dinner. ■

A **cloth** that covers a **table** is called a **tablecloth.** It is shaped like a square, rectangle, or circle.

■ table

tadpole

A **tadpole** is a young frog. **Tadpoles** hatch from eggs. They are tiny and have tails. Some are black, and some are clear.

tail

A **tail** is a part of the body of some animals. **Tails** can be long or short. An animal's **tail** is at the opposite end from its head. ■

■ tail

take

1. To **take** means to move something with your hand. Katy **takes** an apple out of the refrigerator and eats it. My aunt **took** the sock away from the dog. **2.** To **take** also means to bring with you. Avi **takes** books home from the library to read. **3.** To **take** can also mean to ride. Karl **takes** the bus to school in the morning. **4.** To **take** a picture means to use a camera to make a photograph. Dahlia has **taken** three pictures of her brother with her new camera. **5.** To **take** also means that something is needed. It **takes** a lot of practice to play the piano well. **6.** To **take** medicine means to swallow it. The medicine didn't taste good, but I **took** it anyway. —**took, taken**

talent

A talent is something that is easy for you to do well. Raymond has a **talent** for drawing. My **talent** is playing the flute.

> When people have a **talent,** we say they are **talented.** Maia is a **talented** artist.

talk

To **talk** is to speak to someone. Nicole and Jorge **talked** about the chapter we read.

tall

To be **tall** means to stand high above the ground. **Tall** is the opposite of **short.** Large cities have **tall** buildings and monuments. ■

■ **tall**

tame

To be **tame** means for an animal to do what people want. **Tame** animals make good pets.

taste

1. To **taste** is to use your mouth to find out what something is like. Alexa's mother **tasted** the sauce that she made. **2.** To **taste** also means to make your tongue feel some way. Foods **taste** sweet, sour, salty, or bitter. **3.** A **taste** is what something is like when you taste it. Lemons and grapefruits have a sour **taste.** Honey has a sweet **taste.** ■

■ taste

taught

Taught is a form of **teach.** Katharine's parents **taught** her how to take photographs.

taxi

A **taxi** is a car that people pay to ride in. People take **taxis** to go from one place to another.

teach

To **teach** is to give information so that someone can learn. Nadia **taught** me how to whistle. **—taught**

teacher

A **teacher** is a person who teaches other people. Most **teachers** work in schools.

team

A **team** is a group of people who work or play together. In many sports two **teams** play against each other. ■

A person who is on your **team** is your **teammate. Teammates** work together to play the game.

■ **team**

tear

1. A **tear** is a drop of salty liquid that your body makes. **Tears** come out of people's eyes when they cry. **2.** To **tear** is to pull something apart. Lenny **tears** the paper napkin and gives half of it to Mike. My mother **tore** the cloth to make patches for my pants. **3.** A **tear** is a space you can see after something becomes torn. I had to change clothes because there were **tears** in my dress. —**tore, torn**

The **tear** in your eye rhymes with **hear** and **near.** The **tear** in your pants rhymes with **hair** and **pear.**

■ **teddy bear**

teddy bear

A **teddy bear** is a kind of toy. It is soft and looks like a bear. **Teddy bears** can be large or small. ■

teeth

Teeth means more than one **tooth.** People chew food with their **teeth.** ■

■ **teeth**

telephone

A **telephone** is a small machine that lets people talk from far away. **Telephones** use electricity. Some **telephones** use wires and stay in one place. Some **telephones** can be carried with you. ■

■ telephone

telescope

A **telescope** is a tool that helps people see things that are far away. **Telescopes** are made of curved pieces of glass or mirrors inside a tube. People use them to look at the moon and stars. ■

■ telescope

television

A **television** is a machine that uses electricity to show pictures with sounds. A **television** station uses electricity to send the pictures and sounds to **televisions** in people's homes.

> A short way of saying **television** is **TV.** Teddy's favorite movie is on **TV** tonight.

tell

1. To **tell** is to talk about something. After Curtis did a magic trick, he **told** his friends how he did it. **2.** To **tell** also means to know. Susana can **tell** that winter is coming because the days are getting shorter. **3.** To **tell** also means to give information without talking. The clock **tells** the time. This map **tells** us where your street is. —**told**

temperature

The **temperature** of something is how much heat it has. The inside of an oven has a high **temperature.** Ice and snow have low **temperatures.**

ten

Ten is one more than nine. **Ten** is written **10.**
9 + 1 = **10.**

tennis

Tennis is a sport. In **tennis,** people hit a ball back and forth across a wide net. ■

■ **tennis**

tent

A **tent** is a place to sleep when you camp. **Tents** are large pieces of cloth held up by poles in the ground. ■

terrible

Terrible means very bad. Many trees were broken in the **terrible** storm.

■ **tent**

test

1. A **test** is a way to find out how well someone can do something. Teachers often give **tests** in school. **2.** To **test** something is to see if it works well. My parents **tested** the computer in the store before they bought it.

than

Than means that something is being compared to something else. Denny likes summer weather more **than** he likes winter weather.

thank

To **thank** means to tell someone you are glad they did something for you or gave something to you. Ana **thanked** her friends for the cards they gave her when she was sick.

Thanksgiving

Thanksgiving is a holiday that comes in November. People eat dinner with their families on **Thanksgiving.**

that

1. That means one thing you are looking at or talking about and not something else. Ilene put the blue, cotton quilt on her bed. She loves **that** quilt. **2. That** is also used to put two parts of a sentence together. I told my mother **that** the shed was locked.

the

The tells which one. Ramon is very happy. He won **the** school prize for helping his community.

theater

A **theater** is a building where people watch movies or plays. Some **theaters** are very large. ∎

∎ **theater**

their

Their means belonging to them. My sisters couldn't finish **their** homework because they forgot **their** books.

> The word **their** sounds the same as the word **there.**

theirs

Theirs means belonging to them. The students all bought some fish for an aquarium. The fish are **theirs.**

them

Them means more than one person, animal, or thing. There are some birds in Angel's yard. He feeds **them** seeds and bread.

themselves

Themselves means them and nobody else. Babies cannot take care of **themselves.**

then

1. **Then** means at that time. It is cold now. But it was not cold last summer. The weather was warm **then.**
2. **Then** also means next. Paul pulled his sled up the hill. **Then** he rode back down again.

there

1. **There** means at that place. "Where should I put these logs?" Talia asked her father. He pointed to the fireplace. "Please put them down **there,**" he said.
2. **There is** and **there are** mean that something can be found. "**There** is a bee in the car!" Steve shouted.

thermometer

A **thermometer** is a tool that is used to measure temperature. Some **thermometers** show how hot or cold it is outside. Others are used to show the temperatures of people who might be sick. ∎

∎ **thermometer**

these

These means more than one of **this.** If you will carry those chairs, I will carry **these.**

they

They means more than one. Darcy and Penny ran on the beach. Then **they** dug holes in the sand.

they're

They're is a short way to say **they are.** Christine and Alec are not here yet. **They're** coming in ten minutes.

thick

1. Thick means big and heavy. Felix found a board so **thick** he could not hit a nail through it. **Thick** is the opposite of **thin.**
2. To be **thick** also means to be hard to pour. Honey is **thick.** ■

■ **thick**

If something becomes more **thick,** we say that it **thickens.** The tomato sauce **thickened** when my father added flour to it.

thin

1. Thin means having the top and bottom close together. A piece of paper is **thin.** **Thin** is the opposite of **thick. 2. Thin** also means the opposite of **fat.** My uncle lost a lot of weight. He is now **thin. —thinner, thinnest** ■

■ **thin**

thing

1. A **thing** is an object, animal, or plant. You can see many interesting **things** in a museum. **2.** A **thing** can also be what someone does. Patty gave Shelby some of her snack. That was a nice **thing** for her to do.

think

1. To **think** means to use your mind. Sunil **thinks** about what he will do on Saturday. **2.** To **think** also means to believe. Eileen **thinks** she will go to the library on Saturday. Cameron **thought** the movie was funny. **—thought**

third

Third is next after second. The **third** letter of the alphabet is **C.**

thirsty

To be **thirsty** is to need to drink. When you are **thirsty,** your mouth feels dry. **—thirstier, thirstiest**

this

This means one thing and not something else. It is often something that is near you. Sean likes the hat he is wearing. "**This** is my favorite hat," he says.

thorn

A **thorn** is a sharp part that grows on the branch or stem of some plants. Roses have **thorns.**

those

Those means more than one of **that.** I have read these books on the table but not **those** on the couch.

thought

1. **Thought** is a form of **think.** When the teacher asked a question, Spencer **thought** about his answer before he spoke. 2. A **thought** is also something a person thinks about. Noor had many happy **thoughts** about her trip to the country last fall.

thousand

A **thousand** is a number. It is written **1,000.** There are ten hundreds in a **thousand. Thousands** of people went to watch the football game.

thread

Thread is very thin string. It comes in many different colors. People sew clothes with a needle and **thread.** ■

■ thread

three

Three is one more than two. **Three** is written **3.** $2 + 1 = 3.$

threw

Threw is a form of **throw.** Tad **threw** a tennis ball against the barn until his arm got tired.

throne

A **throne** is a special chair that a king or queen sits on. **Thrones** are usually big and fancy. ■

Throne sounds the same as **thrown.**

■ throne

through

Through means from one side to the other. Jess walked **through** a field to get to school. A bird flew into our house **through** an open window.

throw

To **throw** is to make something go through the air. Frederic **throws** the ball, and Katrina catches it. —**threw, thrown** ∎

∎ **throw**

thumb

A **thumb** is a part of the hand. **Thumbs** are short, strong fingers. People have one **thumb** on each hand. ∎

thunder

Thunder is a loud noise in the air. It is made when lightning flashes.

Thursday

Thursday is a day of the week. **Thursday** comes after Wednesday and before Friday.

∎ **thumb**

ticket

A **ticket** is a small piece of paper that lets you enter a place. When Lauren and Aly went to the theater, they bought two **tickets** so they could see the show. We needed **tickets** to get on the airplane.

tie

1. To **tie** is to keep things together with string or rope. Arun keeps his boat **tied** to the dock. **2.** To **tie** also means to make knots in string, rope, or ribbon. Jan **ties** pretty bows on all the gifts. **3.** A **tie** is a kind of clothes. It is a narrow piece of cloth that people wear around their necks. **Ties** come in many different colors. ■

■ **tie**

A **bow tie** is a **tie** that has the shape of a **bow**. People wear **bow ties** at the top of their shirts.

tiger

A **tiger** is a large, wild cat. **Tigers** often have brown or orange fur with black stripes. ■

■ **tiger**

tight

To be **tight** means to be hard to take off or take apart. Doug's boots were **tight** because they were too small for him. **Tight** is the opposite of **loose**.

Tighten means to make something **tight** or **tighter**. Jinko **tightened** her shoelaces so she wouldn't trip.

time

1. Time is how long it takes for something to happen. The past, the present, and the future are all parts of **time.** Cathy lives close to school. It only takes a short **time** for her to walk there. If she has **time,** she always stops at her friend Suzanna's house on the way. **2. Time** is also the hour on the clock when something happens. "What **time** does the show start?" "It starts at eight o'clock." **3.** A **time** is how often something is done. We sang the song once. Then we sang it again. We sang the song two **times.**

tin

Tin is a kind of metal. It is used to make cans, toys, and other things.

tiny

Tiny means very, very small. Ants are **tiny** insects. We use a microscope to look at things that are too **tiny** to see. —**tinier, tiniest**

tire

A **tire** is a round object made of rubber. It covers the outside of a wheel. Cars have four wheels with four **tires.** ■

■ **tire**

tired

To be **tired** is to need rest. Crystal has played basketball all afternoon. Now she is **tired.**

title

A **title** is the name of something you read or see. Books, poems, plays, and paintings all have **titles.** The **title** of the book I am reading now is *Stuart Little.*

to

1. To tells where something goes. Astronauts have flown **to** the moon. **2. To** also means until. The store opens at nine o'clock. It closes at six o'clock. It is open from nine **to** six. **3. To** also tells how something changes. Elijah colored the white page with a blue crayon. He changed the color from white **to** blue. **4. To** is also used to show things that people do. Kara likes **to** swim in the ocean.

toad

A **toad** is an animal that is like a frog. **Toads** have skin that is rough and dry. Frogs like to live in water, but **toads** like to live on land. ∎

∎ **toad**

toast

Toast is bread that has been sliced and heated. **Toast** is brown on both sides. I like **toast** with butter and strawberry jam.

A **toaster** is a machine that makes **toast** from bread.

today

Today means this day. Yesterday came before **today**. Tomorrow comes after **today**.

toe

A **toe** is a thin part at the front of the foot. People have five **toes** on each foot.

together

1. **Together** means with each other. Nina and Maria walked to school **together. 2. Together** also means that two or more parts touch each other or are joined. I sewed the pieces of cloth **together.**

> The opposite of **together** is **apart.** Dave put the pieces of the puzzle **together.** Then Jana took them **apart.**

told

Told is a form of **tell.** Marissa **told** us about her visit to the museum yesterday.

tomato

A **tomato** is a kind of fruit. It is round and red. Ketchup is made from **tomatoes. —tomatoes** ■

■ **tomato**

tomorrow

Tomorrow is the day after today. **Tomorrow** is in the future. If today is Monday, then **tomorrow** will be Tuesday.

tongue

The **tongue** is a part of the mouth. People use their **tongues** to help them eat and speak. Animals have **tongues** too. ■

■ **tongue**

tonight

Tonight is the night between today and tomorrow. Mindy does her homework this afternoon so she can watch television **tonight.**

too

1. Too means also. Whitney can play two instruments. She plays the violin, and she plays the harp **too.**
2. Too also means more than what is good. It is **too** hot to work outside today.

took

Took is a form of **take.** Val **took** her books off the table. Emma and Cynthia **took** the bus to school. Chase **took** pictures of his family with his new camera. It **took** the artist many months to make that statue.

tool

A **tool** is something people use to help them work. Hammers, rakes, knives, and shovels are all **tools.** ∎

> A **toolbox** is a container for carrying or storing small **tools** and other things. Many **toolboxes** have hammers, nails, and scissors.

∎ **tool**

tooth

A **tooth** is a part of your mouth. A **tooth** is hard and white. People chew food with their **teeth. —teeth**

> A **toothbrush** is a small **brush** with a handle. **Toothpaste** is something gooey and thick. People put **toothpaste** on **toothbrushes** to clean their teeth.

top

1. The **top** is the highest part of something. Joanna stored her old toys in a box at the **top** of her closet. **Top** is the opposite of **bottom. 2.** A **top** is also a toy. People play with **tops** by making them spin on a surface.

tore

Tore is a form of **tear.** Zoe **tore** her jacket on a fence on the way home from school.

torn

Torn is a form of **tear.** The cat has **torn** the curtain. There is a tear there now.

tornado

A **tornado** is a very strong wind. It is shaped like a cone that twists in the air. **Tornadoes** can knock down houses and pull trees out of the ground. —**tornadoes** ■

■ **tornado**

touch

1. To **touch** is to feel something with your body. The pillow felt soft when Carrie **touched** it. **2.** To **touch** also means for one thing to be against another so that there is no space between them. The two bowls are **touching.** I will move them apart.

toward

Toward means in the direction of. The ship seemed to grow bigger as it sailed **toward** us. The wind is blowing **toward** the front of the house.

towel

A **towel** is a soft piece of cloth. People use **towels** to dry themselves after they take a bath or go swimming. ■

■ **towel**

town

A **town** is a place where people live and work. Most **towns** are smaller than cities.

toy

A **toy** is an object that people play with. Wood blocks, dolls, and kites are **toys.**

■ **tractor**

tractor

A **tractor** is a large machine with big wheels and a strong engine. Farmers use **tractors** to help prepare the ground to plant vegetables. ■

traffic

Traffic means cars, trucks, and buses on streets or roads. At some times of the day there is a lot of **traffic.** ■

■ **traffic**

A **traffic light** is a machine that tells you what to do when you are driving. A green light means you can go. A red light means you have to stop.

A B C D E F G H I J K L M

trail

A **trail** is a path through a field or forest or across mountains. People walk on **trails** for fun and exercise. ∎

∎ **trail**

trailer

A **trailer** is a large, metal box on wheels. **Trailers** can be pulled by tractors and trucks to carry things. Some people use **trailers** as houses or offices. ∎

∎ **trailer**

train

1. A **train** is a group of railroad cars. **Trains** carry people or heavy loads from one place to another. 2. To **train** means to teach a person or an animal how to do something. Lucy **trained** her dog to sit. My violin teacher was **trained** at a large music school. ∎

∎ **train**

transportation

Transportation is the way you get from one place to another. Cars, trains, airplanes, and boats are all kinds of **transportation.**

trap

1. A **trap** is a way to catch wild animals. Some **traps** are like cages. Other **traps** are nets or holes in the ground. 2. To **trap** is to catch an animal in a trap. Spiders **trap** insects in their webs. —**trapped**

trash

Trash is something people do not want to keep. We picked up the **trash** on the beach. ∎

> A **trash can** is something that you put **trash** in. There were pieces of paper on the floor. I picked them up and put them in the **trash can.**

∎ **trash**

travel

To **travel** means to go and visit another place. Every year Lori's family likes to **travel** to some place they have never seen before.

tray

A **tray** is a flat, shallow container used to carry or hold things. Deepak and his friends carry their lunches on **trays.** ∎

treasure

Treasure is a lot of gold, silver, and jewels. Hundreds of years ago, pirates gathered **treasure** from all over the world.

∎ **tray**

treat

1. A **treat** is something special that you enjoy. One of my favorite **treats** is going to the movies. **2.** To **treat** means to pay for someone else. My uncle **treated** my sisters and me to lunch. **3.** To **treat** also means to act in some way toward a person or animal. The boy across the street **treats** his dog well.

tree

A **tree** is a kind of plant. It has branches and leaves. **Trees** can grow to be very tall. Wood comes from **trees.** Oaks, pines, and palms are different kinds of **trees.**

triangle

A **triangle** is a shape. **Triangles** have three straight sides. Malcolm drew lines between three dots to make a **triangle.** ■

■ **triangle**

> A **triangle** has three sides. Rectangles and squares have four sides.

trick

1. A **trick** is something that seems to happen but really does not. The magician seemed to make a rabbit disappear, but it was just a **trick.** His **tricks** are fun to watch. **2.** To **trick** is to get someone to do something he or she does not want to do. Wayne **tricked** the dog into taking the bitter medicine by hiding it in her food.

tried

Tried is a form of **try.** I **tried** to find the book at the library, but someone had borrowed it.

trip

1. A **trip** is a time when you travel somewhere. Our family went on two **trips** to the mountains last year. **2.** To **trip** means to bump into something with your foot and fall down. Olivia **tripped** on a rock as she was climbing the hill. —**tripped**

trombone

A **trombone** is an instrument. It is a kind of horn. **Trombones** are made of long, metal tubes that fit together. ■

■ **trombone**

trot

To **trot** means to run in a slow way. The horse **trots** in the pasture. —**trotted**

trouble

1. Trouble is something that makes someone sad, angry, or confused. My little brother had **trouble** learning how to tie his shoelaces. **2.** To be in **trouble** means that someone is angry at you. Austin woke up too late. He knew he would be in **trouble** when he got to school.

trousers

Trousers are a kind of clothes. People wear **trousers** over their legs. Most **trousers** have pockets in them.

> Another word for **trousers** is **pants.**

truck

A **truck** is a machine. It is like a very large car that is used to carry heavy loads. Stuart's father has a job driving **trucks.** ■

■ **truck**

true

To be **true** means that something matches the facts that we know. It is **true** that the world is round. It is not **true** that snow is purple.

> The opposite of **true** is **false**. It is **true** that water turns into ice when it gets very cold. It is **false** that 2 + 2 equals 5.

trumpet

A **trumpet** is an instrument. It is a kind of horn. **Trumpets** are made of metal tubes. The sound of a **trumpet** can be very loud. ∎

∎ **trumpet**

trunk

1. A **trunk** is the thick middle part of a tree. The **trunk** of a tree grows up from the ground. Branches grow out of it. Most tree **trunks** are covered with bark. **2.** A **trunk** is also part of an elephant. It is like a very long nose. Elephants can pick up things with their **trunks. 3.** A **trunk** is also a large box. People often store clothes and other things in **trunks.** ∎

∎ **trunk**

trust

To **trust** someone is to believe they will do as they say. Sasha and Valerie are best friends. They **trust** each other not to tell their secrets to anyone else.

truth

The **truth** is what is true. If people do not tell the **truth,** you cannot trust them.

try

1. To **try** is to work to make something happen. Cheryl **tries** to carry the watermelon, but she is too little. 2. To **try** means to do something you never have before. Lou has **tried** different hobbies, but he still likes painting the best. **—tries, tried**

tube

1. A **tube** is a long, hollow piece of metal, glass, rubber, or plastic. Most **tubes** are used to carry liquids or gases from one place to another. 2. A **tube** is also a container that is sealed on one end and has a cap on the other end. There are many **tubes** of toothpaste at the store.

Tuesday

Tuesday is a day of the week. **Tuesday** comes after Monday and before Wednesday.

tug

To **tug** is to pull something for a short time. Paulo **tugs** at his mother's coat when he wants to go home. **—tugged**

A **tugboat** is a kind of boat. It has a very strong engine for pulling and pushing large ships. **Tugboats** are used in harbors where there is not enough room for big ships to move by themselves.

A B C D E F G H I J K L M

tulip

A **tulip** is a kind of flower. It is shaped like a cup. **Tulips** come in many colors. ∎

∎ **tulip**

tunnel

A **tunnel** is a long hole under the ground or under water. Some **tunnels** go through mountains so that people can travel from one place to another. ∎

turkey

1. A **turkey** is a kind of bird. It has a long neck. Some **turkeys** are wild. **2. Turkey** is a kind of meat that comes from a turkey. People often eat **turkey** on Thanksgiving and other holidays. ∎

∎ **tunnel**

turn

1. To **turn** is to move in a circle. The wheels on an automobile **turn** when the automobile moves. **2.** To **turn** is also to move something from being in one direction to being in another direction. Pierre **turned** his head to see who had come into the room. **3.** To **turn** also means to fold, bend, or twist. I **turned** my cap inside out. **4.** To **turn** a page is to move it so you can see the other side. **5.** To take **turns** means that one person goes, and then the other. Pearl and Meg shared a sandwich. First, Pearl took a bite of it. Then Meg did. They took **turns** until the sandwich was gone.

∎ **turkey**

turtle

A **turtle** is a kind of reptile. Turtles can live both in the water and on the land. A **turtle** can pull its head, legs, and tail inside its shell. ■

■ **turtle**

twice

Twice means two times. Sophie liked the movie so much she saw it **twice.**

twig

A **twig** is a small branch. We put **twigs** through our marshmallows so we could roast them in the fire.

twin

A **twin** is one of two children born at the same time to the same parents. Some **twins** look alike. ■

■ **twin**

twist

To **twist** is to turn around and around. Rope is made of pieces of string that are **twisted** together.

> A **twister** is another name for a **tornado. Tornadoes** look like windy cones that **twist** in the air.

two

Two is one more than one. It is the second number when you count. **Two** is written **2.** 1 + 1 = **2.**

ugly

Ugly means not nice to look at. We found some old, **ugly** coats in the attic. **—uglier, ugliest**

umbrella

An **umbrella** is something you use to protect yourself from rain or sun. **Umbrellas** are shaped like upside-down bowls and have long handles. ■

■ **umbrella**

uncle

An **uncle** is the brother of your mother or father. An **uncle** is also your aunt's husband. Fritz has six **uncles.**

under

1. Under means lower than the bottom of something. Water flows **under** a bridge. **2. Under** also means lower than the surface of something. The roots of a plant grow **under** the ground.

> The opposite of **under** is **over.** The ball flew **over** my head and went **under** the porch.

underground

Underground means under the ground. Worms live **underground.**

underline

To **underline** is to draw a line under something. Leon **underlines** his name on the page. People often **underline** things that are important. ■

■ **underline**

understand

To **understand** something means to know it well. Charlotte knows how to read. She **understands** all the words on this page. I **understood** the rules of the game after Lucas explained them to me. —**understood**

underwater

Underwater means below the surface of the water. Javier swam **underwater** to look at the fish. ■

■ **underwater**

uneasy

Uneasy means not feeling safe. Madeline was a little bit afraid to go to school for the first time. She was **uneasy** about it. —**uneasier, uneasiest**

uneven

Uneven means not smooth or straight. It was hard for us to walk in the field. The ground was very **uneven** there.

unhappy

Unhappy means sad. The passengers were **unhappy** when the train arrived late. —**unhappier, unhappiest**

> When **un** is placed in front of a word, it often means **not. Unhappy** means not happy. **Unfair** means not fair.

unicorn

A **unicorn** is an animal in stories. **Unicorns** are not real. A **unicorn** looks like a horse with one long horn on its head. ■

■ unicorn

uniform

A **uniform** is a special kind of clothes. People wear **uniforms** to show that they belong to a group. Police officers, nurses, and sports teams wear **uniforms.** ■

universe

The **universe** is everything in our world and in space put together. The earth, the sun, the moon, and the stars are all part of the **universe.**

■ uniform

unless

Unless means that for one thing to happen, something else must happen. Tess cannot ride on the carousel **unless** she brings money to the park. If she forgets her money, she cannot ride.

untie

To **untie** something means to take the knots out of it. Julian **untied** his shoelaces by himself.

until

Until means that an amount of time has to pass before something happens. We can't go to the party **until** we finish our homework.

unusual

Unusual means not usual. It would be **unusual** to have snow in the summer.

up

1. Up means going from a low to a high place. We went **up** in a balloon. **2. Up** also means at or in a high place. My books are **up** in the closet.

> The opposite of **up** is **down.** The stairs in our house go **up** to the attic and **down** to the basement.

upon

Upon means on. The bird was sitting **upon** the branch. ■

■ **upon**

upset

To be **upset** is to feel angry, hurt, or unhappy. Vanessa was **upset** when she did not get a part in the school play.

upside-down

Upside-down means with the top side down and the bottom side up. The girls were **upside-down** at the playground. Their feet were above their heads. ■

■ **upside-down**

us

Us is a form of **we.** My brother and I walked to the store. At the store we met our aunt. She gave **us** a ride home in her car.

use

To **use** means to do work with something. A carpenter **uses** tools, wood, and nails to build a house.

> To **use** something up means that there is none of it now. We **used** up all the soap when we washed the dog.

useful

Something is **useful** if it helps you do something. Tools are **useful** for fixing and building things.

usual

Something **usual** is something that almost always happens. It is **usual** for it to be hot in the summer.

> **Usually** means almost always. Tanya **usually** rides the bus home from school.

Vv

vacation

A **vacation** is a time when people do not work or go to school. This year our whole family is going on **vacation** to the mountains. **Vacations** are a lot of fun.

valentine

A **valentine** is a special card or gift that you give to someone you like. **Valentine's** Day is a holiday when people give each other **valentines.** Many **valentines** are shaped like hearts.

valley

A **valley** is a long, narrow area of land between hills or mountains. **Valleys** often have rivers or streams that go through them. ■

■ valley

van

A **van** is a long car that looks like a truck. **Vans** are often used to move furniture and other large objects from one place to another.

vanilla

Vanilla is a flavor. It is made from a kind of seed. **Vanilla** is used in ice cream and other desserts.

■ **vegetable**

vegetable

A **vegetable** is a plant or a part of a plant that you can eat. Lettuce, carrots, peppers, and peas are **vegetables.** ■

very

Very means more than what is usual. Bears are big animals. Elephants are **very** big animals.

■ **vest**

vest

A **vest** is a kind of clothes. **Vests** have no sleeves and are worn over a shirt. ■

village

A **village** is a small group of houses and other buildings. **Villages** are not as big as towns. People live and work in **villages.** ■

■ **village**

vine

A **vine** is a kind of plant. **Vines** have long, thin stems that climb on walls and other things.

> Pumpkins and grapes grow on **vines**. A **vine** on which **grapes** grow is called a **grapevine**.

violin

A **violin** is an instrument. **Violins** have four strings. A bow is pulled across the strings to make music. ■

■ violin

visit

To **visit** is to stay somewhere or with somebody for a short time. Our class **visited** the zoo last week. Cliff and Amelia **visit** their grandmother every Sunday.

voice

A **voice** is the sound people make when they speak, sing, or shout. I heard loud **voices** in the other room.

volcano

A **volcano** is an open area on the surface of the earth. **Volcanoes** are often on the top of mountains. Very hot gases and melted rock can flow out of **volcanoes**. —volcanoes ■

■ volcano

volleyball

1. Volleyball is a sport. In **volleyball,** two teams hit a large ball back and forth over a wide net. **2.** A **volleyball** is the large ball used in a game of volleyball. The **volleyballs** and net are in the garage. ■

■ **volleyball**

vote

To **vote** is to choose one person from two or more people for a special job or a prize. We **vote** for people who lead groups such as governments.

> A person who **votes** in an election is called a **voter.** In the election for president of our country, there are millions of **voters.**

vowel

A **vowel** is a kind of letter. A, E, I, O, and U are **vowels.** The letters of the alphabet are either **vowels** or consonants.

voyage

A **voyage** is a long trip to a distant place. People make **voyages** on ships and airplanes.

waffle

A **waffle** is a kind of food. **Waffles** are thin, square cakes. We usually eat them for breakfast.

wagon

A **wagon** is a box that has four wheels and a handle. **Wagons** are used to carry people or things from one place to another. Large **wagons** are sometimes pulled by horses. ■

■ **wagon**

wait

To **wait** means to stay somewhere until something happens. Ernest **waited** ten minutes at the station for the train to come.

wake

To **wake** up means to stop sleeping. Amanda usually **wakes** up early in the morning, but today she **woke** up late. —**woke, woken**

walk

1. To **walk** means to move by taking steps. Mara helps her little brother to **walk.**
2. A **walk** is when you go somewhere by walking, especially for fun. Nat likes to go for **walks** on the beach. ■

wall

1. A **wall** is a side of a room. Most rooms have a ceiling, a floor, and four **walls. 2.** A **wall** is something that is built to keep one place apart from another. The farmer built a stone **wall** around his field. ■

■ walk

want

To **want** something means that you would like to have it. Abigail **wants** a trumpet more than anything else.

■ wall

war

A **war** is a fight between countries or groups of people in the same country. Many people die in **wars.**

warm

Warm means not very hot. When spring comes, it starts to get **warm** outside.

> The opposite of **warm** is **cool.** It was **warm** in our apartment, so we went to the park where it was **cool.**

warn

To **warn** means to say that something bad or dangerous might happen. The principal **warned** us that it might snow during our class trip.

was

Was is a form of **be.** Yesterday I **was** late for school. Today I will be early.

wash

To **wash** something means to clean it with soap and water. Every Thursday afternoon it is Yolanda's turn to **wash** her family's car. ∎

∎ **wash**

wasn't

Wasn't is a short way to say **was not.** Isaac went to Manny's house to see him, but he **wasn't** there.

watch

1. To **watch** means to look at something to see what it will do. Cindy **watched** her father while he fixed the baby's crib. **2.** A **watch** is a small clock that you wear on your wrist. Meryl has two **watches.** ∎

∎ **watch**

water

Water is a kind of liquid. It is clear, and it has no taste. People, plants, and animals need **water** to live.

watermelon

A **watermelon** is a large fruit. **Watermelons** are green outside and red and sweet inside. ■

■ **watermelon**

wave

1. To **wave** means to move your hand from side to side. Alejandro **waves** hello when he sees his cousins.

2. A **wave** looks like a long bump that moves through the water in a lake or an ocean. Our boat went up and down on the **waves.**

Some things that look like **waves** are called **wavy.** My friend Sarah has long, **wavy** hair.

wax

Wax is something used to make candles and crayons. It melts easily when it is heated. Bees make one kind of **wax.** Other **waxes** are made from plants or oil. ■

■ **wax**

way

1. A **way** is how you get from one place to another. We took the long **way** home.

2. A **way** also means how something is or how something is done. Alicia was acting in a funny **way.** There is an easy **way** to finish the puzzle.

we

We is a word you use when you speak about yourself and one or more other people. My brothers and I are going to the library. **We** want to borrow some books.

weak

1. Weak means not strong. I am too **weak** to lift that heavy box. **2. Weak** also means easy to break. There are many cracks in that wall. It looks very **weak.**

> To **weaken** means to make **weak** or **weaker.** The settlers were **weakened** by their long journey.

wear

1. To **wear** something means to have it on your body to cover or protect you. When it is cold outside, Jade **wears** a coat, a hat, boots, and gloves. **2.** To **wear** out means to get old and not work well. The tires on our car **wore** out, so we had to buy new ones. —**wore, worn**

weather

Weather is what it is like outside. When the **weather** is warm, Bud likes to go to the lake. When the **weather** is cold, he likes to ski.

web

A **web** is a group of threads that a spider makes. Spiders make **webs** to catch insects to eat. ■

■ web

wedding

A **wedding** is a time when two people marry. My sister carried flowers at two **weddings** last summer.

Wednesday

Wednesday is a day of the week. **Wednesday** comes after Tuesday and before Thursday.

weed

A **weed** is a plant that grows where it is not wanted. My grandmother pulls **weeds** from her garden every day in the summer.

week

A **week** is an amount of time. There are seven days in one **week.** There are 52 **weeks** in one year.

> If something happens every **week,** we say that it happens **weekly.** Sydney visits her grandparents **weekly.**

weigh

To **weigh** means to measure how heavy something is. At the supermarket, my mother **weighed** carrots on a scale. ∎

∎ **weigh**

> When we **weigh** something, we find out its **weight. Weight** is how heavy something is. Roger finds out his **weight** at the doctor's office.

welcome

1. To be **welcome** means that someone is glad to see you. We tried to make our new neighbors feel **welcome. 2.** You're **welcome** means that someone is happy to have done something for someone else. We say "You're **welcome**" to someone who says "Thank you."

well

1. A **well** is a deep hole in the ground. Most **wells** are dug to get water, oil, or gas. **2. Well** means in a good way. Esther plays the violin **well.** Everyone likes to listen to her. **3. Well** also means healthy. Antonio stayed home because he was sick. When he is **well,** he will go back to school. ■

■ **well**

we'll

We'll is a short way to say **we will. We'll** see dolphins at the aquarium.

went

Went is a form of **go.** Sometimes Aidan and Randy go places together. Last Saturday they **went** bowling.

were

Were is a form of **be.** Eliot and Kris will be home today. They **were** away on vacation last week.

we're

We're is a short way to say **we are.** My sisters and I are very good at sports. **We're** also good at painting and drawing.

weren't

Weren't is a short way to say **were not.** Oliver and Howard **weren't** hungry after they ate pizza for dinner.

west

West is a direction. The sun sets in the **west. West** is the opposite of **east.** ∎

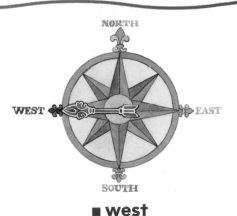

∎ **west**

wet

Wet means covered with water or full of water. Brooke got **wet** when she walked in the rain. —**wetter, wettest** ∎

> The opposite of **wet** is **dry.** Our dog was **wet** after her bath. We rubbed her with a towel until she was **dry.**

∎ **wet**

we've

We've is a short way to say **we have. We've** lived in our house for two years.

whale

A **whale** is a very large animal. It lives in the ocean, but it is not a fish. **Whales** are mammals.

> There are many kinds of **whales.** The **blue whale** is the largest animal in the world.

N O P Q R S T U V **W** X Y Z 367

what

1. **What** is used to ask questions about people and things. **What** are you having for dinner? **What** book are you reading? 2. **What** also tells which thing. We learned **what** happened in the story. We wondered **what** was inside the backpack.

whatever

Whatever means anything or everything. Sara eats **whatever** her father cooks for her.

wheat

Wheat is a kind of plant. The seeds of **wheat** are made into flour. **Wheat** is used to make cereal. ■

■ **wheat**

wheel

1. A **wheel** is a round object. **Wheels** turn to help machines move or work. 2. To **wheel** means to move something that has wheels. I **wheeled** my bicycle into the garage. ■

> A bicycle has two **wheels.** A car has four **wheels.** Some trucks have eight or more **wheels.**

■ **wheel**

when

1. **When** is used to ask questions about time. **When** does the basketball game start? 2. **When** means at what time. All the snow melts **when** the weather gets warm.

where

1. Where is used to ask questions about a place. **Where** did the cat go? **2. Where** also means at what place. Sachi found the key on the table **where** her brother had left it.

which

1. Which is used to ask questions about one person or thing in a group. **Which** of these coats is yours? **Which** girl is your friend? **2. Which** also means the one that. We saw two books about whales and bought the longer one, **which** looked more interesting.

while

1. While means during what time. Mason went to the store **while** it was open. **2. A while** is a small amount of time. We played for a **while,** and then we went home.

whisper

To **whisper** means to speak in a soft voice. People **whisper** in a library so they won't bother other people.

whistle

1. To **whistle** means to make a musical sound by blowing air through your teeth or lips. Many people learn to **whistle** songs. **2. A whistle** is a very small instrument that you blow into. **Whistles** make a noise like a bird.

A **dog whistle** is a special kind of **whistle.** People cannot hear the noise that it makes, but **dogs** can. **Dogs** can hear some noises that people cannot.

white

White is a color. It is a very light color. This page is printed on **white** paper.

who

1. **Who** is used to ask questions about a person. **Who** knocked on the door? 2. **Who** tells which person. The man **who** works in the movie theater is very friendly.

whoever

Whoever means any person. **Whoever** runs the fastest will win the race. My parents said to invite **whoever** I wanted to play games with us.

whole

Whole means all together. Our **whole** class went to the science museum to see fossils.

> The word **whole** sounds the same as the word **hole.** The **whole** class watched as the **hole** was dug for a new school.

who's

1. **Who's** is a short way to say **who is. Who's** in the kitchen? 2. **Who's** is also a short way to say **who has. Who's** been to the zoo?

whose

Whose tells who something belongs to. The teacher found a glove that someone had lost. She wanted to know **whose** glove she had found.

why

Why is a word people use when they ask about or explain what makes things happen. **Why** do birds fly south for the winter? Luanne doesn't know **why** so many students were absent from school today.

wicked

Wicked means very bad and mean. The **wicked** king took land and money from the people.

wide

1. Wide means having a lot of space between the two sides. The truck carried a very **wide** load. **2. Wide** tells how far something is from side to side. The island is three miles **wide.** ■

■ **wide**

width

Width is how wide something is. The **width** of Darla's paper is eight inches.

wife

A **wife** is a married woman. The **wives** of my uncles are my aunts. —**wives**

wig

A **wig** is an object made from hair that may or may not be real. You wear **wigs** on your head. The clown wore a funny purple **wig.** ■

■ **wig**

wild

Wild means not usually cared for or kept by people. Lions and tigers are **wild** animals.

will

Will tells about something in the future. Hermione **will** go to the pool with Eleanor tomorrow. —**would**

willing

Willing means that you agree to do something. My sister was **willing** to lend me her skirt.

win

To **win** means to finish first or to do the best in a game or a race. I always **win** when I play checkers with my brother. —**won** ∎

∎ win

> The opposite of **win** is **lose.** Yesterday we played Skylar's team in soccer. Her team **won,** and our team **lost.**

wind

Wind is air that moves. Strong **winds** blew the tree down.

> If there is a lot of **wind,** we say that it is **windy.** During a storm, it is usually very **windy.**

windmill

A **windmill** is a kind of machine. The power of the wind makes it work. Some **windmills** bring up water from the ground. Some help make electricity. ∎

∎ windmill

window

A **window** is an open place in a wall. It lets light and air into a room. **Windows** usually have glass in them. ▪

▪ **window**

wing

A **wing** is a long part that helps something to fly. All birds have **wings.** Bats and many insects also have them. Most airplanes have two **wings.** ▪

winter

Winter is a season. It comes after autumn and before spring. **Winter** can be very cold in some places.

> The days of **winter** are called **wintertime.** Shauna likes to build a snowman during the **wintertime.**

▪ **wing**

wipe

To **wipe** means to rub something so that it is clean or dry. Mitzi **wiped** the wet desk with a towel.

wire

A **wire** is a piece of metal. It looks like a long string and is easy to bend. Electricity moves through **wires.** ▪

wise

Wise means very smart. **Wise** people have learned many things, and they often know the right thing to do.

▪ **wire**

wish

1. A **wish** is something that you hope will happen. Rachel made a **wish** when she threw pennies into the well. **2.** To **wish** means to hope that something good will happen. Hal **wishes** that he could find a hidden treasure.

witch

A **witch** is a woman who has magic powers in stories. We dressed like **witches** for the costume party.

with

1. With means together. I went to the store **with** my sister. Jolie's hamburger came **with** onions on it. **2. With** tells what something has. A giraffe is an animal **with** a long neck. **3. With** can also tell what you use to do something. Hunter dug a hole **with** a shovel.

without

1. Without means not having. People cannot live **without** air and food. **2. Without** means not with someone or something else. Casey walks to school alone. She goes **without** anyone else.

wives

Wives means more than one **wife.**

wizard

A **wizard** is a man who has magic powers in stories. The **wizards** in the movie had long, white hair and pointed hats.

woke

Woke is a form of **wake.** Thomas **woke** up and got dressed for school.

woken

Woken is a form of **wake.** It is nine o'clock, but Jacques has not **woken** up yet.

wolf

A **wolf** is a kind of animal. It looks like a large dog. **Wolves** search for food in groups. —**wolves** ■

■ **wolf**

woman

A **woman** is a grown, female person. A girl grows up to be a **woman.** The **women** in our family all have long hair. —**women**

won

Won is a form of **win.** My sister's soccer team **won** most of its games this year.

> The word **won** sounds like the word **one.**

wonder

To **wonder** means to think about something that you are curious about. I **wonder** what I will be when I grow up.

wonderful

Wonderful means very good. Giorgio thought the book he just finished reading was so **wonderful** that he lent it to his sister.

won't

Won't is a short way to say **will not.** Rose **won't** be seven years old until next spring.

wood

1. **Wood** is what trees are made of. It is used to make houses, furniture, and paper. 2. The **woods** is a place where a lot of trees grow. We went for a walk in the **woods.** ■

If something is made from **wood,** we say that it is **wooden.** Natasha sat on a **wooden** chair.

■ **wood**

woodpecker

A **woodpecker** is a kind of bird. **Woodpeckers** have hard, sharp bills. The bills can make holes in trees to get insects for food.

wool

Wool is the hair that grows on sheep and some other animals. **Wool** is used to make yarn and cloth for clothes and blankets. Many sweaters are made of **wool.** ■

■ **wool**

word

A **word** is a sound or a group of sounds that means something. People speak **words** to share their thoughts with other people. Letters are symbols people use for **words.**

wore

Wore is a form of **wear.** Everybody in the play **wore** a funny costume and a wig.

work

1. Work is the energy you use to do or to make something. Digging a hole is hard **work. 2. Work** is also what someone must do. Some people earn money for their **work.** Colin's mother is a scientist. She loves her **work. 3.** To **work** means to do work. Claudia is writing a book. She **works** on it every day. **4.** To **work** also means to do what something is made to do. After the radio fell on the floor, it did not **work.**

> A **worker** is a person who **works.** Sherry and Heather are pilots. They **work** hard at their jobs. They are good **workers.**

world

The **world** is the place where everyone lives. Our **world** is made of land, water, and air.

worm

A **worm** is a very small animal. It has a long, soft body and no legs. Many **worms** live in the ground. ■

■ **worm**

worn

Worn is a form of **wear.** Cody's jacket is new. He has not **worn** it before today.

> When something has been **worn** a lot, it can become **worn-out.** It cannot be **worn** anymore. My **worn-out** slippers have holes in them.

worry

To **worry** means to feel that something bad can happen. My parents **worry** sometimes if I am late coming home. —**worries, worried**

worse

Worse means very bad but not as bad as the worst. Yesterday it rained. Today the weather was **worse.** It rained and snowed. **Worse** is the opposite of **better.**

worst

Worst means worse than any other. Dwight did not like the soup his brother made at all. He thought it was the **worst** thing he had ever tasted. **Worst** is the opposite of **best.**

would

Would is a form of **will.** Damon said yesterday that he **would** go swimming with us today.

wouldn't

Wouldn't is a short way to say **would not.** The cat **wouldn't** come down from the tree.

wrap

To **wrap** means to cover with something such as paper or cloth. People usually **wrap** holiday presents and tie them with ribbons and bows. Michaela and her friend **wrapped** themselves in big towels. —**wrapped** ■

■ **wrap**

wrinkle

A **wrinkle** is a crooked line on something.
Wrinkles are places where the surface of
something is folded. Our dog has many
wrinkles in his skin. ■

> If something has a lot of **wrinkles,** we say
> that it is **wrinkled.** If you throw your shirts
> on the floor, they will become **wrinkled.**

■ **wrinkle**

wrist

A **wrist** is a part of the body. It is between your hand
and your arm. You wave your hands by bending
your **wrists.**

write

1. To **write** means to make letters and words with a
pencil, a pen, or a computer. My cousin **wrote** her
name in big letters across the page. Leslcy has **written**
a letter to her friend Emilio. **2.** To **write** means to
make a book, poem, play, or something else for
people to read. Some people also **write** for magazines
and newspapers. —**wrote, written**

wrong

1. Wrong means not correct. Margo gavc the **wrong**
answer to the teacher's question. The teacher told
her the right answer. **2. Wrong** also means the way
something should not bc. Jonathan knew it was **wrong**
to lie to his teacher.

wrote

Wrote is a form of **write.** Morgan **wrote** the date at the
top of the page.

x-ray

1. An **x-ray** is a kind of energy. It can pass through objects. Doctors use **x-rays** to take photographs of the inside of the body. **2.** An **x-ray** is also the photograph that we can look at after x-rays are used. My father can see his heart and lungs on the **x-ray** of his chest.

xylophone

A **xylophone** is an instrument. It is made of a row of wood rectangles that are different sizes. **Xylophones** make music when they are hit with small hammers. ■

■ **xylophone**

Yy

yard

1. A **yard** is an amount of length. One **yard** is the same as three feet. A **yard** is almost as long as a meter. **2.** A **yard** is also an area of land around a house. Many **yards** are covered with grass. ■

■ **yard**

yarn

Yarn is a kind of string. It is made from wool, cotton, or other threads that are twisted together. **Yarn** is used to make sweaters and socks.

yawn

To **yawn** is to open your mouth wide and take a deep breath. People **yawn** when they are tired.

year

A **year** is an amount of time. There are 12 months in one **year.** Sabrina has gone to my school for two **years.**

Most **years** are 365 days long. In some **years,** there are 366 days. These years are called **leap years.**

yell

To **yell** means to shout. The hockey game was very exciting. We **yelled** for our team.

yellow

Yellow is a color. Bananas and lemons are **yellow.**

yes

Yes means that you agree. Audrey asked Noreen to come to her house after school. Noreen said, "**Yes,** I would like to come."

yesterday

Yesterday is the day before today. It snowed **yesterday.** Today the ground is covered with snow.

yet

Yet means up to this time. The movie has not started **yet.** It will start in five minutes.

yolk

A **yolk** is the yellow part of an egg. **Yolks** are food for an animal when it is inside an egg.

you

You is a word that is used when one person speaks to another person or other people. I like **you.** Do **you** like to dance? **You** are the best friends I have ever had.

you'll

You'll is a short way to say **you will.** Let's play this new board game. I think **you'll** like it.

young

To be **young** means to have been alive only a short time. Babies are very **young** people. ■

> The opposite of **young** is **old.**

■ **young**

your

Your means belonging to you. That is **your** house.

you're

You're is a short way to say **you are. You're** tall for your age. **You're** a great group of actors.

yours

Yours means belonging to you. That cup is **yours.** This one is mine.

yourself

Yourself means you and nobody else. Did you earn that money **yourself**?

you've

You've is a short way to say **you have. You've** got a nice smile.

yo-yo

A **yo-yo** is a kind of toy. It is a round piece of wood or plastic with a string tied to it. The **yo-yo** goes up and down on the string. Some people can do tricks with **yo-yos.** ■

■ **yo-yo**

zany

To be **zany** means to be funny in an unusual way. Tenisha invents **zany** games that make me laugh.

zebra

A **zebra** is an animal. It looks like a small horse. **Zebras** have black and white stripes.

zero

Zero is a number. It is written **0.** 1 + **0** = 1. One hundred is written with a one and two **zeroes.** —**zeroes**

zest

Zest means extra flavor. Those spices give **zest** to soup.

zigzag

Zigzag means first going one way and then another, again and again. The truck followed a **zigzag** path down the hill.

zip

1. To **zip** means to close with a zipper. Tessa **zips** her jacket when it is cool outside. **2.** To **zip** also means to move very fast. Joshua **zipped** down the street on his bicycle. —**zipped**

zipper

A **zipper** is used to hold parts of clothes together. **Zippers** are made of plastic or metal. They have two rows of little bumps that look like teeth. These rows fit together when the **zipper** is closed. ∎

∎ **zipper**

zone

A **zone** is an area that is special because of where it is or how it is used. People must be careful when they drive in a school **zone.**

zoo

A **zoo** is a place where animals are kept. Sometimes they stay in cages. You can see lions, tigers, and elephants at some **zoos.**

A person who works at a **zoo** is called a **zookeeper. Zookeepers** feed the animals. They also clean the places where the animals live.

zoom

To **zoom** means to move suddenly and very fast. The rocket **zoomed** into the sky.

zucchini

A **zucchini** is a kind of vegetable.
Zucchinis are long and green. ■

■ **zucchini**

Here are examples of different ways to spell vowel and consonant sounds.

Short Vowel Sounds

Short a

Short **a** (as in **at**) is often spelled **a**:

act	cap
bad	glass
bag	fast
began	flash

Short **a** may be spelled **au**:

laugh

cap

Short e

Short **e** (as in **pet**) is often spelled **e**:

best	hen	spend
desk	insect	step
egg	leg	tell
fed	mess	them
fresh	neck	wet

desk

Short **e** is sometimes spelled **ea**:

bread	instead	read (in the past)
dead	leather	spread
feather	meant	treasure
head	measure	weather

Short **e** may also be spelled with these letters:

a	any, many	**u**	bury
ai	said	**ue**	guess
ie	friend		

Short i

Short **i** (as in **pit**) is often spelled **i**:

big	ink	sick
bin	lid	sister
disk	lip	wish
fist	miss	with
fit	ring	zip

feather

Short **i** is sometimes spelled **y**:

gym

Short **i** may also be spelled with these letters:

e	pretty	u	busy
			business
o	women	ui	build
			building

Short o

Short **o** (as in **hot**) is often spelled **o**:

body	monster
copy	pop
costume	rock
knot	solid

Short **o** may be spelled **a**:

watch

Short u

Short **u** (as in **nut**) is often spelled **u**:

brush	hunt	must
bucket	luck	puppy
bus	lump	rung
butter	much	summer
fun	mud	tub
hug		

Short **u** may also be spelled **o**:

color	love	some
done	month	son
from	mother	tongue
honey	nothing	

In some words, short **u** is spelled **ou**:

double	touch
rough	trouble

Short **u** may also be spelled with these letters:

a	was
oe	does
oo	blood, flood

costume

brush

honey

Long Vowel Sounds

Long a

Long **a** (as in **ate**) is often spelled **a**. Many words that end in **a-consonant-e** have a long **a** sound.

able	radio	strange
made	rake	take
male	safe	tape
page	same	wave

radio

Long **a** may also be spelled with these letters:

ai		**ay**		**ea**		**ey**	
	aid		hay		break		they
	daisy		maybe		great		
	grain		played		steak		
	paid						
	pail			**ei**	eight		
	painter				neighbor		
	raise				weigh		
	wait				weight		

Long e

Long **e** (as in **see**) is often spelled **e**. Many words that end in **e** or **e-consonant-e** have a long **e** sound.

be	me	evil
she	he	these

tree

Long **e** may also be spelled **ee**:

bee	freeze
cheese	seed
deep	teeth
feel	tree
feet	week

Long **e** may also be spelled **ea**:

bead	leave
clean	please
east	seat
heap	speak
leaf	teacher

leaf

Long **e** may also be spelled with these letters:

eo	people	**ie**	believe	**i**	piano	**y**	family
			piece		ski		hurry
							pretty

Long i

Long **i** (as in **ice**) is often spelled **i**. Many words that end in **i-consonant-e** have a long **i** sound.

describe	hide	like	size
dime	I	mine	smile
find	iron	nice	write
fire	ivy	pint	

smile

Long **i** may also be spelled **y** or **y** with another letter:

y	by	**ey**	eye	**ye**	dye
	fly				goodbye
	my	**uy**	buy		
	rhyme				
	xylophone				

Long **i** is sometimes spelled **i** plus one or more silent consonants:

igh	flight	**is**	island
	sigh		

xylophone

Long o

Long **o** (as in **go**) is often spelled **o**. Many words that end in **o-consonant-e** have a long **o** sound.

both	joke	robe
fold	lone	rode
home	note	so
hope	owe	those

Long **o** may be spelled **oa**:

coat	loan	road
loaf	loaves	soap

Long **o** may also be spelled **ow**:

below	know	throw
grow	show	yellow

loaves

Long **o** may be spelled **oe:**

> toe

Long u

Long **u** (as in **use**) is often spelled **u**. Many words that end in **u-consonant-e** have a long **u** sound.

computer	music
cute	uniform

Long **u** may also be spelled in these ways:

ew few   **eau** beautiful   **oo** zoom

Other Vowel Sounds

The sound of **a** in **all** may be spelled with these letters:

al	talk	**au**	caught	**aw**	awful	**ough**	fought
	walk		saucer		crawl		ought
			taught		jaw		thought
all	call				paw		
	fall				saw		
	small				straw		
	tall				yawn		

saucer

The vowel sound in **how** may be spelled in these ways:

ow	clown	**ou**	about
	cow		house
	flower		our
	now		proud
	powder		round
	towel		

The vowel sound in **good** may be spelled in these ways:

oo	book	**u**	bull
	hood		full
	look		put
	took		pull
	wood		

wood

The vowel sound in **moon** may be spelled in these ways:

oo		o		u		oe	
	cool		lose		June		canoe
	food		move		ruby		shoe
	loose		to		truth		
	rooster		who		tulip	**ui**	fruit
	smooth		whose				suit
	soon			**ou**	group		
	too	**ew**	blew		soup	**ue**	blue
	tooth		flew		through		glue
	troop		grew		you		true

The vowel sound in **joy** may be spelled in these ways:

oy		oi	
	cowboy		boil
	enjoy		noise
	toy		oil

rooster

Consonant Sounds

Some consonant sounds have more than one spelling.
Here are some to remember.

The sound of **f** as in **fun** may be spelled in these ways:

f		ff		gh		ph	
	after		different		enough		phone
	fall		off		laugh		
	if				rough		
	life						
	perfect						

The sound of **j** as in **jam** may be spelled in these ways:

j		g		dg	
	injure		energy		edge
	jelly		ginger		judge
	jog		imagine		
	jump		magic		
	object		page		

The sound of **ch** as in **much** may be spelled in these ways:

ch		tch	
	bunch		catch
	chalk		scratch
	child		stretch
	choose		watch
	rich		
	touch	**ti**	question

stretch

The sound of **k** as in **kick** may be spelled in these ways:

k		**c**		**ck**	
	keep		because		back
	park		car		hockey
	sky		helicopter		rocks
	speak		macaroni		
	woken		picnic	**ch**	school
	wrinkle		uncle		

macaroni

The sound of **r** as in **red** may be spelled in these ways:

r, rr				**rh**	
	border		our		rhinoceros
	borrow		ran		rhyme
	far		spring		
	green		story	**wr**	wrap
	hurry		tree		wrist
	more		work		write

The sound of **s** as in **say** may be spelled in these ways:

s, ss		**c**		**sc**	
	base		cent		muscle
	disappear		city		science
	fast		dance		scissors
	loose		December		
	miss		nice	**st**	castle
	pants		pencil		listen
	sit		princess		whistle

pants

The sound of **sh** as in **ship** may be spelled in these ways:

sh		**ti**	
	push		dictionary
	shut		direction
	wash		pollution
s	sugar	**ci**	magician
	sure		special
		ch	machine

wash

SPECIAL NAMES FOR WORDS

Words have special names that tell how they are used.

A **noun** is a word that names a person, a place, or a thing. In these examples, the nouns are underlined.

- The <u>dog</u> dug a <u>hole</u> in the <u>yard</u>.
- My <u>sister</u> wrote a <u>book</u> about <u>horses</u>.
- <u>Basketball</u> is my favorite <u>sport</u>.

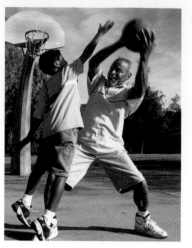

A **proper noun** is the name of a person, place, or thing. Proper nouns begin with a capital letter.

Names of people	George Washington
Names of pets	Tabby
Names of cities or countries	New York
Names of days of the week	Sunday
Names of months	September
Names of holidays	Thanksgiving
Names of languages	English

basketball

A **pronoun** is a word that can take the place of a noun. A pronoun names the same person, place, or thing as the noun it stands for. The words **I, you, he, she, it, we,** and **they** are pronouns. In each of these examples, the noun and the pronoun that takes its place are underlined.

- <u>Ava</u> read the book. <u>She</u> enjoyed the story.
- Bees make <u>honey</u>. <u>It</u> is very sweet.

A **verb** is a word that names an action. In these examples, the verbs are underlined.

- The cat <u>jumped</u> over the fence.
- Dale <u>caught</u> the ball and <u>threw</u> it to my brother.

bee

An **adjective** is a word that tells about a person, a place, or a thing. In these examples, the adjectives are underlined.

- The <u>little</u> child began to cry.
- The library was very <u>quiet</u>.
- The car was <u>clean</u> after we washed it.

WORDS THAT SOUND ALIKE

Many words sound alike but do not have the same spelling or the same meaning. These words are called **homophones.** For example, **one** is a number and **won** is a form of the word **win.** The words **one** and **won** are spelled differently and have different meanings, but they sound alike when you say them out loud.

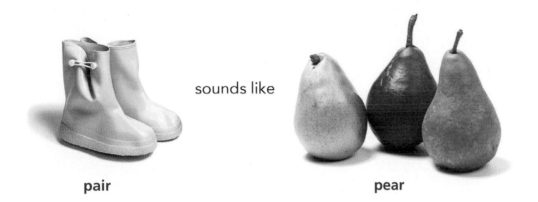

pair   sounds like   pear

Here are some examples of other words that sound alike in this dictionary.

ate	eight	knew	new	sew	so
bare	bear	knight	night	son	sun
be	bee	knot	not	their	there
blew	blue	know	no	threw	through
buy	by	mail	male	to	too, two
cent	sent	meat	meet	wait	weight
dear	deer	one	won	way	weigh
eye	I	pair	pear	weak	week
flour	flower	peace	piece	wear	where
for	four	plain	plane	which	witch
heal	heel	right	write	wood	would
hear	here	road	rode		
hole	whole	sea	see		

COMPOUND WORDS

Many words are made up of two shorter words joined together. These are called **compound words.** Here are some examples from this dictionary.

afternoon	grownup	popcorn
backpack	homework	railroad
bathtub	horseshoe	rainbow
birthday	jellyfish	scarecrow
cowboy	keyhole	shoelace
doorbell	lighthouse	sidewalk
everywhere	newspaper	something
fireplace	nobody	toothbrush
flashlight	outside	tugboat
gingerbread	pancake	underground
grasshopper	playground	

fireplace

The compound words in the list below are made up of short words given in this dictionary. Can you tell what they mean?

corn + bread = cornbread	mouse + trap = mousetrap
dish + towel = dishtowel	paint + brush = paintbrush
doll + house = dollhouse	pine + cone = pinecone
farm + land = farmland	rain + drop = raindrop
grape + vine = grapevine	sail + boat = sailboat
hair + brush = hairbrush	tool + shed = toolshed
moon + light = moonlight	wheel + chair = wheelchair

pinecone

A **contraction** is also a way of joining two words together. Contractions are short ways of writing two words. An **apostrophe** (') takes the place of a letter or letters that have been taken out.

can't = cannot	they're = they are
don't = do not	we're = we are
I'm = I am	you've = you have

COMMON WORD GROUPS

Mammals

ape	fox	panda
bat	giraffe	pig
bear	goat	puppy
beaver	hamster	rabbit
calf	hippopotamus	raccoon
camel	horse	rat
cat	kangaroo	rhinoceros
cattle	kitten	seal
cow	leopard	sheep
cub	lion	skunk
deer	mice	squirrel
dog	monkey	tiger
dolphin	moose	whale
donkey	mouse	wolf
elephant	ox	zebra

rabbit

Insects

ant	caterpillar	mosquito
bee	cricket	moth
beetle	fly	
butterfly	grasshopper	

grasshopper

Birds

chicken	hen	robin
crow	ostrich	rooster
duck	owl	swan
eagle	parrot	turkey
goose	peacock	woodpecker
hawk	penguin	

Other Animals

alligator	frog	toad
crab	lobster	turtle
crocodile	snail	
dinosaur	snake	

Instruments

drum	horn	violin
flute	piano	xylophone
guitar	trombone	
harp	trumpet	

drum

Time

calendar	minute	watch
clock	month	week
hour	second	year

clock

Seasons

spring	winter
summer	fall

Months

January	May	September
February	June	October
March	July	November
April	August	December

Days

Sunday	Thursday
Monday	Friday
Tuesday	Saturday
Wednesday	

Number Words

zero	0	five	5	ten	10
one	1	six	6	hundred	100
two	2	seven	7	thousand	1,000
three	3	eight	8	million	1,000,000
four	4	nine	9		

skate

Sports

baseball	skating
basketball	soccer
bowling	swimming
football	tennis
hockey	volleyball

Parts of the Body

arm	foot	nail
back	hair	neck
bone	hand	nose
brain	head	shoulder
cheek	heart	stomach
chest	heel	toe
chin	jaw	tongue
ear	knee	tooth
elbow	leg	teeth
eye	lung	wrist
face	mouth	
finger	muscle	

face

Furniture

bed	crib	sofa
bench	couch	table
chair	desk	

Family

aunt	grandfather	parent
brother	grandmother	sister
cousin	grandparent	son
daughter	husband	uncle
father	mother	wife

Colors

black	green	red
blue	orange	white
brown	pink	yellow
gray	purple	

colors

Shapes

circle	oval	star
cone	rectangle	triangle
diamond	square	

Clothes

apron	glove	slipper
belt	hat	sneaker
bib	helmet	sock
boot	hood	suit
bowtie	pajamas	sweater
cap	pants	tie
cape	shirt	trousers
coat	shoelace	vest
dress	shoes	

belt

Foods

apple	grapefruit	pepper
banana	gravy	pie
bean	ham	pineapple
beef	hamburger	pizza
berry	hot dog	plum
bread	ice cream	popcorn
butter	jam	potato
cake	jelly	pudding
candy	ketchup	pumpkin
carrot	lemon	rice
cereal	lettuce	sandwich
cheese	lime	sauce
cherry	macaroni	soup
chocolate	marshmallow	spice
cookie	meat	steak
corn	milk	sugar
cream	mustard	tomato
dessert	onion	turkey
doughnut	orange	vegetable
egg	pancake	waffle
fish	pea	watermelon
fruit	peach	wheat
gingerbread	peanut butter	
grape	pear	

carrot

soup

Land and Water

beach	jungle	river
cave	lake	sea
continent	marsh	shore
desert	meadow	stream
field	mountain	swamp
forest	ocean	valley
harbor	plain	
hill	pond	

desert

Transportation

airplane	carriage	sled
automobile	fire engine	submarine
bicycle	helicopter	train
boat	jet	truck
bus	motorcycle	tugboat
canoe	rocket	wagon
car	ship	

rocket

Jobs

actor	engineer	nurse
artist	farmer	pilot
astronaut	firefighter	police
author	fisherman	president
baker	grocer	principal
barber	guard	sailor
blacksmith	judge	scientist
carpenter	librarian	singer
coach	magician	teacher
cook	mayor	zookeeper
doctor	musician	

Amounts and Distances

foot	mile
gallon	ounce
gram	pint
inch	pound
kilometer	quart
meter	yard

carpenter

PAIRS OF OPPOSITES

absent	present	loose	tight
asleep	awake	loud	soft
back	front	love	hate
backward	forward	male	female
beautiful	ugly	many	few
before	after	minus	plus
below	above	morning	evening
best	worst	narrow	wide
better	worse	neat	messy
big	small	new	old
borrow	lend	north	south
buy	sell	odd	even
cheap	expensive	on	off
clean	dirty	open	close
cold	hot	plain	fancy
comfortable	uncomfortable	possible	impossible
day	night	quiet	loud
deep	shallow	rich	poor
down	up	right	wrong
early	late	safe	dangerous
east	west	same	different
easy	hard	shout	whisper
empty	full	slow	fast
entrance	exit	smooth	rough
evil	good	start	finish
far	near	strong	weak
fat	thin	tall	short
frown	smile	thick	thin
good	bad	tight	loose
hard	soft	together	apart
here	there	top	bottom
in	out	true	false
inside	outside	under	over
large	small	up	down
left	right	warm	cool
less	more	wet	dry
light	heavy	wild	tame
little	big	win	lose
long	short	young	old

JUST FOR FUN: WORD CHALLENGES

1. Sometimes two short words can be joined to form a longer word. Match each word in column A with a word in column B to form a **compound word** that is in your dictionary.

A	B
after	room
high	melon
score	board
bath	ball
base	case
water	rise
sun	noon
suit	bow
rain	chair

2. Find the words that **rhyme**.

- Find a word on page 121 that rhymes with **sun**.
- Find a word on page 24 that rhymes with **tree**.
- Find a word on page 152 that rhymes with **mouse**.
- Can you find two words that rhyme with **two** and begin with the letter d?
  (Hint: The words are on pages 83 and 87.)

3. **Synonyms** are words that mean the same thing. Say the missing word or fill in the blank.

A word on page 254 that means the same as **gift** *is* _____.

A word on page 139 that means the same as **glad** *is* _____.

A word on page 69 that means the same as **sofa** *is* _____.

4. The words in the dictionary are in **ABC order**. Can you list these words in ABC order?

scissors, knife, fork, spoon, dish, cup, pitcher

whale, camel, ape, hawk, turkey, woodpecker, cat

kite, chalk, marble, crayon, teddy bear, sled, bicycle

Now see if you can find these words in your dictionary. Use the **guidewords** at the top of the pages to help you.

5. Match the word in column A with its **opposite** in column B. Look up these words in your dictionary.

A	B
shout	crooked
early	spend
high	forget
asleep	entrance
straight	late
exit	find
save	low
lose	wet
remember	awake
dry	whisper

PICTURE CREDITS

The following source abbreviations are used throughout the credits: AB/Albano Ballerini, COR/Corbis, COR-RF/Corbis Royalty-free, EVC/Eva Vagreti Cockrille, GI/Getty Images, GI-RF/ Getty Images Royalty-free, HMH/© Houghton Mifflin Harcourt Digital Studio, MF/Masterfile, MF-RF/Masterfile Royalty-free, PD-GI/Photodisc-Getty Images, PF/Phoebe Ferguson, PR/Photo Researchers, Inc., SS/SuperStock, Inc., and SS-RF/SuperStock, Inc. Royalty-free.

Frontmatter credits
tiger cub GI-RF, Martin Harvey paint palette PD-GI, Ryan McVay pinwheel Creativ Studio Heinemann crayons GI-Stockdisc Classic dinosaur EVC dive PD-GI, Jeff Maloney orange EVC dishes AB hug SS-RF, RubberBall grow PD-GI grew PD-GI thin EVC team RS-RF, SW Productions PictureArts Corp.

Letter opener credits
(Letter opener picture credits are arranged in order of the photographs in the openers from left to right.)

Apples: GI, Brand X Pictures, Burke/Triolo Productions; GI, Foodpix, Trevor Pearson; PD-GI, Siede Preis; GI, Brand X Pictures, Burke/Triolo Productions
Balloons: SS-RF, Stockdisc; HMCO; GI-RF, Digital Vision; HMCO
Clocks: SS-RF, Exactostock; HMCO; HMCO; SS-RF, Westend61
Drums: PD-GI; PD-GI; HMCO; PD-GI
Eagles: GI-RF, Digital Vision; GI, Gallo Images, Heinrich van den Berg; PR, James Zipp; GI-RF, Digital Vision
Flowers: PD-GI; PD-GI; GI, Brand X Pictures, Burke/Triolo Productions; GI, The Image Bank, Davies and Starr
Grapes: PD-GI; PD-GI; PD-GI, Ryan McVay; GI, Foodpix, John E. Kelly
Hats: HMCO; COR, Rick Gayle Studio; GI, Thinkstock; GI, Brand X Pictures, Burke/Triolo Productions
Insects: PD-GI, Don Farrall; COR, Scott Smith; COR; Shutterstock, Leighton Photography & Imaging
Jars: HMCO; HMCO; HMCO; HMCO
Kites: HMCO; Courtesy of intothewind.com; Shutterstock, Alice Kirichenko; Courtesy of intothewind.com
Leaves: PD-GI; PD-GI; PD-GI; GI, The Image Bank, Jody Dole
Monkeys: PD-GI; PD-GI; GI, Taxi, Jonathan and Angela; GI, National Geographic, Roy Toft
Nuts: PD-GI; GI, Foodpix, Eisenhut & Mayer; GI, Foodpix, Eisenhut & Mayer; PD-GI
Owls: COR, Tim Davis; SS, age fotostock; GI; Dorling Kindersley, Frank Greenaway
Penguins: GI-RF, Fuse; SS, James Urbach; GI-RF, Digital Vision; COR
Quilts: Index Stock Imagery RF, Scott Berner; COR, Roman Soumar; Alamy RF, Ruth Black; PD-GI, Photolink
Rabbits: GI, Taxi, American Images, Inc.; SS, age fotostock; Alamy, Juniors Bildarchiv; PD-GI
Socks: HMCO; HMCO; HMCO; HMCO
Turtles: SS, age fotostock; PR, Millard H. Sharp; GI, Stockdisc Classic; PD-GI, Jules Frazier
Umbrellas: Shutterstock, Petr Malyshev; COR, Zefa, Sergio Pitamitz; PD-GI, Michael Matisse; HMCO; HMCO
Valentines: Shutterstock, Cristy; GI, Photonica, Lenora Gim; COR; HMCO
Wheels: HMCO; PD-GI; COR-RF; SS, Richard Cummins
X-rays: PR, Scott Camazine; PD-GI, Jim Wehtje; PD-GI, Keith Brofsky; PR, Scott Camazine
Yarns: HMCO; GI, Brand X Pictures, Burke/Triolo Productions; HMCO; HMCO
Zebras: COR, Kevin Schafer; PR, Mitch Reardon; COR, Frank Lane Picture Agency, Terry Whittaker; GI, Martin Barraud

A-Z text credits
above age fotostock RF, David Oxberry **across** COR-RF **after** (note) GI-RF, ThinkStock **against** AB **airplane** COR, W. Deuter/zefa **alike** Robertstock.com RF, BananaStock **alone** PD-GI **along** PD-GI **anchor** EVC **ant** EVC **ape** Fotolia RF **apron** SS-RF, ThinkStock **aquarium** SS-RF, Francisco Cruz **armor** EVC **around** COR, James P. Blair **arrow** COR, Peter Johnson **artist** SS, age fotostock **asleep** SS, NaturePL **astronaut** PD-GI **attic** GI, The Image Bank, Dennis Novak **automobile** PR, Margaret Zwiazek **awake** PF **ax** EVC **baby** SS, age fotostock **backpack** GI, Bruce Rogovin **backward** GI-RF, Andersen Ross **bag** AB **bake** (note) PD-GI **ball** Robertstock.com RF, BananaStock **balloon** COR-RF **barber** PD-GI, Adam Crowley **barn** SS-RF, Ron Chapple Photography **baseball** PD-GI **baseball** (note) COR, Chase Swift **basketball** SS-RF, BlueMoon Stock **bat** EVC **bath** age fotostock, Ariel Skelley **beach** COR, Richard Klune **beak** EVC **bear** GI-RF, Comstock Images **beaver** PR, Tom McHugh **bee** EVC **behind** GI, Herman Agopian **bell** COR, Richard Cummins **bend** Index Stock Imagery RF, RubberBall Productions **beside** PR, Richard Hutchings **between** COR, Ariel Skelley **bicycle** Imagestate RF **bill** SS, age fotostock **bird** (note) GI-RF, Michael Matisse **bite** Alamy RF, Catalin Petolea **blacksmith** Alamy, Pat & Chuck Blackley **blanket** EVC **block** Robertstock.com RF, William McKellar PictureArts Corp. **blow** PR, Jim Corwin **board** SS, age fotostock **boat** COR, Neil Rabinowitz **boil** COR, Paul Seheult **bone** COR, Paul A. Souders **boot** SS, Lisette Le Bon **border** Alamy, John Glover **borrow** (note) HMH **both** Robertstock.com RF, BananaStock **boulder** SS, All Canada Photos **bow** Alamy RF, Mike Kemp **bowl** AB **braces** SS, Arlene Sandler **braid** PF **branch** COR, Tim McGuire **bread** COR, K. Hackenberg/zefa **breakfast** (note) GI-RF, PhotoAlto, Isabelle Rozenbaum & Frederic Cirou **brick** ISI-RF, Jeffrey Blackman **bridge** SS-RF, BananaStock **broom** COR-RF **brush** Robertstock.com RF, Steve Allen PictureArts Collection **bubble** SS, Powerstock **build** GI-RF, Paul Burns, Digital Vision **building** SS, age fotostock **bull** GI-RF, Brand X Pictures **bus** SS, age fotostock **bush** COR, Patrick Johns **butterfly** GI-RF, Don Johnston **button** PD-GI **caboose** SS, age fotostock **cactus** GI-RF, Digital Vision, Visions of America, Joe Sohm **call** GI-RF, Bruce Laurance **camel** Susan Ley Photography **camp** GI-RF, Chris Robbins **can** PD-GI **candy** (note) age fotostock RF, Ingeborg Knol **canoe** Alamy RF, imac **cap** SS-RF, David Muscroft **cape** PF **carousel** COR, Roger Chester **carpenter** (note) PD-GI **carriage** COR, Neil Rabinowitz **carrot** PD-GI **carry** GI-RF, Ariel Skelley, Blend Images **castle** SS-RF, Exactostock **caterpillar** PD-GI **caught** COR-RF **cave** SS **chair** SS-RF, RubberBall Productions **chair** (note) PD-GI, C Squared Studios **chalk** MF, Rommel **chase** GI-RF, Stockdisc **checkers** SS-RF, SOMOS **cheese** SS-RF, Fancy Collection **cherry** EVC **chicken** COR, Angela Hampton **chimney** COR, Kevin R. Morris **chin** PF **choose** SS-RF, Purestock **circle** EVC **city** SS, age fotostock **clap** COR, LWA-Dann Tardif **claw** EVC **clay** PR, Southern Living **clear** GI, Chris Cheadle **climb** Alamy, Ashley Cooper **closet** MF, Zoran Milich **cloud** COR-RF, L. Clarke **coat** HMH **coin** PD-GI **collect** (note) HMH **color** SS, age fotostock **computer** PhotoEdit, Richard Hutchings **cone** PD-GI **container** PD-GI, Burke-Triolo Productions **cook** PD-GI, Buccina Studios **corn** EVC **costume** COR, John Henley **cotton** SS **cover** GI, Rita Maas **cowboy** Alamy RF, Lisa Dearing **crack** SS, Steve Vidler **crawl** SS-RF, Kwame Zikomo **crib** PD-GI, C Squared Studios **crocodile** Alamy, James Caldwell **crooked** GI, Gandee Vasan **crowd** SS-RF **crown** GI, AFP **crutch** COR, Jim Craigmyle **cub** PR, Michel & Christine Denis-Huot **cup** HMH **curly** PF **curve** PD-GI, John A. Rizzo **daisy** SS, age fotostock **dam** PR, Calvin Larsen **dandelion** EVC **deer** PD-GI **dentist** COR, Steve Jay Crise **design** Robertstock.com, S. Piumatti **desk** PF **diamond** EVC **dig** MF-RF **dinosaur** EVC **direction** EVC **dirt** SS, age fotostock **dish** AB **dive** GI-RF, Jeff Maloney **dock** Alamy, Steve P. **doctor** PR, Blair Seitz **dog** SS **donkey** COR, George McCarthy **door** GI, Steven Nilsson **dragon** EVC **dress** GI, The Image Bank, Elizabeth Zeschin **drink** GI-RF, Brand X Pictures **drop** GI-RF, David Sacks **drum** PD-GI **dry** SS, Angelo Cavalli **duck** PR, Tony

Camacho **duck** (note) GI, Tony Evans, Timelapse Library **dust** Index Stock Imagery RF, Fogstock **eagle** SS, age fotostock **earth** PD-GI **east** EVC **edge** GI, Greg Ceo **egg** PD-GI **elbow** GI-RF, Barbara Penoyar **electricity** (note) PD-GI **elephant** PD-GI **empty** COR-RF **engine** COR-RF, Jim Zuckerman **entrance** PR, John G. Ross **equal** AB **exciting** GI, The Image Bank, ATABOY **exercise** SS, age fotostock **expand** PF **explore** COR-RF **face** PD-GI **factory** COR-RF **fair** COR, Nik Wheeler **fan** Robertstock.com, Ron Jaffe Photography, Camerique Inc. **fancy** GI-RF, Scott T. Baxter **farm** GI, Richard Price **feather** EVC **feed** GI-RF, image100 **feel** SS, Francisco Cruz **fence** PR, W. Cody **festival** PR, Lawrence Migdale **field** GI-RF, Holly Cohn **fill** PF **firefighter** GI, The Image Bank, Stuart Dee **fireworks** COR, Otto Rogge **fish** SS, Carlos Davila **fisherman** SS, age fotostock **flag** PR, Rafael Macia **flashlight** COR, David Woods **flat** PF **flock** GI, Mula Eshet **flood** Robertstock.com, J. Whitmer **flour** Shutterstock, Wiktory **flower** COR, O'Brien Productions **flute** GI, Nicola Sutton **fly** EVC **fog** SS-RF, Penny Adams **fold** AB **foot** EVC **football** GI, Joe McBride **forest** Fotolia RF, Pakhnyushchyy **fossil** GI, altrendo nature **fox** GI, Randy Green **frog** PR, Rod Planck **frost** SS, age fotostock **frown** PF **frozen** SS, age fotostock **fruit** SS, age fotostock **full** AB **fur** PD-GI **gallon** EVC **game** (note) HMH **garden** Alamy, Holmes Garden Photos **gate** GI, Stuart McCall **giant** SS, Travel Pix Ltd. **gingerbread** EVC **giraffe** COR-RF **glass** (note) SS-RF, Francisco Cruz **globe** PD-GI **glove** EVC **goat** Alamy, WILDLIFE GmbH **goldfish** COR, Robert Pickett **goose** COR, Julie Habel **grandfather** (note) COR-RF **grape** PD-GI **grass** GI-RF, Brand X Pictures **grasshopper** EVC **greenhouse** COR, Joseph Sohm **grin** SS **group** GI, Ariel Skelley **guard** COR-RF **guide** (note) COR, Jim Craigmyle **guitar** PD-GI **half** EVC **hall** GI-RF, Thomas Barwick **ham** SS-RF, Sadik Demiroz **hammer** AB **hamster** PR, Carolyn A. McKeone **hand** (note) HMH **handle** EVC **hang** SS, age fotostock **harbor** COR, Hubert Stadler **harp** GI, Greg Ceo **hat** Alamy, Blend Images **hatch** COR, Jonathan Blair **hawk** PR, Jim Zipp **head** (note) Ken Karp **heavy** COR, Norbert Schaefer **heel** PF **helicopter** SS, age fotostock, **helmet** Robertstock.com, B. Bridge **herd** Alamy RF, F1online digitale Bildagentur GmbH **high** GI, Julia Fullerton-Batten **hill** COR, Owen Franken **hippopotamus** COR, Staffan Widstrand **hive** COR, Paul A. Souders **hold** SS-RF, ThinkStock **hole** SS **hollow** AB **honey** SS-RF, Niamh Baldock **hook** EVC **horn** SS, age fotostock **horse** COR, John Sommers **horse** (note) PD-GI **hose** EVC **house** COR, John Henley **hug** SS-RF, RubberBall Productions **huge** EVC **hump** SS, age fotostock **hut** COR, Paul Almasy **ice** SS **ice** (note) PD-GI, C Squared Studios **ice cream** PD-GI, C Squared Studios **igloo** age fotostock, Yvette Cardozo **ill** GI, Britt Erlanson **ink** GI, Leland Bobbe **insect** EVC **inside** GI, Wendy Ashton **instrument** COR, Chris Rogers **iron** AB **island** COR, Lawson Wood **ivy** Jupiterimages RF **ivy** (note) iStockphoto.com, Judy Picciotto **jacket** GI-RF, Chase Jarvis **jelly** (note) PD-GI **jellyfish** SS, Robert Huberman **jet** COR, George Hall **jog** GI, Al Bello **join** COR, Ariel Skelley **juggle** COR, Michael S. Yamashita **juice** SS-RF, Pixtal **jump** (note) SS, age fotostock **jungle** COR, Gavriel Jecan **junk** COR-RF, Radius Images **kangaroo** PD-GI **kettle** AB **key** MF, Artiga Photo **kick** GI, Mike Powell **kite** GI-RF, ThinkStock **kitten** PD-GI **knight** SS **knot** HMH **koala** COR-RF **ladder** PF **lake** SS, age fotostock **lamb** GI, The Image Bank, Brett Froomer **lantern** SS-RF, ThinkStock **laugh** SS, age fotostock **laundry** PD-GI **lead** age fotostock, Alvaro Leiva **leaf** PR, John Kaprielian **leash** COR-RF, Tom Grill **leather** GI-RF, Brand X Pictures **lemon** EVC **lemon** (note) PD-GI, C Squared Studios **leopard** GI, David Tipling **lettuce** PD-GI **library** Alamy, Sally and Richard Greenhill **lick** COR-RF **lift** COR, Nancy Ney **light** PD-GI **lightning** PD-GI **lime** EVC **lion/lioness** COR, Paul A. Souders **list** EVC **listen** GI-RF, Tom Grill **loaf** PD-GI **lobster** PR, Andrew J. Martinez **lock** PD-GI **lock** (note) GI, David Woolley **log** Robertstock.com, ACE Photo Agency **long** COR-RF **loud** (note) SS, Kwame Zikomo **low** GI, Jasper James **lumber** SS, age fotostock **lunch** AB **macaroni** COR-RF **machine** SS, age fotostock **magic**

(note) GI, Arthur Tilley **magnet** AB **make** PF **maple** Alamy RF, Todd Muskopf **marble** PD-GI **march** Alamy, Paul Maguire **marsh** SS, age fotostock **mask** SS, Robert Huberman **meadow** SS, age fotostock **meal** AB **measure** PF **mess** PF **microscope** SS-RF, Exactostock **middle** SS, age fotostock **mirror** SS-RF, Image Source **mix** Index Stock Imagery RF, ThinkStock **model** SS, age fotostock **money** (note) PD-GI **monkey** GI-RF, Pierre Arsenault **monument** PD-GI **moon** COR-RF **mosquito** EVC **moth** PR, Biophoto Associates **motorcycle** Alamy, Mark Jenkins **mountain** SS, Philip & Karen Smith **mouse** Alamy, Juniors Bildarchiv **mud** SS, age fotostock **music** (note) PD-GI **mustard** PD-GI **narrow** PD-GI **neat** COR, Carlos Dominguez **neck** PF **needle** PD-GI, C Squared Studios **neighbor** COR, Ed Bock **nest** COR-RF **net** EVC **newspaper** COR, Brian Leng **night** PD-GI **north** EVC **note** EVC **nurse** GI, Richard Price **nut** PR, Jean-Paul Chassenet **oak** EVC **octopus** SS, age fotostock **office** Alamy RF, Juice Images **oil** HMH **onion** SS-RF, FoodCollection **opposite** SS, age fotostock **orchestra** GI, Oliver Benn **ostrich** COR, Kevin Schafer **oval** EVC **oven** COR-RF, Reed Kaestner **owl** PD-GI **pack** PF **pail** PD-GI **paint** GI-RF, Digital Vision **pair** HMH **palm** PF **pancake** AB **panda** GI, The Image Bank, James Balog **pants** GI-RF, RubberBall Productions **paper** (note) PD-GI, David Toase **parade** PR, Lawrence Migdale **parrot** Alamy-RF, imagebroker **party** COR, Hutchings Stock Photography **patch** GI, Evan Sklar **path** SS, age fotostock **paw** COR, Gunter Marx Photography **peacock** COR-RF **peanut** COR-RF **pear** HMH **peek** GI, M. Llorden **penguin** PR, Kevin Schafer **pepper** PD-GI **pet** COR, Carl & Ann Purcell **piano** COR, A. Inden/zefa **pick** COR-RF, Nick Dolding, cultura **picnic** COR, Ariel Skelley **piece** GI, Judd Pilossof **pig** PD-GI **pile** GI, Greg Ceo **pineapple** PD-GI **pipe** PD-GI, Travel Ink **pitcher** HMH **pizza** PD-GI, John A. Rizzo **planet** GI-RF, StockTrek **plant** SS, age fotostock **playground** Alamy, David R. Frazier Photolibrary **plum** GI-RF, Creative Crop, Digital Vision **pocket** GI-RF, Jupiterimages **point** PD-GI **pole** GI, George Grall **pony** PD-GI **pool** Robertstock .com, ACE Photo Agency **popcorn** AB **porch** GI-RF, Digital Vision, Stewart Cohen **pot** GI, Sang An **pour** PF **present** PD-GI **prize** COR, Peter Beck **propeller** COR, Neil Rabinowitz **puddle** GI, Pauline Cutler **pull** COR, John Henley **pumpkin** COR-RF **puppy** COR-RF, Stan Fellerman **push** Michael Schmitt Photography **raccoon** PR, Jeffrey Lepore **race** GI-RF, Deborah Jaffe **radio** COR-RF **raft** COR, Ales Fevzer **railroad** SS, age fotostock **rainbow** COR-RF, Wayne Green **rake** MF, Michael Mahovlich **reach** GI, Betsie Van Der Meer **read** GI-RF, Digital Vision **rectangle** EVC **refrigerator** AB **reptile** EVC **rhinoceros** GI-RF, Steve Allen **ribbon** EVC **rice** EVC **ride** GI, Hamish Blair **ring** GI **rink** GI, Medford Taylor **river** GI, Stan Navratil **road** GI, The Image Bank, Eric Meola **roast** COR, Ariel Skelley **robin** GI, altrendo nature **robot** PR, Mauro Fermariello **rocket** NASA **roof** GI-RF, Rob Melnychuk **rooster** PD-GI **rope** GI-RF, Doug Menuez **rose** GI, David Reffalt **rug** Alamy RF, Greg Wright **run** GI-RF, Stockdisc **sack** GI, Joern Rynio **sail** SS, George Glod **same** PD-GI, Travel Ink **sand** Michael Schmitt Photography **sandwich** HMH **saucer** AB **saw** COR, Michael Keller **scale** COR-RF **scarecrow** GI, Stephen St. John **scissors** HMH **score** (note) COR-RF **seal** Alamy, David Lyons **seat** SS, age fotostock **seed** GI-RF, Isabelle Rozenbaum **seesaw** GI, Steve Smith **sew** PF **shadow** GI, Clive Mason **shake** (note) EVC **shallow** GI, Danita Delimont **shark** COR, Tim Davis **sharp** PR, Voisin **sheep** PD-GI **shell** (note) PD-GI **shell** GI-RF, Digital Vision **ship** SS **shirt** PD-GI **shoe** (note) GI, LifeStock **shoot** PR, Lawrence Migdale **shop** GI-RF, TRBfoto **shore** COR, Danny Lehman **shoulder** GI, Nancy Brown **shovel** PD-GI **sidewalk** GI-RF, ThinkStock **sign** PD-GI **silver** AB **sing** (note) GI-RF, Image Source **skate** COR-RF **skate** (note) PD-GI, C Squared Studios **ski** Alamy, Catherine Esmeralda **skirt** GI, Paul Conrath **skunk** PD-GI **sled** HMH **sleep** COR, Jose Luis Pelaez **sleeve** GI, The Image Bank, Steven Biver **slice** COR-RF, Ocean **smile** SS-RF, ThinkStock **snake** COR-RF, Jack Goldfarb, Design Pics **sneaker** HMH **snow** COR, P. Pet/zefa **snow** (note) COR, K. Hackenberg **soap** GI-RF, Image Source **soccer** GI-RF, Fuse **sock** EVC **soil** GI, Bob

Thomas **soup** AB **south** EVC **space** PD-GI **spider** COR, Herbert Kehrer/zefa **spot** SS, Gary Neil Corbett **spread** COR, Roy Morsch/zefa **square** EVC **squeeze** COR-RF **squirrel** GI, The Image Bank, Paul McCormick **stable** GI, The Image Bank, Nicolas Russell **stairs** GI-RF, Comstock Images **star** GI, The Image Bank, Pete Turner **station** SS, age fotostock **statue** GI-RF, Digital Vision, Jon Arnold **steam** AB **steel** GI-RF, Hisham F. Ibrahim **step** COR-RF **stick** COR, Renee Lynn **stone** Alamy, Jason Lindsey **storm** PR, Jim Edds **stove** SS-RF, ThinkStock **straight** SS, age fotostock **straw** GI, Jeff Cadge **stream** GI-RF, Toy Sweet **street** (note) GI, Silvia Otte **stretch** COR-RF **string** GI-RF, Stockdisc **stripe** PR, B. Jones & M. Shimlock **submarine** COR, George Hall **subway** COR, Art Stein **suds** GI, Steve Cohen **suit** GI, Carl Posey **suitcase** GI-RF, Siede Preis **sunrise** GI-RF, Radius Images **surprise** (note) PD-GI **swan** GI-RF, Andrew Ward **sweater** age fotostock RF, RubberBall Productions **swim** GI, Ron Chapple **swing** COR, Michael S. Yamashita **symbol** (note) GI-RF, Burke-Triolo Productions **syrup** AB **table** GI-RF, Digital Vision **tail** PD-GI **talent** (note) GI, Bill Losh **tall** GI, Roy Rainford **taste** COR, LWA, Dann Tardif **team** Robertstock.com RF, SW Productions PictureArts Corp. **teddy bear** PD-GI **teeth** GI, Ryan McVay **telephone** GI-RF, Jack Hollingsworth **telescope** COR, Phil Schermeister **tennis** COR, Chuck Savage **tent** COR-RF **theater** GI, Wayne Eastep **thermometer** GI-RF, Siede Preis **thick** EVC **thin** EVC **thread** AB **throne** COR, Massimo Listri **throw** COR, Scott Wohrman **thumb** GI, The Image Bank, Ross Whitaker **tie** Robertstock.com RF, BananaStock **tiger** SS-RF, COR **tight** (note) Robertstock.com RF **tire** EVC **toad** COR-RF, Jack Goldfarb, Design Pics **toast** (note) GI-RF, Burke-Triolo Productions **tomato** PD-GI **tongue** GI-RF, GK Hart & Vikki Hart **tool** EVC **tooth** (note) PD-GI **tornado** COR, Aaron Horowitz **towel** GI, Anne Ackermann **tractor** SS, age fotostock **traffic** SS, Angelo Cavalli **trail** COR, Ashley Cooper **trailer** Alamy, Sunpix Travel **train** Alamy, Sophotographie **trash** GI, Michael Kelley **tray** GI, Yellow Dog Productions **triangle** EVC **trombone** PF **truck** GI-RF, Fuse **trumpet** COR, Chuck Savage **trunk** AB **tug** GI-RF, James Lauritz **tulip** PD-GI **tunnel** SS, Wilburn

D. Murphy **turkey** GI, altrendo images **turtle** Alamy RF, CY Chan **twin** Alamy, COR, Flirt **umbrella** GI, Steve Satushek **underline** PF **underwater** PR, Alexis Rosenfeld **unicorn** EVC **uniform** COR, Ariel Skelley **upon** Alamy RF, William Leaman **upside-down** GI, Mike Powell **valley** SS, age fotostock **vegetable** PD-GI **vest** GI, Stephen Simpson **village** SS, age fotostock **vine** (note) Robertstock.com, R. Kord **violin** GI-RF, Peter Dazeley **volcano** Fotolia RF, Marco Regalia **volleyball** Digital Railroad RF **wagon** COR-RF **walk** MF, Ariel Skelley **wall** GI, altrendo travel **wash** PR, Blair Seitz **watch** PF **watermelon** Fotolia RF **wave** GI, The Image Bank, Ron Levine **wax** EVC **web** SS, age fotostock **weigh** SS-RF, COR **well** EVC **west** EVC **wet** GI, Marina Jefferson **wheat** EVC **wheel** SS, age fotostock **wide** SS-RF, Visions of America **wig** GI-RF, Hisham F. Ibrahim **win** GI, Jim Cummins **windmill** Fotolia RF **window** COR-RF **wing** PD-GI, Alan and Sandy Carey **wire** SS, age fotostock **wolf** Alamy RF, Lisa Dearing **wood** EVC **wood** (note) PD-GI **wool** SS, age fotostock **worm** EVC **wrap** PD-GI **wrinkle** GI-RF, Life On White **xylophone** PF **yard** COR, W. Deuter/zefa **young** PR, Ursula Markus **yo-yo** COR-RF **zipper** GI, Lifestock **zoo** (note) COR-RF **zucchini** Bernadette Lau

Backmatter credits
cap SS-RF, David Muscroft **desk** PF **feather** EVC **costume** PF **brush** RS-RF, Brand X, Steve Allen PictureArts Collection **honey** AB **radio** COR-RF **tree** EVC **leaf** PD-GI **smile** SS-RF, Thinkstock **xylophone** PF **loaves** PD-GI **saucer** AB **wood** EVC **rooster** PD-GI **stretch** COR-RF **macaroni** COR-RF **pants** GI-RF, Rubberball Productions **wash** GI-RF, Image Source **basketball** SS-RF, BlueMoon Stock **bee** EVC **pair** HMCO **pear** HMCO **fireplace** COR-RF, David Papazian **pinecone** EVC **rabbit** PD-GI **grasshopper** EVC **drum** PD-GI **clock** GI-RF, George Diebold **skate** COR-RF **face** GI-RF, Caroline Schiff **colors** SS, age fotostock **belt** COR, Paul A. Souders **carrot** PD-GI **soup** AB **desert** GI-RF, Bruce Heinemann, Stockbyte **rocket** NASA **carpenter** PR, Bill Aron **between** COR, Ariel Skelley